Gender and Sexuality in Education and Health

Highlighting the voices less commonly showcased to the public – voices of young people, parents and social and health practitioners – this book comments on gender and sexuality in the contexts of formal and informal education, peer cultures and non-conformity, social sustainability and equal rights.

At a time of mounting conservatism globally – when broader issues of equity and justice around sexuality and gender in education and health have come under attack – it is critical that health workers, social service practitioners and educators share approaches, stories and data across these spaces to advocate for informative, inclusive approaches to sex, gender and sexuality education in an effort to speak back to the conservative voices which currently dominate policy spaces.

The chapters in this book were originally published as a special issue of *Sex Education*.

Jacqueline Ullman is a Senior Lecturer in Adolescent Development, Behaviour and Wellbeing at Western Sydney University, Australia. Her primary research focus is the schooling experiences of sexuality and gender diverse students and LGBTQI inclusivity across primary and secondary classrooms. She is on the editorial board of the *Journal of LGBT Youth* and *Gender and Education*. She is also the co-editor of *Understanding Sociological Theory for Educational Practices* (with Ferfolja and Jones Diaz, 2015; 2018).

Tania Ferfolja is Associate Professor in Social and Cultural Diversity at Western Sydney University, Australia. Her research focuses on sexuality and gender diverse subjectivities in education. She is the lead editor of *Understanding Sociological Theory for Educational Practices* (with Ullman and Jones Diaz, 2015; 2018), author of *Crossing Borders: African Refugees, Teachers and Schools* (2010) and co-editor of *From Here to Diversity: The Social Impact of Lesbian and Gay Issues in Education in Australia and New Zealand* (with Robinson, 2002).

Gender and Sexuality in Education and Health

Advocating for Equity and Social Justice

Edited by
Jacqueline Ullman and Tania Ferfolja

LONDON AND NEW YORK

First published 2018
by Routledge
2 Park Square, Milton Park, Abingdon, Oxon, OX14 4RN, UK

and by Routledge
711 Third Avenue, New York, NY 10017, USA

Routledge is an imprint of the Taylor & Francis Group, an informa business

© 2018 Taylor & Francis

All rights reserved. No part of this book may be reprinted or reproduced or utilised in any form or by any electronic, mechanical, or other means, now known or hereafter invented, including photocopying and recording, or in any information storage or retrieval system, without permission in writing from the publishers.

Trademark notice: Product or corporate names may be trademarks or registered trademarks, and are used only for identification and explanation without intent to infringe.

British Library Cataloguing in Publication Data
A catalogue record for this book is available from the British Library

ISBN13: 978-1-138-49345-2

Typeset in MyriadPro
by diacriTech, Chennai

Publisher's Note
The publisher accepts responsibility for any inconsistencies that may have arisen during the conversion of this book from journal articles to book chapters, namely the possible inclusion of journal terminology.

Disclaimer
Every effort has been made to contact copyright holders for their permission to reprint material in this book. The publishers would be grateful to hear from any copyright holder who is not here acknowledged and will undertake to rectify any errors or omissions in future editions of this book.

Contents

Citation Information		vii
Notes on Contributors		ix
	Introduction: Gender and sexuality in education and health: voices advocating for equity and social justice *Tania Ferfolja and Jacqueline Ullman*	1
1	Dogma before diversity: the contradictory rhetoric of controversy and diversity in the politicisation of Australian queer-affirming learning materials *Barrie Shannon and Stephen J. Smith*	8
2	'Is it like one of those infectious kind of things?' The importance of educating young people about HPV and HPV vaccination at school *Cristyn Davies, Susan Rachel Skinner, Tanya Stoney, Helen Siobhan Marshall, Joanne Collins, Jane Jones, Heidi Hutton, Adriana Parrella, Spring Cooper, Kevin McGeechan and Gregory Zimet, for the HPV.edu Study Group*	22
3	Teacher positivity towards gender diversity: exploring relationships and school outcomes for transgender and gender-diverse students *Jacqueline Ullman*	42
4	That's so homophobic? Australian young people's perspectives on homophobic language use in secondary schools *Karyn Fulcher*	56
5	Knowing, performing and holding queerness: LGBTIQ+ student experiences in Australian tertiary education *Andrea Waling and James A. Roffee*	68
6	'That happened to me too': young people's informal knowledge of diverse genders and sexualities *Paul Byron and Jessie Hunt*	85

CONTENTS

7 Responsibilities, tensions and ways forward: parents' perspectives on
children's sexuality education 99
Kerry H. Robinson, Elizabeth Smith and Cristyn Davies

8 Gender and sexuality diversity and schooling: progressive mothers speak out 114
Tania Ferfolja and Jacqueline Ullman

9 Young people, sexuality and diversity. What does a needs-led and
rights-based approach look like? 129
Simon Blake in conversation with Peter Aggleton

Index 137

Citation Information

The chapters in this book were originally published in *Sex Education*, volume 17, issue 3 (May 2017). When citing this material, please use the original page numbering for each article, as follows:

Introduction
Gender and sexuality in education and health: voices advocating for equity and social justice
Tania Ferfolja and Jacqueline Ullman
Sex Education, volume 17, issue 3 (May 2017) pp. 235–241

Chapter 1
Dogma before diversity: the contradictory rhetoric of controversy and diversity in the politicisation of Australian queer-affirming learning materials
Barrie Shannon and Stephen J. Smith
Sex Education, volume 17, issue 3 (May 2017) pp. 242–255

Chapter 2
'Is it like one of those infectious kind of things?' The importance of educating young people about HPV and HPV vaccination at school
Cristyn Davies, Susan Rachel Skinner, Tanya Stoney, Helen Siobhan Marshall, Joanne Collins, Jane Jones, Heidi Hutton, Adriana Parrella, Spring Cooper, Kevin McGeechan and Gregory Zimet, for the HPV.edu Study Group
Sex Education, volume 17, issue 3 (May 2017) pp. 256–275

Chapter 3
Teacher positivity towards gender diversity: exploring relationships and school outcomes for transgender and gender-diverse students
Jacqueline Ullman
Sex Education, volume 17, issue 3 (May 2017) pp. 276–289

Chapter 4
That's so homophobic? Australian young people's perspectives on homophobic language use in secondary schools
Karyn Fulcher
Sex Education, volume 17, issue 3 (May 2017) pp. 290–301

CITATION INFORMATION

Chapter 5
Knowing, performing and holding queerness: LGBTIQ+ student experiences in Australian tertiary education
Andrea Waling and James A. Roffee
Sex Education, volume 17, issue 3 (May 2017) pp. 302–318

Chapter 6
'That happened to me too': young people's informal knowledge of diverse genders and sexualities
Paul Byron and Jessie Hunt
Sex Education, volume 17, issue 3 (May 2017) pp. 319–332

Chapter 7
Responsibilities, tensions and ways forward: parents' perspectives on children's sexuality education
Kerry H. Robinson, Elizabeth Smith and Cristyn Davies
Sex Education, volume 17, issue 3 (May 2017) pp. 333–347

Chapter 8
Gender and sexuality diversity and schooling: progressive mothers speak out
Tania Ferfolja and Jacqueline Ullman
Sex Education, volume 17, issue 3 (May 2017) pp. 348–362

Chapter 9
Young people, sexuality and diversity. What does a needs-led and rights-based approach look like?
Simon Blake in conversation with Peter Aggleton
Sex Education, volume 17, issue 3 (May 2017) pp. 363–369

For any permission-related enquiries please visit:
http://www.tandfonline.com/page/help/permissions

Notes on Contributors

Peter Aggleton is Scientia Professor of Education and Health at the University of New South Wales, Sydney, Australia.

Simon Blake is the Chief Executive of the National Union of Students, based in London, UK.

Paul Byron is an Associate Lecturer in the Department of Sociology at Macquarie University, Sydney, Australia.

Joanne Collins is a Research Officer in Paediatrics and Reproductive Health and a member of the Women's and Children's Health Network at the University of Adelaide, Australia.

Spring Cooper is Associate Professor in the Department of Community Health and Social Sciences at the City University of New York, NY, USA.

Cristyn Davies is a Research Associate in the Discipline of Paediatrics and Child Health, and Western Sydney Sexual Health Centre, University of Sydney, Australia.

Tania Ferfolja is Associate Professor in Social and Cultural Diversity at Western Sydney University, Australia.

Karyn Fulcher is a graduate student based at the Australian Research Centre in Sex, Health and Society, La Trobe University, Melbourne, Australia.

Jessie Hunt is based at the Sydney Medical School, University of Sydney, Australia.

Heidi Hutton is a Researcher based at the Telethon Kids Institute at the University of Western Australia, Perth, Australia.

Jane Jones is a Researcher based at the Telethon Kids Institute at the University of Western Australia, Perth, Australia.

Helen Siobhan Marshall is Associate Professor of Vaccinology and a member of the Women's and Children's Health Network at the University of Adelaide, Australia.

Kevin McGeechan is a Lecturer in Biostatistics in the School of Public Health at the University of Sydney, Australia.

Adriana Parrella is a Research Fellow in the Discipline of Paediatrics, and a member of the Women's and Children's Health Network at the University of Adelaide, Australia.

Kerry H. Robinson is Professor in the Sexualities and Genders Research Network at the Western Sydney University, Australia.

NOTES ON CONTRIBUTORS

James A. Roffee is a Senior Lecturer in Criminology in the School of Social Sciences at Monash University, Melbourne, Australia.

Barrie Shannon is a PhD candidate in Sociology and Anthropology at the University of Newcastle, Australia.

Susan Rachel Skinner is Associate Professor in the Discipline of Paediatrics and Child Health at the University of Sydney, Australia.

Elizabeth Smith is a Research Fellow in the Living with Disability Research Centre at LaTrobe University, Melbourne, Australia.

Stephen J. Smith is a Teaching Fellow in Sociology and Anthropology at the University of Newcastle, Australia.

Tanya Stoney is a Researcher based at the Telethon Kids Institute at the University of Western Australia, Perth, Australia.

Jacqueline Ullman is a Senior Lecturer in Adolescent Development, Behaviour and Wellbeing at Western Sydney University, Australia.

Andrea Waling is a Research Associate at the Australian Research Centre in Sex, Health and Society, LaTrobe University, Melbourne, Australia.

Gregory Zimet is Professor of Pediatrics and Clinical Psychology at Indiana University, Bloomington, IN, USA.

INTRODUCTION

Gender and sexuality in education and health: voices advocating for equity and social justice

Background

In Australia, sexual health and sexuality education in relation to young people are not well integrated and education and health systems appear to function, in the main, independently of each other. This is perplexing, considering the known benefits of cooperative work for young people's sexual health and relationship knowledge, critical understandings and practices. Despite the apparent disjuncture, pockets of innovative, inspirational and integrated perspectives and programmes that pursue equity and justice in relation to these areas do exist across public, private and community spheres.[1] This themed issue of *Sex Education*, entitled *Gender and Sexuality in Education and Health: Advocating for Equity and Social Justice,* derives from the Australia Forum for Sexuality, Education and Health[2]'s inaugural conference, Equity and Justice – in Gender, Sexuality, Education and Health, held in Sydney, Australia in 2015. The conference sought to stimulate greater national and local connections between the education and sexual health sectors and to provide a rallying point for the formation of strategic alliances for positive sexual health outcomes among young people.

The peer-reviewed papers arising from the conference and available in this special issue have been developed and published at a time of mounting conservatism globally, when broader issues of equity and justice around sexuality and gender in education and health have come under attack. Archaic patriarchal and conservative discourses position thinking and approaches that advocate for equity and rights, as radical, leftist, and a threat to traditional family values and 'the way things should be'. As researchers and tertiary educators with a combined 30 years of experience in the fields of equity and diversity in relation to gender and sexuality, it is alarming to witness how understandings about sexuality, sexuality and gender diversities, and sexual health and relationships, have been at the very least stalled and, in many cases, regressed at the national level in many nations. Internationally, for example, this is demonstrated by the recent decision of the Russian parliament to decriminalise domestic violence (Stanglin 2017); by US President Donald Trump's recent revocation of guidelines on transgender toilets in schools that permitted 'students to use the bathrooms matching their chosen gender identity' which had been enabled by the previous administration (ABC 2017); and by the same president's reinstatement of a 'global gag rule that bans US-funded groups around the world from discussing abortion' (ABC 2017), impacting women's sexual and reproductive health and rights across many nations that rely on international funding to survive. Such retrograde measures not only undermine the rights, education and sexual health of individuals who are already highly vulnerable, they constitute discourses that convey regressive messages about sex, gender and sexuality impacting young people's access and the development of their subjective experiences with longer term implications on social cohesion.

Australia, too, is party to a similar conservative backlash that undermines principles of equity and justice. In terms of the intersections of gender, sexuality, health and education with young people, this backlash has recently played out in protracted, emotive and misinformed ways largely through divisive media campaigns and political interference in school education. For example, in 2015 in New South Wales, the State Minister for Education banned from viewing in schools, an award-winning PG-rated documentary, *Gayby Baby*, which documented Australian children's lives in lesbian- and gay-headed families (see Shannon and Smith this issue). Similarly, the *Safe Schools Coalition Australia* (SSCA) (henceforth referred to as 'Safe Schools'), an initiative to educate about gender and sexuality diversities to create deeper understanding and social harmony, experienced a cut in federal government funding after lobbying for its abolition by vocal Christian groups and conservative politicians. Traditional and social media hysteria and misinformation served to galvanise the movement through what initial analysis has found to be the use of hyperbolic, violent and graphic language that demonises difference and naturalises heterosexual and cis-gendered people as the only un-pathologised subjectivities for an authentic humanity. As a result, only one Australian state, Victoria (where the programme originated), is resisting federal directives to cease the work and is instead continuing with implementation, albeit in a different form. More myopic, however, is the state of New South Wales where gender theory, applied in the Safe Schools resource materials, has recently been banned from classrooms. According to media reports, 'Students will no longer be taught that gender is a "social construct" or that sexuality is "nonbinary", occurring on a continuum and "constantly changing"'. Rather, the education minister sitting at the time when the Safe Schools debate was being most fiercely debated, ordered a review into the 'scientific underpinning' of the material (Urban 2017). Such a ban portends a move towards a back-to-basics approach that positions sexuality and gender as biological, fixed and given – a position that fails to explain or validate the diversity present in the world – including in schools – or the fact that gender performance, for instance, is a product of history, time, place and culture.

The divisions perpetuated by such events, including the concomitant vocal and visible hysteria presented both in and by the media, contribute to discourses that potentially erode sexuality and gender education and, by extension, the sexual health and relationships knowledge of young people. As we see it, in the current Australian sociopolitical context, the loudest voices critiquing education and health promotion in the areas of gender and sexuality are those that receive the most mainstream media attention. Such voices promote messages of censure and foreclosure, bolstered, more often than not, by rhetoric purporting moral superiority and righteousness. These messages, disseminated through social and traditional media outlets and spread through popular culture across public and political spaces, negatively impact schools, and the work that teachers can do in terms of educating young people as such work becomes risky business (Cumming-Potvin and Martino 2014; Smith et al. 2011). As a result, teachers remain silent and these silences discursively constitute and reinforce what is perceived as 'normal' and acceptable in relation to sex, gender and sexuality. Such silences, for instance, are apparent in the national Health and Physical Education national curriculum, which contains few directives for the teaching of sexual health and almost no mention of sexuality and gender diversities (Ullman and Ferfolja 2014). This opaque approach enables schools to meet the needs of the school communities

– presumably to avoid community offence and backlash. However, one needs to ask, whose voices are heard in and by these communities, and whose subjectivities are thereby validated? History informs us that schools and schooling near inevitably fall on the side of conservatism and caution; so what might such a climate herald for the future sexual health of young people?

Papers in this issue

In this special issue, we aim to highlight the voices less commonly showcased to the public: voices of young people, parents, and the social and health practitioners who work in these politicised spaces. Here, these voices comment on gender and sexuality in the contexts of formal and informal education, peer cultures and non-conformity, social sustainability and equal rights.

We begin with a paper by Barrie Shannon and Stephen Smith who provide a critical examination of the politicisation of queer-affirming teaching resources through the lens of two recent media 'controversies': the showing of the *Gayby Baby* film at a New South Wales high school and the federal examination of the SSCA's teaching resource *All of Us*. The authors outline a social and political Australian climate in which such public debate is possible, particularly in light of – what appears to be, at least on the surface – clear directives for teachers to 'acknowledge and affirm' sexuality and gender diversity within federal curriculum documentation (ACARA 2015). By unpacking the rhetoric of the 'diversity discourse' employed both by the media as well as within the national curriculum, Shannon and Smith offer a critical voice that highlights the contradictory and damaging quality of superficial curricular and policy inclusions without pedagogical substance and clear federal support.

We continue with a set of two papers presenting outcomes related to young people's experiences of their teachers' intended and, perhaps, unintended curricular inclusions. These papers demonstrate the varied ways in which teachers' words, attitudes and framings matter, and how these are shaped by their own relevant professional development. Looking at a preventive education strategy for sexually transmitted infections, Cristyn Davies, in collaboration with colleagues from across the public health sector, presents an evaluation of an educational intervention trialled as part of Australia's National HPV (Human Papillomavirus) Vaccination Program. The authors, employing a randomised control trial design, investigated the impacts of the teaching intervention for students in their early years of high school; the intervention included a guide for educators, lesson plans and associated resources, and targeted nearly 7000 students across two Australian states. Students from intervention schools showed significant knowledge gains related to the causes, impacts and protections against HPV. Focus group data showcased the voices of young people and their educators, highlighting teachers' appreciation of clear guidelines and resources as well as the subsequent impact of comprehensive, preparatory materials on students' sense of comfort and positivity about the vaccination process.

In the case of messages regarding sexuality and gender diversity, educators often communicate their positionality indirectly either in conjunction with or, as is often the case for these topics, in lieu of formalised curricular inclusions. Jacqueline Ullman's paper examines the impact of in/direct messages from teachers on transgender and gender diverse students' school well-being and sense of connection to their secondary schooling environments. Using cohort data from her *Free2Be?* survey of over 700 sexuality and gender diverse teenagers

(Ullman 2015), Ullman investigates the relationships between gender diverse students' perceptions of their teachers' positivity regarding diversity of gender expression and various measures of their school well-being. The predictive nature of perceived teacher positivity on students' sense of connection to the schooling environment foregrounds the student perspective illustrating that, regardless of how teachers view their practices in relationship to sexuality and gender diversity, students' perceptions are of critical importance to their sense of school community belonging.

In line with this focus on the voices of young people with regards to inclusivity and sexuality/gender diversity, the three papers that follow provide insights into peer cultures across educational settings, including secondary, tertiary and within out-of-school, informal spaces. These papers highlight students' learning away from, and perhaps in direct contrast to, their educators' directives. In the first of these, Karyn Fulcher explores students' peer group use of homophobic language in secondary school environments. Fulcher begins by outlining the prevalence of such language and the challenges faced by educators working to eradicate its use. Some of this challenge can be explained in part, she contends, by educators' framing of this language as always 'homophobic' in nature – that is, indicative of a fear or hatred of same-sex attracted individuals. Based on her analysis of interviews and online forums with a cohort of heterosexual-identifying young adults, she advocates for a reframing of such language by educators, which considers the function of such language within students' peer group settings and uses this information to examine related systemic issues, such as the policing of gender norms.

Andrea Waling and James Roffee likewise provide an examination of students' use of marginalising language in their research into LGBTQI + peer groups in Australian tertiary settings as a method of establishing in group/out group boundaries with respect to an 'authentic' queerness. Using interview data from 16 sexuality and gender diverse university students, the authors illustrate tensions experienced by young people whose presentation, identity and experiences are positioned as 'lacking' by other members of their university's LGBTQI + peer community. Their paper highlights the challenges faced by all LGBTQI + students within a heteronormative society and a degree of reaffirmation of these exclusionary processes as evidenced via peers' reported homo/transnormative identity policing.

Through their analysis of auto-biographical accounts of their experiences working as youth peer educators and health workers, Paul Byron and Jessie Hunt further examine youth peer cultures, making a case for the affordances – in the forms of both information and emotional support – provided by informal learning practices for sexuality and gender diverse young people. Beginning from the premise that schools are contested sites for information sharing related to sex, gender and sexuality, Byron and Hunt present a series of anecdotes which highlight sexuality and gender diverse young people's information sharing practices in the absence of adult, formal educators, both in social media spaces and during face-to-face encounters. Their paper foregrounds the expert voices located in these informal learning experiences, calling into question what is thought to be 'known' about students' capabilities with regards to supporting peers' lived experiences.

Recent media controversies surrounding curricular inclusions and resources in the area of sex, sexuality and relationships education have privileged a vocal minority of parents/carers of school-aged children who advocate for children's protection from 'irrelevant' and 'dangerous' information, and which seek to make invisible 'non-normative' sexualities and gender identities. In the two papers that follow, the authors foreground perspectives from a larger subset of this population in efforts to better understand what parents want and expect out of their children's Health and Physical Education curriculum. In the first of these Kerry Robinson, Elizabeth Smith and Cristyn Davies present survey, interview and focus group data from primary school parents across two Australian states, the overwhelming majority of whom felt that sexuality education was relevant and important during the primary years of schooling. Parents who supported such inclusions highlighted their children's right to information – both in order to learn about their bodies and also to respond to relevant media portrayals of intimacy and relationships. Most of the cohort of surveyed parents further agreed that such education should be collaborative in nature including both parents and trained educators through the primary school. Though in the minority, some parents stood in opposition to sexuality education for primary school students, fearing their ability to process or understand information that might not be relevant or age-appropriate for their developmental stage, and the paper presents a useful analysis of these discourses in the light of the construction of childhood innocence.

Tania Ferfolja and Jacqueline Ullman continue with the theme of parental perspectives – this time, with a focus on the inclusion/exclusion of curriculum content and approaches that address gender and sexuality diversities in the classroom. Their paper, drawn from their broader qualitative state-based study (see Ullman and Ferfolja 2016), concentrates on the complex and multifaceted perceptions and experiences of mothers living and schooling their children in an enclave of Sydney where gender and sexuality diversities are visibly present and celebrated. Their findings illustrate that these women overwhelmingly support gender and sexuality diversity content inclusions in their child's schooling; despite this, they simultaneously felt that the schools in which their children are being educated, provide little tangible support for, or education about, gender and sexuality diversity across curricula, policy or practical approaches. Clearly, more research is required in this area as a fear of parental backlash and a belief that parents do not want this work to be done in schools is frequently used by schools, teachers and conservative politicians as key reasons for avoiding or omitting such topics. Such invisibility, however, continues to work against the well-being of many young people.

Finally, this special issue concludes with a conversation between Simon Blake, OBE and Sex Education Editor-in-chief, Professor Peter Aggleton. Simon's work in the sexual health and education sectors and the collaborative models that he has built across education, health and social care in the UK, offers educators, practitioners and researchers in these fields in Australia and beyond, positive ideas for integration and inclusion for the health and well-being of all children and young people. Simon speaks of the importance of a needs-led, rights-based approach in creating positive and empowering learning experiences to facilitate educational change. His innovations have had far-reaching effects and need to be considered in other spaces where what may be read as a controversial and limiting policy backgrounds prevail. His achievements give us hope for what may be achieved and, we believe, give us hope for future change in bringing together the health and education sectors for the benefit of future generations.

In response to the conservative political climate and subsequent regressive policy revisions across the health and education sectors, we believe strength can only be found through interdisciplinary collaboration. Our collective resistance and advocacy is enhanced by a goal shared across the diversity of our expert perspectives: to support the sexual health and well-being of young people, through education, visibility and inclusion, as they navigate their relationships and their own embodied selves. In the current climate, it is critical that health workers, social service practitioners and educators share approaches, stories and data across these spaces to advocate for informative, inclusive approaches to sex, gender and sexuality education in efforts to speak back to the conservative voices which currently dominate policy spaces. We hope that you will find this special issue of *Sex Education* useful, inspirational and reflective of some of the voices which continue to be marginalised by politicised framings of the topics discussed therein.

Notes

1. The *Talking Sexual Health* resource for secondary schools (Ollis and Mitchell 2001) is an especially brilliant example of an outcome of the type of cross-disciplinary work we are referring to here.
2. The *Australian Forum for Sexuality, Education and Health*, founded in 2012, aims to connect researchers, practitioners, community and policy leaders from the fields of sexuality, education and health, to develop and consolidate networks, and to undertake collaborative initiatives in relation to the intersections of these fields.

Acknowledgements

The authors would like to thank the contributors to the special issue and the many practitioners and educators who participated in the inaugural national conference of the *Australia Forum for Sexuality, Education and Health* from which these papers derive. Further, we would like to acknowledge and thank the following organisations who provided financial and in-kind support for this conference, without which neither the conference, nor by extension, this special edition, would have been possible: the Australian Research Centre in Sex, Health and Society; The Ian Potter Foundation; the University of New South Wales' Practical Justice Initiative; and lastly, the conference hosting institution, Western Sydney University.

References

ABC News Online. 2017. "Trump Revokes Guidelines on Transgender Bathrooms in Schools." February 25. Accessed http://www.abc.net.au/news/2017-02-23/trump-revokes-guidelines-on-transgender-bathrooms/8295482

ACARA (Australian Curriculum, Assessment and Reporting Authority). 2015. *The Australian Curriculum: Foundation to Year 10, Health and Physical Education, Student Diversity*. Accessed http://v7-5.australiancurriculum.edu.au/health-and-physical-education/student-diversity

Cumming-Potvin, Wendy, and Wayne Martino. 2014. "Teaching about Queer Families: Surveillance, Censorship, and the Schooling of Sexualities." *Teaching Education* 25 (3): 309–333.

Ollis, Debbie, and Anne Mitchell. 2001. *Talking Sexual Health: A Teaching and Learning Resource for Secondary Schools*. Melbourne: La Trobe University, The Australian Research Centre in Sex, Health and Society.

Smith, Anthony, Marisa Schlichthorst, Anne Mitchell, Jenny Walsh, Anthony Lyons, Pam Blackman, and Marian Pitts. 2011. *Sexuality Education in Australian Secondary Schools 2010* [Monograph Series No. 80]. Melbourne: La Trobe University, The Australian Research Centre in Sex, Health and Society.

Stanglin, Doug. 2017. "Russian Parliament Votes 380-3 to Decriminalise Domestic Violence." *The Sydney Morning Herald*, January 29. Accessed http://www.smh.com.au/lifestyle/news-and-views/news-features/russian-parliament-votes-3803-to-decriminalise-domestic-violence-20170128-gu0q86.html

Ullman, Jacqueline, and Tania Ferfolja. 2014. "Bureaucratic Constructions of Sexual Diversity: 'Sensitive', 'Controversial' and Silencing." *Teaching Education* 26 (2): 145–159.

Ullman, Jacqueline. 2015. *Free to Be?: Exploring the Schooling Experiences of Australia's Sexuality and Gender Diverse Secondary School Students*. Penrith: Centre for Educational Research, School of Education, Western Sydney University.

Ullman, Jacqueline, and Tania Ferfolja. 2016. "The Elephant in the (Class)Room: Parental Perceptions of LGBTQ-Inclusivity in K-12 Educational Contexts." *Australian Journal of Teacher Education* 41 (10): 15–29.

Urban, Rebecca. 2017. "Gender Theory Banned in NSW Classrooms." *The Australian*, February 9. Accessed http://www.theaustralian.com.au/national-affairs/education/gender-theory-banned-in-nsw-classrooms/news-story/eeb40f3264394798ebe67260fa2f5782

Tania Ferfolja and Jacqueline Ullman

Dogma before diversity: the contradictory rhetoric of controversy and diversity in the politicisation of Australian queer-affirming learning materials

Barrie Shannon and Stephen J. Smith

ABSTRACT

This paper discusses contradictory imperatives in contemporary Australian pedagogy – the notions of 'controversy' and 'diversity' as they relate the subjects of genders and sexualities. It is a common view that both gender and sexuality are important organising features of identity, society and politics. Consistent effort is made in the Australian educational context to combat discrimination, prejudice against sexually, and gender 'diverse' people. However, the state's commitment to diversity policies must be balanced with a secondary focus on appeasing those who are hostile to non-heteronormative expression, or who view such expression as inherently 'political' in nature and therefore inappropriate for the school setting. Australia has arguably demonstrated this dilemma recently in two notable controversies: an intervention in planned school screenings of *Gayby Baby*, a documentary exploring the experience of children in same-sex families, and media furore over the trans-positive *All of Us* teaching kit. Using these case studies, this paper explores the competing imperatives of controversy and diversity, commenting on the tendency for the lives and experiences of LGBTIQ people becoming consequently politicised. To do so, is arguably detrimental to the meaningful participation of LGBTIQ people as social citizens.

Introduction

Gender and sexuality are very often relegated to the domain of the personal and private; and yet they lie at the heart of many of our public conversations and form 'some of our most pressing sociocultural and political debates' (Alexander 2008, 1). These debates, in turn, serve as 'key components of how we conceive ourselves personally, organise ourselves collectively, and figure ourselves politically' (Alexander 2008, 1). Sexuality is of primary importance in the creation of individual and collective identity and a 'prime connecting point between body, self-identity and social norms' (Giddens 1992, 15). The 'varied ways in which narratives of intimacy, pleasure, the body, gender, and identity become constructed and disseminated personally, socially and politically' (Alexander 2008, 1) are connected through 'complex discourses, and political formations mediated through ideological investments' (Alexander 2008, 1).

Within the educational context, provision for the discussion of gender and sexuality at any real level of critical engagement is limited in contemporary Australian school curricula. Any direct exploration of issues related to human sexuality tends to be limited to specific areas of the curriculum that deal with health, biology and sport (Shannon and Smith 2015). The focus of this curriculum perspective, however, rarely provides sufficient opportunities for a more nuanced discussion of gender and sexuality-related issues, such as intimacy, eroticism, sexualities, gender roles and ethics, which form the basis for a more sophisticated knowledge and understanding of gender and sexuality.

Despite the widespread invisibility of queer-affirming content, state and territory governments expend significant effort attempting to provide 'support' for sexual and gender diversity in the form of policies and best practice documents. This paper considers issues of diverse sexualities and genders, and demonstrates how such diversities, rather than being readily embraced, instead form the basis for ongoing controversy in educational contexts.

From a Foucauldian perspective, discourse is a praxis that 'systematically forms the objects of which they speak' (Foucault in Ball 1990, 2, 5) and which is reinforced through its 'material base in established social institutions and practices' (Weedon 1987, 100). According to Weedon (1987, 21), it is in language, as the basis for the 'constitution of discourse and subjectivities' (Ferfolja 2013, 161), where meaning is produced, and it is in language where 'actual and possible forms of social organisation and their likely social and political consequences are defined and contested' (Weedon 1987, 21). Ferfolja warns that 'the power of language and its ability to perpetuate discrimination should not be underestimated' (Ferfolja 2013, 161). In terms of the way in which gay men and lesbians are positioned, she further argues (Ferfolja 2013, 161) that comments which might be construed as relatively harmless in its effects by its speaker may, in fact, serve to bolster 'the power of the discriminatory discourses', the intention of which being to maintain the privileged heteronormative status quo.

At this point, it is important to interrogate some of the language that will be used in this paper. Discourses about the rights, health and welfare of people who identify as lesbian, gay, bisexual, transgender, intersex and queer (LGBTIQ), or any other diverse expression of sexuality or gender, often employ umbrella terms such as 'queer'. Terms such as queer is used, often for semantic purposes, in order to capture a group that consists a wide range of identifying experiences and meanings. In contrast, some queer academics may indeed use terms such as 'queer' as a form of strategic essentialism (Spivak 1989) that facilitates collective political advocacy for those outside of the heteronorm.

This phenomenon has been the subject of a central criticism that gender theorists and transgender academics have sought to mount. Ansara (2010) has critiqued the 'coercive queering' of transgender and gender diverse people in academic literature; the 'lumping in' of gender diverse people under umbrella terms such as LGBTIQ and 'queer' despite a lack of meaningful focus on these specific groups. Throughout this paper, the term queer will be used to refer to people who defy heteronormative conventions of sexuality and gender presentation. Queer-affirming learning materials, then, are educational tools designed for classroom use that openly embrace LGBTIQ issues, and that aim to facilitate critique of heteronormativity.

Two recent sagas in Australia have demonstrated a poignant example of the state's commitment to fostering 'diversity' through the use of queer-affirming learning materials being superseded by their need to handle controversy as a form of 'risk management'. The first example this paper will employ as a brief case study is the documentary film *Gayby Baby*, a film that chronicles the lives of children living with same-sex parents. The film was 'banned' in New South Wales (NSW) schools in 2015 by a ministerial decree in response to conservative media backlash. The second is the negative media reaction to the *All of Us* teaching kit, which was developed by LGBTIQ youth network Minus18 and the Safe Schools Coalition. The teaching kit comprehensively addresses queerness, and specifically, transgender issues. The moral panic surrounding *All of Us*, which was broadly referred to as the 'Safe Schools' controversy, has generated persistent public discussion about whether schools are an appropriate setting for criticism of sex and gender roles.

The paper further seeks to expose both the overt and covert heterosexualised processes at work, and to demonstrate how those processes deride attitudes towards 'atypical' sexual practices, gender presentations and family arrangements. The paper will reveal what is seen as a 'neoliberalisation' of diversity; a continuing reassembly of hegemonic masculinity that renders diversity and inclusion justifiable only when the diverse subject willingly assimilates into existing economic and social practice.

Rhetoric of 'controversy' and 'diversity'

Diversity discourse

The term diversity is variously used in a number of Australian state and territory government educational policy documents (ACARA 2015; MCEETYA 2008), but nowhere is it clearly defined. Diversity is paradoxically understood within the Australian Curriculum to encompass individual students' 'diverse capabilities' (ACARA 2015). 'All students have diverse learning needs and, regardless of a student's circumstances, all students should be afforded the same opportunities and choices in their education and their diversity catered for through personalised learning' (ACARA 2015). What differentiates students and makes them diverse are their 'current levels of learning, strengths, goals and interests', as well as their degree of physical and mental (dis)ability, whether they fall into the gifted and talented group or whether English is their first or additional language (ACARA 2015).

It is important to note here the meeting of the nation's Ministers of Education in 2008, which resulted in the publication of the Melbourne Declaration on Educational Goals for Young Australians. The document argues that the role of education is to equip students with an 'appreciation of and respect for social, cultural and religious diversity', a 'sense of self-worth, self-awareness and personal identity', 'personal values' and 'respect for others' (MCEETYA 2008, 4; 9; 5; italics added). The Melbourne Declaration, however, as with the other relevant documents already mentioned, does not provide a concrete definition of 'diversity'.

Further to this discussion, the Australian Health and Physical Education (F-10) curriculum document states that that it seeks to value diversity 'by providing for multiple means of representation, action, expression and engagement' (ACARA 2015). The document reiterates the abovementioned criteria for a 'diverse' student, but to this list is added '[s]ame-sex attracted and gender-diverse students'. '[I]t is crucial', the document states, 'to acknowledge and affirm diversity in relation to sexuality and gender in Health and Physical Education' (ACARA 2015). Teaching programmes are expected to recognise 'the impact of diversity on students' social worlds, acknowledge and respond to the needs of all students, and provide more meaningful and relevant learning opportunities for all students' (ACARA 2015), while all school communities shoulder the responsibility to ensure that teaching programmes are 'relevant to the lived experiences of all students' (ACARA 2015).

Interestingly, the requirement that schools provide an affirmation for all kinds of diversity can create contradictions in policy. In the South Australian context, for example, teachers are guided to acknowledge sexual and gender diversity, while delivering sex education in a 'sensitively and developmentally appropriate' (Shannon and Smith 2015, 646) way that also considers cultural and religious 'diversities' as well. Shannon and Smith (2015) continue that 'the South Australian curriculum does not, however, define sensitivity, nor does it reveal the standards by which children are judged to be "developmentally" prepared for any particular aspect of the sexuality education curriculum', creating a confusing conundrum for school administrators, teachers and indeed students.

A support document for the current NSW Personal Development, Health and Physical Education (PDHPE) curriculum highlights the importance of acknowledging 'sexual diversity', providing information to facilitate teaching activities that educate on homophobia, discrimination and negative effects on queer students (NSW Department of Education and Communities 2011). Sexuality is described as being 'diverse', 'fluid' and 'dynamic', involving not only a person's sexual behaviour but also their sexual orientation and identity. The NSW PDHPE Teaching Sexual Health webpage, which was decommissioned during the writing of this paper, points to a number of ways in which schools can challenge recognised assumptions and negative community values, attitudes and expectations in order to cater positively for students. The online document stresses the need 'to teach students about respecting and celebrating diversity' in such a way as to provide students 'with more effective options for explaining their world' (NSW Department of Education and Communities 2011). In terms of the major concerns of this paper, the document states that it is the responsibility of schools to 'ensure that sexual diversity is acknowledged'. Provision is made for 'examples that are gender and sexually diverse when representing families and significant relationships' in teaching and learning activities which 'use a range of scenarios, not just heterosexual characters' (NSW Department of Education and Communities 2011). A clear silence in this document and throughout education policy more broadly, is the lack of attention given to trans and gender non-conforming students (Ullman and Ferfolja 2015). Despite the claims in the *Teaching Sexual Health* resource that sexuality is fluid and is broader than just an individual's sexual behaviour, diversity is afforded quite a narrow discursive definition. Here, diversity refers specifically to gay and lesbian students; the privilege of 'acknowledgment' and 'celebration' is not specifically extended to students whose diversity goes further than same-sex attraction.

Sexualities, genders and controversy

The key to the appropriate integration of sexualities and genders into schools as discursive places is a renewed focus on the critical exploration of sexuality, gender and power within the school curricula (Jones 2011; Shannon and Smith 2015). However to do so at school is not a simple task, as notions of controversy and community anxiety permeate contemporary debate (Shannon and Smith 2015). Critical exploration of sexual diversity is rare, 'due to [its] positioning as sensitive or too controversial for school communities' (Ferfolja 2013, 162). Such positioning results in what Ferfolja (2013, 162) describes as the perpetuation of 'silence in relation to these issues: first through the removal of the child so they are not exposed to the information; and second, by ensuring that teachers' work is monitored, essentially dis-couraging teachers from broaching difficult knowledges'. Indeed, teachers perpetuate silence on 'controversial' or 'political' issues out of a fear of backlash and moral panic, among other factors (Carrion and Jensen 2014; Johnson, Sendall, and McCuaig 2014).

One strategy to expand the range students' discursive options is to present queer lives through their lived experiences of family and identity, and their everyday decisions and activities. On the one hand, such a strategy provides opportunities for the legitimate claiming of subject and voice, whilst, on the other, opponents might regard such actions as naïve expressions of identity politics. Activists might call for a more radical approach, arguing that to propagate a cultural narrative of deep-down sameness and similarity depoliticises ques-tions of identity into merely personal struggles, cordoning off the personal as a realm totally separate from the political (Queirolo 2013). It is from the position of privilege which dominant heteronormative discourses bestow heterosexual power and authority. To present alterna-tives to the heterosexist understandings of family, property, marriage, sex, gender and sex-uality is to question and challenge that position of privilege.

The following case studies, which clearly validate Ferfolja's (2013) findings, demonstrate how attempts to overcome the silence and to expose students to a presentation of alternative sexualities and family structures can be suppressed.

Gayby Baby and Safe Schools

The ban on Gayby Baby

Gayby Baby (2013) is a documentary film directed by Maya Newell that portrays the lives of four young children of same-sex couples. The insight into the children's lives the film provides encapsulates the dreams, fears and aspirations of youth on the verge of puberty, stumbling to find their own place in the world. The children navigate their lives alongside their parents; gay and lesbian couples who themselves face certain degrees of uncertainty and vulnera-bility, embodying a very public rejection of gendered norms. The film serves a transformative role, challenging the notion of what constitutes the modern Australian family, and how and by whom it should be defined. It sets up the notions and conventions of heteronormativity for serious criticism, by presenting a personalised tale of each of the protagonists as a 'living, moving portrait of same-sex families that offers a refreshingly honest picture of the value systems that really count in modern life' (Marla House 2015).

The documentary champions the 'legitimacy' and health of these families by adopting the very techniques which opponents of marriage equality and same-sex parenting use to rationalise their prejudiced arguments against social change. It provides a platform for the voices of real children and their lived experiences into the current national dialogue on the personal and political issue of marriage equality and same-sex parenting, signifying a groundbreaking departure from traditional 'adults-only' discourse.

Following *Gayby Baby's* success at various national and international film festivals, a large, female single-sex school in Sydney's inner-western suburbs invited Newell, one of the school's alumnae, to screen the film. The screening was scheduled to coincide with Wear it Purple Day, an annual awareness event for the well-being of young LGBTIQ people. Before the date of its anticipated screening, however, the film found itself at the centre of a contro-versy that first appeared on the front page of the Sydney tabloid newspaper, *The Daily*

Telegraph on Wednesday, the 26th of August 2015. Headlined 'Gay class uproar', the issue was accompanied by a comment piece entitled: 'Gay push should be kept out of schools'. It was reported that there had been a 'backlash from parents' opposed to the film's screening, who were 'outraged' that their daughters were being subjected to 'propaganda'.

The *Gayby Baby* controversy was soon picked up by most mainstream print, television and radio media outlets in NSW. A local Presbyterian Minister alleged on Sydney radio station 2UE that the school '[was] trying to change people's minds by promoting a gay agenda' by 'promoting a political agenda in direct contradiction of the Department [of Education] guidelines' (2UE 954 AM 2015). The then NSW Education Minister Adrian Piccoli further told *The Daily Telegraph* that 'the government expects schools to remain apolitical places and that schools must comply with all departmental policies' (Akerman 2015). The school in question, however, attempted to assure the media that students had not been compelled to attend the screening, nor to be involved in the Wear it Purple Day celebrations that were taking place at the same time.

As media interest escalated, Piccoli presented an extraordinary ministerial decree enforcing a statewide ban on the screening of the documentary during school hours. Piccoli's ministerial memorandum, which was issued to all state schools on Wednesday, the 26th of August, 2015, demanded that *Gayby Baby* not be shown in school time so that it does not impact on the delivery of planned lessons. 'This film,' Piccoli argued, 'is not part of the curriculum and that's why I have made that direction' (McDougall 2015). The then-NSW State Premier, Mike Baird, said he supported the ban and that 'tolerance' should be taught outside of class hours (Bagshaw 2015a).

Minister Piccoli's decision to ban the viewing of the documentary during school hours calls into question the motives for the decision, and the reasoning behind banning students from viewing a film, especially when considering that the themes of embracing diversity in gender and sexuality lie at the core of various NSW governmental policy documents. Indeed, the main assumption underpinning this action is, according to the Minister, that schools ought to be 'apolitical' places, and that non-normative sexual and gender expression are therefore 'political'. The comparative responses from the NSW Liberal (centre-right) Government and the opposing perspective presented by the leader of the Victorian Labor (centre-left) Government suggests that the political and social justice agendas of the respective governments had some degree of influence on the decision-making processes in regards to the banning (or praising) of the film.

The banning of the film calls into the question the capacity for individuals to participate in the democratic project, our 'conceptions of ourselves as individuals and as citizens in a pluralistic democracy' (Alexander 2008, 3), and the attempts of politicians to limit information about genders and sexualities in the public school system. The episode, which received widespread national and international media attention, demonstrates vividly Dennis Altman's argument that '[s]exuality is an area of human behavior, emotion and understanding which is often thought of as "natural" and "private", even though it is simultaneously an area of constant surveillance and control' (2002, 2).

All of Us *teaching kit and* Safe Schools

The Safe Schools Coalition is a 'national network of organisations working with schools to create safer and more inclusive environments for same sex attracted, intersex and gender diverse students, staff and families' (FYA 2016). With the support of the Safe Schools Coalition, Melbourne-based LGBTIQ youth advocacy network Minus18 published *All of Us*, a teaching and learning resource which sought to broach the topics of sexuality and gender diversity in the classroom. The resource (Bush et al. 2015) claims that it is a 'collection of short videos and teaching activities designed… to assist students in understanding gender diversity, sexual diversity and intersex topics', in line with the Health and Physical Education component of the Australian Curriculum. The rationale behind the *All of Us* project is to bring these issues to the forefront of classroom discussion, rather than allowing them to remain invisible. The resource explores gender and sexuality by using the stories of real LGBTIQ-identifying young people, in order to both humanise the issues, and to give students insight into their lived experiences.

Minus18 had also produced a separate set of resources named 'OMG I'm Queer', 'OMG My Friend's Queer' and 'OMG I'm Trans'. These were developed by young LGBTIQ-identifying people involved in Minus18, and sought to support young people who are currently dealing with queer issues on a personal level. They contain personal anecdotes and advice about sex, sexuality and gender presentation, moderated by experts associated with Minus18. The 'OMG I'm Trans' resource, for example, discussed the safest and most comfortable ways that a gender-questioning young person may 'bind' or 'tuck', referring to the cosmetic concealment of the breasts and penis respectively. These tips are aimed at empowering young transgender people to alleviate dysphoria in a safe way (Minus18 2016).

The *All of Us* and OMG resources were assembled in order to address the wealth of research that shows the disproportionate rates of depression, suicidality and other mental illness among LGBTIQ youth in Australia. Reports such as *Writing Themselves In 3* (Hillier et al. 2010) have demonstrated the unique issues faced by young same-sex attracted and gender diverse young people. The Safe Schools Coalition and Minus18 have also drawn on the *From Blues to Rainbows* report, the first broad-scale Australian research that specifically focuses on the mental health and well-being of transgender and gender diverse young people (Smith et al. 2014).

The subject matter of the *All of Us* resource, and particularly the OMG resources, was interpreted by right-wing commentators as patently political in nature. It was argued in the media and indeed within Parliament that all of the above-described programmes intended to subscribe young people to left-wing ideology rather than to prevent bullying. This controversy and the set of teaching resources, including *All of Us* and the OMG resources, have since become known as 'Safe Schools', resulting in the brunt of the media backlash being directed at the Safe Schools Coalition. Far-right Senator Cory Bernardi told Sky News (2016) that he believed Safe Schools dealt in 'intimidating and bullying kids into conforming to what is the homosexual agenda', and that the teaching materials were 'straight out of Marx 101'. Former Prime Minister Tony Abbott publicly agreed with Bernardi's view, describing the programme as 'social engineering' (Anderson 2016). In response to the criticism from the right wing of his own party, Prime Minister Malcolm Turnbull ordered a 'review' of the Safe Schools programme, which eventually recommended that the programme continue with amendments.

The moral panic extended further than the Australian Parliament, although it was largely limited to Christian Right lobby groups. For example, the director of the Australian Christian Lobby, Lyle Shelton, posted on his blog stating that 'the cowardice and weakness of Australia's [politicians] … is causing unthinkable things [Safe Schools] to happen, just as unthinkable things happened in Germany in the 1930s' (Koziol 2016). Similar emotionally and politically charged language featured in the headlines of various right-leaning news outlets, describing the programme variously as a 'push' by predatory adults, indicative of some gay 'agenda' (Bita 2016; Sky News 2016). Far-right political parties such as The Christian Democratic Party, Family First and Australian Christians adopted the criticisms of Safe Schools''radical' gender ideology as central to their campaigns for the 2016 Federal Election. Interestingly, the conservative media furore appeared to have the opposite of the intended effect; 32 new schools had become Safe Schools by registering with the Safe Schools Coalition through the peak period of the controversy (Medhora 2016).

Neoliberalisation of 'diversity' and the politicisation of queer-affirmation

Problematising 'diversity'

In a pluricultural society such as that of modern Australia, the question of the concept of diversity and its many representations and manifestations depends on a number of different and current social, political and economic imperatives. Whilst Morrish and O'Mara (2011, 974) tell us that 'diversity is "good"', they recognise that, as a term, it is somewhat nebulous, 'a signifier of everything and yet nothing; it is conveniently unspecific'. It is often within this discourse of 'diversity' that efforts to acknowledge and include non-normative social, cultural, ethnic, gendered or sexual subjects in the educational context occur. Morrish and O'Mara's (2011) description suggests that the rhetoric of 'diversity' and its use as a tool of social cohesion and inclusion is potentially laden with often unhelpful ideological assumptions.

The notion of diversity carries with it the connotation that something is being either implicitly, or explicitly, compared to and/or contrasted with some real or imagined 'norm'. Both sexual and gender diversity, for example, are constructed against the backdrop of heteronormativity. By implication, heterosexuality and gender-conformity are at least implicitly identified as the 'norm' and as being in direct contrast to 'diverse forms' of other identities, practices or behaviours. It can be argued, then, that any discussion of diversity entails the intentional identification of differences radiating from a central 'norm', rather than from shared similarities. As such, in any effort to 'normalise' the whole spectrum of real, lived genders and sexualities, a new vocabulary, coupled with a seismic shift in the rhetoric and entrenched assumptions, needs to be forged. The rhetoric associated with sexual or gender diversity in the Australian educational context is demonstrative of this concept.

What constitutes diversity, and indeed acceptable forms of diversity, remain dictated by a patently neoliberal and heteronormative hegemony. An individual may only be 'diverse' within the parameters that hegemony will allow before that individual is discursively distanced, silenced or even pathologised. It is therefore imperative that the contemporary socio-economic and political framework of neoliberalism, which stresses homogeneity, privacy and personal responsibility, be directly challenged in favour of a pedagogical position that will at once consolidate the principles and ethos of acceptance, respect and true inclusivity into school curricula.

An appraisal of the language and silences in relevant government policy and school curricula suggest that the 'tolerance' of student diversity is extended as far as this diversity can be assimilated into contemporary social, cultural and economic narratives. The reticence of teaching resources to explicitly normalise gender non-conformity in particular can perhaps be explained by a difficulty in parsing these issues in traditional neoliberal sameness discourses. In the context of sexuality in schools, the tendency for LGBTIQ people to be portrayed as 'just like' their heterosexual and cisgender counterparts has been criticised (Harris and Farrington 2014; Peterson 2013; Riggs and Due 2013). While underpinned by a well-meaning focus on equality, discourses of sameness such as this take much needed critical attention away from the differences between the lived experiences and histories of queer people as a whole. Such critical attention is of primary importance if the presence of sexuality in the curriculum is to facilitate any notion of social justice.

When attempts are made to assimilate LGBTIQ people into existing social structures, rather than to challenge these structures to become broader, LGBTIQ people are not afforded the equal degree of social citizenship extended to their heterosexual and cisgender counterparts. Rather, LGBTIQ people are expected to be washed of their social and political complexities in order to be 'tolerated' within the contemporary gendered hegemony. Framing the discussion of diversity in terms of gender and sexuality as differences to be 'respected' or 'tolerated' is to downplay the heterosexist dogma that continues to dominate the public perception of sexuality. The perspective presented in the various curriculum documents that have been discussed problematise queer issues: 'homophobia' and 'tolerance' are topics that need to be addressed, rather than those of 'heterosexist domination' and 'queer liberation', for example. Any changes to that perception will come about only if dominant notions of sex, sexuality and gender are challenged through critical reflection on the legitimacy of alternative understandings of sex, gender and sexuality.

Ferfolja (2013, 159) writes that even though anti-discrimination legislation at state, territory and federal levels aims to further the rights of LGBTIQ people, these attempts are little more than a 'veneer of growing acceptance and visibility' (Ferfolja 2013, 160). Indeed, a certain 'tension' continues to exist between 'appreciation/celebration and discrimination towards lesbians and gay men' in Australia (Leonard et al. 2010, 1). Historically, Ferfolja continues (2013, 159), gay men and lesbian women have been 'derided, harassed, silenced and made invisible ... through social, cultural and political institutions, including education, where particular understandings of sexual subjectivities are produced'.

Ferfolja's (2013) argument here can be observed in the contemporary media and political portrayal of transgender people. Transgender figures such as retired Olympic athlete Caitlyn Jenner, actress Laverne Cox, and Australian military officer Cate McGregor have enjoyed considerable career success and celebrity despite a long history of structural violence and discrimination towards gender non-conforming people. Despite this 'veneer' of acceptance, as Ferfolja (2013) has described it, transgender issues suffer significant hurdles in terms of political, legislative and educational integration. Existing outside of traditional gendered arrangements still manages to arouse anxiety and controversy, despite a general trend towards 'acceptance' of sexual and gender non-conformity. This phenomenon sees diversity 'tolerated'; however, moves to enshrine this tolerance or to make a stronger push toward embracing nonconformity are perhaps a bridge too far for institutional frameworks of gender dominance. Benign 'diversity' discourse becomes cast as political advocacy at this line, a concept that runs counter to the foundational objectives of contemporary neoliberalism.

Politicisation of queer lives

The events leading to the banning of the screening of the *Gayby Baby* film provide a demonstration of the way in which the legitimacy of same-sex subjectivities and relationships, 'positioned within the dominant discourse of heterosexuality' (Ferfolja 2013, 160), can be undermined, eroded and ultimately silenced. Minister Piccoli's directive to NSW public schools to prohibit the screening of *Gayby Baby*, and indeed conservative political figures' condemnation of Safe Schools, carries with it a clear and unambiguous message. To call for a prohibition of queer content in one's official capacity as an elected representative, with its discursive connotations of prohibition, injunction, and/or legal forbidding, demonstrates how the power of language as praxis can tell us not only *what* to think, but *how* to think. Furthermore, it demonstrates the political nature of rhetoric, 'involving a dialectical interaction engaging the material, the social and the individual … with language as the agency of mediation' (Berlin 1997, 692). The implication here is that the political figures involved in opposing the material in the discussed case studies did so because of their content having been deemed inappropriate during for the educational setting. Such comments, at the very least, disparage the content of *Gayby Baby* and Safe Schools and their recognition of sexually diverse relationships and non-heteronormative family structures, while positioning the issues explored in the resources as either too sensitive or too controversial for schooling communities to broach (Britzman and Gilbert 2004).

The politicisation of queer lives is facilitated by discourse that aligns same-sex attraction and gender non-conformity with a broad range of taboo sexual topics. In doing so, critics of programmes such as *All of Us* are able to employ 'child politics' (Baird 2008) in order to galvanise opposition by portraying exposure to concepts such as sexual and gender non-conformity as a danger to the prototypical figure of a vulnerable child, and by extension, children in the wider community. Child politics were employed extensively during the Safe Schools saga, and used specifically to attack the *From Blues to Rainbows* report, which underpinned all of the materials produced by the Safe Schools Coalition and by Minus18. A report that appeared in the right-wing newspaper *The Australian* claimed that 'vulnerable teenagers as young as 14, including some who had suicidal thoughts, were secretly interviewed without parental knowledge about their gender and sexuality by a university research team with links to the Safe Schools programme' (Urban and Brown 2016). The language used here clearly sets a tone of parental deception and child exploitation, and further targets the team of researchers who have contributed to Safe Schools. The paper quotes the *From Blues to Rainbows* report, acknowledging that parental permission was not sought in order to avoid 'outing' young people who did not wish to be publicly identified as transgender or gender diverse. However, the paper itself continues to build a narrative that children are innately gendered and asexual beings, and that exposure to concepts such as gender, sex and sexuality ought to be closely regulated.

An analysis of the discussed controversies reveals a number of entrenched issues related to diversity and its vague definition (verbal, intellectual and physical), as well as how legitimacy and normalcy are widely perceived. The incidents, and the media attention they gained, demonstrate the creation of a demonised, aberrant construct – the non-normative, non-gendered individual. This results in the overt politicisation of matters of gender, sexuality and identity. The language and rhetoric used by the political representatives and advocates, especially Minister Piccoli, Senator Bernardi and Mr Shelton, and indeed their failure to challenge morality discourse within mainstream media, facilitated the creation of a 'folk devil' empowered by the commentators' use of flagrant and at times vacuous discourse.

The suppression of genders and sexualities in the classroom is not solely facilitated by morality discourse based on traditional social conservatism and religious views, however.

An over-reliance on secularism, science and 'facts' appears to be limiting the extent to which teachers are willing or able to explore sexual subjectivities in the curriculum. Rasmussen (2010, 710) provides a criticism at the contemporary secular and scientific approaches to sex education, which she argues are 'steeped in particular value judgements about what constitutes a quality sex education'. Drawing on Rasmussen's work, Lamb (2013) problematizes progressives' reliance on 'facts' in determining quality sex education, arguing that there is rarely any critical exploration of what constitute 'facts' or which worldviews underpin them. A fact-based approach to sex education encourages 'objective', tangible information, such as anatomy, reproduction, pregnancy and sexually transmitted infections, which comfortably coalesce with heteronormativity. Conversely, exploration of intangible social and sexual subjectivities are discouraged by a framework that relies on provable facts to produce its legitimacy. By focussing on facts, sex education curricula privilege heteronormative subjectivities, providing them a solid, rational ground upon which they can be based. Any deviation from this foundation of heteronormative rationality then begins to tread into the uneasy waters of controversy and political advocacy.

Conclusion

The socialisation of young people, and their guidance towards their fullest participation in society is in large part the responsibility of their schooling. That schools are able to provide opportunities and forums to comfortably discuss and embrace non-normative expression is paramount to ensuring that an equitable level of social citizenship is granted to all, regardless of their personal, social, religious, ethic or sexual characteristics and identities. This is particularly important for students who identify as LGBTIQ, as their histories and lived experiences continue to be debated in a very heated and public way.

Consultation, collaboration, and fostering critical thinking skills is therefore paramount for effective school-based programmes which meaningfully address issues of sexuality and gender diversity. If we are to accept the premise that sexuality and gender are both primary organising features of our society, and have significant impact on our political and social participation, we need to recognise that young people are not exempt from this. It is only right that they be well-educated and able to parse sexuality in both their public and private lives, and also be prepared to relate to others whose characteristics may not necessarily fall in line with their own.

Due to acts of politicisation, both subtle and overt, queer subjectivities struggle for representation and inclusion in public institutions that are heralded as 'neutral' and 'secular'. Unfortunately, the reticence of institutions to address issues relevant to queer young people delivers a negative blow to their legitimacy as sexual and gendered beings, and to their sense of belonging in the community. This sense of alienation that young queer Australians experience is a key factor in explaining their disproportionate rates of depression, anxiety and suicidal ideation (Hillier et al. 2010). It is clear that in Australia, and indeed in all places that seek to enshrine the necessary protections and concessions for trans and gender diverse young people at school, unflinching political will is required.

However, the public attention on the *Gayby Baby* and Safe Schools sagas has provided something of an education for Australia, and arguably worked in favour of a progressive agenda in certain ways. As mentioned, many more Australian schools have become accredited Safe Schools since the sagas began, than have withdrawn from the programme (Medhora

GENDER AND SEXUALITY IN EDUCATION AND HEALTH

2016); and the massive media exposure that the *All of Us* resources received would have helped them to reach many more trans and gender questioning young people than they perhaps otherwise would have. In response to the *Gayby Baby* 'ban', the film's directors formulated a teaching kit to accompany the film that 'provides lesson ideas and plans about different types of families, including single parents, same-sex parents, and Indigenous kinship families' (Sainty 2016). At the time of writing, the 'ban' on *Gayby Baby* still stands. Despite the ban, the film has since been shown at certain schools in NSW accompanying the teaching kit, as a specific part of those schools' curricula (Sainty 2016). Interestingly, reports based on freedom of information requests have shown that the majority of Department of Education complaints regarding *Gayby Baby* were in protest to the ministerial decree that banned the film (Bagshaw 2015b).

In view of these developments, perhaps it is time for us to avoid equating controversy with failure. Critique of deep-seated beliefs about sexuality, gender and morality in a society that is simultaneously obsessed with and enraged by the sexualisation of youth is unlikely ever to be a simple task. The themes in *Gayby Baby* have asked an important question that has so far been absent in debates about sexuality, gender and civics: what do the kids think? As researchers continue to listen to the voices of young same-sex attracted and gender nonconforming Australians, it is important that policy-makers and indeed politicians to follow suit if we are to make the changes that strong, expert-led research is telling us we need.

Disclosure statement

No potential conflict of interest was reported by the authors.

References

2UE 954 AM. 2015. *Presbyterian Minister Mark Powell from the Cornerstone Church Strathfield Talks to 2UE about Burwood Girls High School and Gayby Baby*. Sydney: Fairfax Media. https://www.rewindradio. com/2ue/presbyterian-minister-mark-powell-from-the-cornerstone-church-strathfield-talks-to-2ue-about-burwood-girls-high-school-and-gayby-baby

Akerman, P. 2015. "Gay Push Should Be Kept out of School." *The Daily Telegraph*. http://blogs.news. com.au/dailytelegraph/piersakerman/index.php/dailytelegraph/comments/gay_push_should_be_kept_out_of_schools/

Alexander, J. 2008. *Literacy, Sexuality, Pedagogy: Theory and Practice for Composition Studies*. Logan: Utah State University Press.

Altman, D. 2002. *Global Sex*. Chicago, IL: University of Chicago Press.

Anderson, S. 2016. "Tony Abbott Calls for Safe Schools 'Social Engineering Program' to Be Axed." *ABC Online*. Accessed July 1, 2016. http://www.abc.net.au/news/2016-03-01/abbott-calls-for-end-to-safe-schools/7209766

Ansara, Y. G. 2010. "Beyond Cisgenderism: Counselling People with Non-Assigned Gender Identities." In *Counselling Ideologies: Queer Challenges to Heteronormativity*, edited by L. Moon, 167–200. Aldershot: Ashgate.

ACARA (Australian Curriculum Assessment Authority). 2015. *Student Diversity*. http://www. australiancurriculum.edu.au/studentdiversity/student-diversity-advice

Bagshaw, E. 2015a. "Gayby Baby: Education Minister Adrian Piccoli and Premier Mike Baird Ban Film without Seeing It." *The Sydney Morning Herald*. Sydney: Fairfax Media. http://www.smh.com.au/national/education/gayby-baby-education-minister-adrian-piccoli-and-premier-mike-baird-ban-film-without-seeing-it-20150827-gj8rut.html

GENDER AND SEXUALITY IN EDUCATION AND HEALTH

Bagshaw, E. 2015b. "Gayby Baby: Complaints against Ban Outnumber Complaints against Film." *The Sydney Morning Herald*. Sydney: Fairfax media. http://www.smh.com.au/national/education/gayby-baby-complaints-against-ban-outnumber-complaints-against-film-20151104-gkqesx.html

Baird, B. 2008. "Child Politics, Feminist Analyses." *Australian Feminist Studies* 23 (57): 291–305.

Ball, S., ed. 1990. *Foucault and Education: Disciplines and Knowledge*. London: Routledge.

Berlin, J. 1997. "Rhetoric and Ideology in the Writing Class." In *The Norton Book of Composition Studies*, edited by S. Miller, 667–684. New York: Norton & Company.

Bita, N. 2016. "Activists Push Taxpayer-funded Gay Manual in Schools." *The Australian*. Accessed March 15, 2016. http://www.theaustralian.com.au/national-affairs/education/activists-push-taxpayerfunded-gay-manual-in-schools/news-story/4de614a88e38ab7b16601f07417c6219

Britzman, D., and J. Gilbert. 2004. "What Will Have Been Said about Gayness in Teacher Education." *Teaching Education* 15 (1): 81–96.

Bush, C., R. Ward, J. Radcliffe, M. Scott, and M. Parsons. 2015. *All of Us*. Melbourne: Safe Schools Coalition and Minus18.

Carrion, M., and R. E. Jensen. 2014. "Curricular Decision-Making among Public Sex Educators." *Sex Education* 14 (6): 623–634.

Ferfolja, T. 2013. "Sexual Diversity, Discrimination and 'Homosexuality Policy' in New South Wales' Government Schools." *Sex Education* 13 (2): 159–171.

FYA (Foundation for Young Australians). 2016. "Who We Are." *Safe Schools Coalition*. Accessed July 1, 2016. http://www.safeschoolscoalition.org.au/who-we-are

Giddens, A. 1992. *Transformation of Intimacy: Sexuality, Love and Eroticism in Modern Societies*. Stanford, CA: Stanford University Press.

Harris, A., and D. Farrington. 2014. "It Gets Narrower': Creative Strategies for Re-broadening Queer Peer Education." *Sex Education* 14 (2): 144–158.

Hillier, L., T. Jones, M. Monagle, N. Overton, L. Gahan, J. Blackman, and A. Mitchell. 2010. *Writing Themselves in 3*. Melbourne: La Trobe University, Australian Research Centre in Sex, Health and Society.

Johnson, R., M. Sendall, and L. McCuaig. 2014. "Primary Schools and the Delivery of Relationships and Sexuality Education: The Experience of Queensland Teachers." *Sex Education* 14 (4): 359–374.

Jones, T. 2011. "A Sexuality Education Discourses Framework: Conservative, Liberal, Critical and Postmodern." *American Journal of Sexuality Education* 6 (2): 133–175.

Koziol, M. 2016. "Australian Christian Lobby Likens Gay Marriage and Safe Schools to 'Unthinkable' Nazi Atrocities." *Sydney Morning Herald*. Accessed July 1, 2016. http://www.smh.com.au/federal-politics/federal-election-2016/australian-christian-lobby-likens-gay-marriage-and-safe-schools-to-unthinkable-nazi-atrocities-20160531-gp8ff2.html

Lamb, S. 2013. "Just the Facts? The Separation of Sex Education from Moral Education." *Educational Theory* 63 (5): 443–460.

Leonard, W., D. Marshall, L. Hillier, A. Mitchell, and R. Ward. 2010. *Beyond Homophobia: Meeting the Needs of Same-sex Attracted and Gender Questioning (SSAGQ) Young People in Victoria. A Policy Blueprint*. Melbourne: La Trobe University, Australian Research Centre in Sex, Health and Society.

Marla House. 2015. *Gayby Baby*. http://thegaybyproject.com/

McDougall, B. 2015. "Burwood Girls High School: Anger over Gay Parenting Documentary 'Gayby Baby.'" *The Daily Telegraph*. http://www.dailytelegraph.com.au/news/nsw/burwood-girls-high-school-anger-over-gay-parenting-documentary-gayby-baby/story-fni0cx12-1227498780623?sv=ea3bfecb943a6008f3ad172aeeb77a6e

Medhora, S. 2016. "Safe Schools Program: 32 More Schools Sign up and Only One Leaves after Furore." *The Guardian Australia*. Accessed February 3, 2017. https://www.theguardian.com/australia-news/2016/mar/11/safe-schools-32-more-schools-sign-up-and-only-one-leaves-after-furore

(MCEETYA) Ministerial Council on Education, Training and Youth Affairs. 2008. *Melbourne Declaration on Educational Goals for Young Australians*. Melbourne: MCEETYA.

Minus18. 2016. "OMG I'm Trans." *Minus18*. Accessed July 1, 2016. https://minus18.org.au/index.php/resource-packs/omg-i-m-trans

Morrish, L., and K. O'Mara. 2011. "Queering the Discourse of Diversity." *Journal of Homosexuality* 58 (6–7): 974–991.

NSW Department of Education and Communities. 2011. *Teaching Sexual Health: Sexual Diversity*. http://www.curriculumsupport.education.nsw.gov.au/sexual_health/inclusive/diversity.htm

Peterson, C. 2013. "The Lies That Bind: Heteronormative Constructions of 'Family' in Social Work Discourse." *Journal of Gay & Lesbian Social Services* 25 (4): 486–508.

Queirolo, C.J. 2013. "We Have Never Been Queer: The De-politicization of Queer Activism." *Wetlands Magazine*. University of Puget Sound. http://wetlandsmagazine.com/2013/09/20/we-have-never-been-queer-the-de-politicization-of-queer-activism-by-c-j-queirolo/

Rasmussen, M. 2010. "Secularism, Religion and 'Progressive' Sex Education." *Sexualities* 13 (6): 699–712.

Riggs, D., and C. Due. 2013. "Moving beyond Homonormativity in Teacher Training: Experiences from South Australia." *Sex Education* 13 (S1): 99–112.

Sainty, L. 2016. "Banned 'Gayby Baby' Film to Be Shown in Schools." *Buzzfeed News*. Accessed February 3, 2017. https://www.buzzfeed.com/lanesainty/gayby-baby

Shannon, B., and S. J. Smith. 2015. "'A Lot More to Learn than Where Babies Come From': Controversy, Language and Agenda Setting in the Framing of School-based Sexuality Education Curricula in Australia." *Sex Education* 15 (6): 641–654.

Sky News. 2016. "Safe Schools Promotes Homosexual Agenda." *Sky News Online*. Accessed July 1, 2016. http://www.skynews.com.au/news/top-stories/2016/02/25/safe-schools-promotes–homosexual-agenda-.html

Smith, A., T. Jones, R. Ward, R. Dixon, A. Mitchell, and L. Hillier. 2014. *From Blues to Rainbows: The Mental Health and Well-Being of Gender Diverse and Transgender Young People in Australia*. Melbourne: La Trobe University, Australian Research Centre in Sex, Health and Society.

Spivak, G. C. 1989. *In Other Worlds: Essays in Cultural Politics*. New York: Routledge.

Ullman, J., and T. Ferfolja. 2015. "Bureaucratic Constructions of Sexual Diversity: 'Sensitive', 'Controversial' and Dilencing." *Teaching Education* 26 (2): 145–159.

Urban, R., and G. Brown. 2016. "Parents in Dark over Uni Sex Survey Linked to Safe Schools." *The Australian*. Accessed February 3, 2017. http://www.theaustralian.com.au/national-affairs/education/parents-in-dark-over-uni-sex-survey-linked-to-safe-schools/news-story/c43050a03326ab1fb6a96f5bef796dee

Weedon, C. 1987. *Feminist Practice and Poststructuralist Theory*. Oxford: Blackwell.

'Is it like one of those infectious kind of things?' The importance of educating young people about HPV and HPV vaccination at school

Cristyn Davies, Susan Rachel Skinner, Tanya Stoney, Helen Siobhan Marshall, Joanne Collins, Jane Jones, Heidi Hutton, Adriana Parrella, Spring Cooper, Kevin McGeechan, Gregory Zimet, for the HPV.edu Study Group

ABSTRACT

The National Human Papillomavirus (HPV) Vaccination Program in Australia commenced in 2007 for girls and in 2013 for boys, using the quadrivalent HPV [4vHPV] vaccine. In Australia, students are primarily vaccinated en masse, on school grounds, after parental/guardian consent is obtained. Students most often receive little, or no, education at school about HPV or HPV vaccination prior to immunisation. There is also some uncertainty about where young people can and should obtain reliable information about the vaccine, outside of school. We conducted a cluster randomised controlled trial of a complex intervention in schools. This study aimed to improve: (1) student knowledge about HPV vaccination; (2) psycho-social outcomes and (3) vaccination uptake. In this paper, we briefly outline our educational intervention and discuss its implementation by educators including facilitators and barriers. We also discuss the study findings pertaining to student knowledge about HPV and HPV vaccination and their attitudes to vaccination across control and intervention schools. Study results showed students in intervention schools demonstrate greater knowledge and understanding of HPV and HPV vaccination. Greater knowledge and understanding of HPV and HPV vaccination appeared to promote positive attitudes towards vaccination and supported confidence with vaccination.

Introduction

The National HPV Vaccination Program in Australia commenced school delivery in April 2007 for girls and February 2013 for boys, using the quadrivalent human papillomavirus (HPV) [4vHPV] vaccine. In Australia, students (aged 11–14 years) are primarily vaccinated as a group, on school grounds, after parental/guardian consent has been obtained. HPV vaccination is free of charge for students and is Commonwealth Government funded. Secondary schools distribute consent forms with an information brochure to all parents/guardians of eligible students. However, students most often receive little, or no, education about HPV or HPV vaccination prior to immunisation. Despite media awareness campaigns, there is also some uncertainty about where young people can and should obtain reliable information about the vaccine.

In this paper, we provide some brief background about HPV and HPV vaccination. We then discuss the limited knowledge and understanding many young people have about HPV and HPV vaccination based on our earlier research. Next, we outline our study aims and methodology, which included a cluster randomised controlled trial of a complex intervention in secondary schools and a process evaluation. We then briefly outline our theoretical framework, which was based on a broad psychosocial model. We also present our educational intervention and its relationship to the Australian (national and state-based) school curricula, and provide an overview of the implementation of our education intervention by educators (teachers and/or school nurses). Drawing on both quantitative and qualitative data, we discuss the findings related to student knowledge about HPV and HPV vaccination and their attitudes to vaccination. We also discuss the facilitators and barriers to teaching the education intervention in schools. Finally, we discuss the implications of these findings for schools, and specifically educators who teach health education to secondary students.

Background

HPV and HPV vaccination

HPV infection, if persistent, can cause cancers of the cervix, vulva, vagina, penis, anus and oropharynx. The two most prevalent cancer-causing genotypes are HPV16 (3.2% in healthy women) and HPV18 (1.4% in healthy women).[1] According to data from the Australian Institute of Health and Welfare (AIHW), in Australia in 2015, new cervical cancer cases affected 885 women, while 395 people were newly affected with anal cancer (AIHW 2016).[2] All cervical cancer is considered to be due to HPV infection (with HPV 16 and 18 causing at least 70%) (Trottier and Burchell 2009). At least 90% of anal cancer is associated with HPV (Trottier and Burchell 2009). HPV has been recognised as contributing to some cancers of the head and neck particularly cancers affecting the oropharynx (20–50% associated with HPV depending on study and site of cancer) which includes the base of the tongue, the tonsils and the upper throat (AIHW 2014; Trottier and Burchell 2009). All penile cancers are associated with HPV (mainly HPV 16) (Trottier and Burchell 2009). In 2005, there were 69 cases of penile cancer, which is rare, diagnosed in Australia (Grulich et al. 2010). The National HPV Vaccination Program in Australia uses the quadrivalent HPV [4vHPV] vaccine, which protects against two major HPV genotypes: 16 and 18 that are responsible for 70%–80% of cervical cancers (de Sanjosé et al. 2013), and also genotypes 6 and 11 which cause about 90% of genital warts (Garland et al. 2007).[3]

In Australia, young people aged 11–14 years (year 7 or 8 in secondary school depending on jurisdiction) are vaccinated as part of the School-based Immunisation Program (SBIP). The HPV vaccine is offered alongside other vaccines in the national school vaccination programme (e.g. Diphtheria, Tetanus and Pertussis (DTaP) booster and varicella vaccines). The Australian National HPV Vaccination Program Register reported that for girls turning 15 years in 2015, 85.6% received HPV dose 1, 83% received HPV dose 2 and 77.4% received HPV dose

3 (National HPV Vaccination Program Register). National coverage has increased from an average of 73% for 3-doses in 2014 when this study was undertaken, to 77.4% in 2015. It is also worth noting that coverage varies across states, with some states such as South Australia and Western Australia (where this study was undertaken) and Tasmania reporting coverage lower than the national average. In boys, coverage is lower at a national average of 60% for 3-dose completion by 15 years in 2014. To achieve a comprehensive reduction in HPV disease burden at a population-level, vaccination uptake needs to be consistently high (Regan et al. 2007; Tabrizi et al. 2012; Drolet et al. 2015; Skinner et al. 2015a).[4] HPV vaccines are now recommended as part of vaccination programmes for girls in many countries (Markowitz et al. 2012), and more recently some countries have extended this recommendation to boys. Implementation of HPV vaccination programmes varies considerably by country, as do vaccination coverage levels (Drolet et al. 2015; Wigle, Fontenot, and Zimet 2016). Generally, school-based programmes tend to have higher coverage than non-school based programmes (Marshall et al. 2013).

Limited knowledge and understanding about HPV and HPV vaccination

Many young people have limited or no understanding of the vaccines they receive, including the HPV vaccine, or the diseases they are intended to prevent (Cooper Robbins, Bernard, McCaffery, Garland, et al. 2010; Bowyer et al. 2013; Davies and Burns 2014; Burns and Davies 2015; Skinner et al. 2015b; Kelly-Hanku et al. 2017). Research in Australian schools indicates that young people's understanding, self-efficacy and involvement in decision-making about the HPV vaccine are low, while vaccination-related fear and anxiety are high (Cooper Robbins, Bernard, McCaffery, and Skinner 2010; Burns and Davies 2015). Australian girls offered the vaccine as part of the school programme had limited, or no understanding about HPV, HPV vaccination, their future risk of cervical cancer and other sexually transmitted infections (Cooper Robbins, Bernard, McCaffery, et al. 2010; Burns and Davies 2015; Cooper et al. 2016). Knowledge of HPV and vaccination has been found to be even lower in Australian boys than girls (Agius 2010). Poor understanding about HPV and the HPV vaccine has also been linked to heightened anxiety on vaccination day (Cooper Robbins, Bernard, McCaffrey, et al. 2010; Burns and Davies 2015).

Informed young people are in a better position to make decisions about their health and well-being (Davies and Burns 2014; Burns and Davies 2015). Young people are unlikely to learn about HPV and HPV vaccination without structured and effective education (Cooper et al. 2016). Expecting parents/guardians to educate young people is also unlikely to be effective as their own knowledge about HPV and HPV vaccination can also be very limited (Marshall et al. 2007, 2013), and, as with sex education more broadly (Davies and Robinson 2010; Robinson and Davies 2014, 2017) they also experience barriers such as embarrassment about discussing the sexually transmitted nature of the virus with their child (Cooper Robbins et al. 2011). Young people's access to accurate, research-based information about HPV and HPV vaccination is a critical component of their sex education, contributing to healthy sexual citizenship and the development of their sexual literacy (Davies and Robinson 2010; Illes 2012; Robinson 2013). They have a right to information that they can understand about their health and health care, which is an ethical imperative to ensure informed consent (Children's Hospitals Australasia's 2011).

Study aims

Against the background described above, this study aimed to improve: (1) student knowledge about HPV vaccination; (2) psycho-social outcomes and (3) vaccination uptake. We discuss our findings for our first study aim, and attitudes to HPV vaccination, which is a component of our second study aim.

Methods

We conducted a multi-centre cluster randomised controlled trial (RCT) of a complex intervention in 40 secondary schools with 6965 secondary students from 2012 to 2014 (Skinner et al. 2015a). In medicine, RCTs are considered the most rigorous way of determining whether a cause-effect relation exists between treatment and outcome, and for assessing the cost-effectiveness of a treatment (Sibbald and Roland 1998). Generally, the unit of control in a RCT is an individual subject (patient). In a cluster RCT, groups of subjects (such as schools) are randomised to receive an intervention or act as a control (usual practice) rather than individual subjects (such as students) (Sibbald and Roland 1998). See Figure 1.

Sample

Forty schools were randomly allocated to intervention (21 schools, 3806 students) or control (19 schools, 3159 students). Intervention schools received the complex intervention which included an intervention for young people (education and distraction); a shared decisional support tool for parents and young people and logistical strategies (consent form return strategies, in-school supplementary HPV vaccination team visits, targeting students who have missed a dose of the vaccine, and vaccination-day guidelines).

Setting

The study was conducted in Western Australia (WA) and South Australia (SA) with schools stratified by Government, Catholic, and Independent sectors and geographical location.

Participants

Students in their first year of high school (year 8 in participating states), key school personnel (teachers, principals, school nurses), immunisation nurses and parents/guardians participated in the study. In 2013, boys were vaccinated in year 9 as part of the HPV catch-up programme and participated in our study in selected schools.

Recruitment

A stratified random sample of schools was invited to participate in the HPV.edu study. Those who accepted were then randomly allocated to intervention or control. Schools were recruited via a study invitation letter sent to the school principal with telephone follow-up by study staff. Purposive sampling across school sectors and intervention and control groups

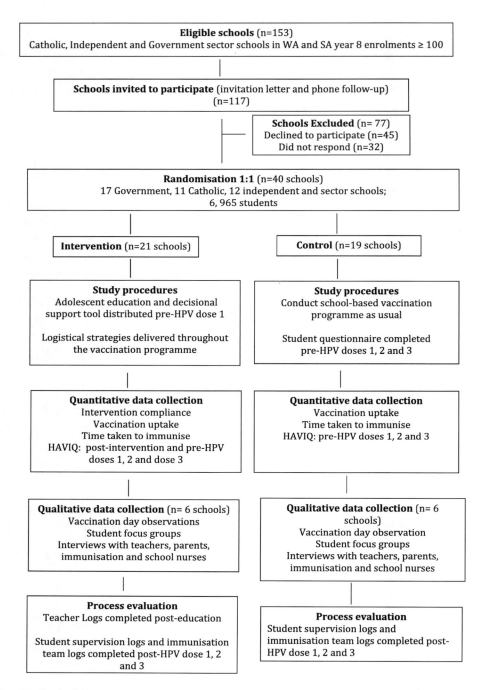

Figure 1. Study design.

(5 control, 6 intervention) was used to subsequently recruit 11 case study schools from the study sample for the qualitative component of the study.

Intervention

Schools that were randomly allocated to the intervention group were provided with study educational materials (see Education Resources about HPV and HPV vaccination below) and were advised to use the materials at around the time the consent forms were distributed and before the first dose of vaccine was administered. Each educator (teacher and/or school nurse) was invited to complete a log documenting lesson type, student year group, number of students in attendance at the HPV.edu lesson, sex of students, lesson time spent educating students about HPV and HPV vaccination, educational resources used, number of students that received the magazine, number of students that undertook the student questionnaire, kinds of questions asked by students about HPV and HPV vaccination, educator confidence with responding to student questions, and educator comments and suggestions regarding the education resources. Control schools followed usual practice, without these educational materials.

Theoretical framework

The conceptualisation and design and of our study was informed by a broad-based biopsychosocial model, which recognises that young people who are offered the vaccine are individuals acting in a social world that includes their school and community, to inform the intervention development (Wight, Abraham, and Scott 1998). We also drew on widely recognised theories of behaviour change, including the Health Belief Model (HBM) (Strecher and Rosenstock 1997), the Theory of Planned Behaviour (TPB) (Ajzen 2012) and Social Cognitive Theory (Luszczynska and Schwarzer 2005), which have been used successfully in health promotion programmes including the promotion of immunisation. For a more detailed description of the relationship between behaviour change theories and our education resources, please see our intervention constructs and strategies for young people for the education intervention (Cooper et al. 2016).

Data collection

Our mixed methods evaluation design was implemented to explore, in-depth, possible mechanisms for any observed effect of the intervention on knowledge of HPV and HPV vaccination, as well as change in a range of psychosocial outcomes, such as fear and anxiety relating to HPV vaccination and HPV vaccination uptake. The study included a quantitative evaluation (validated student survey) and a qualitative component (17 focus groups with 111 students, 22 interviews with parents, 11 interviews with school personnel, 10 immunisation team interviews and 20 school observation logs of vaccination day processes). The student survey, called HPV Adolescent Intervention Questionnaire (HAVIQ) was undertaken pre-dose 1, 2 and 3 of the HPV vaccine. Interviews and focus groups were undertaken postdose 2 until after dose 3 of the vaccine. We also developed fidelity logs for teachers undertaking the education intervention with students, for immunisation nurses on vaccination day, and for school personnel supervising vaccination day.

Data analysis

We developed and validated the HAVIQ to determine changes in knowledge about HPV and vaccination. Items in this measure were developed from existing HPV vaccine questionnaires, the results of our own preliminary qualitative research, and an expert panel of academics working in related fields. A short series of factual questions were asked of students, relating to information that had been provided in the educational materials, with options of agree/ disagree/ don't know. We collapsed the incorrect response with don't know to dichotomise the response for each item for each student. We then calculated a mean percentage of correct responses for students in intervention schools, and compared this to the mean percentage of correct responses for students in control schools. Statistical tests included two-sample t-tests with appropriate adjustment for clustering.[5]

We also conducted semi-structured focus groups and interviews, which were digitally recorded, transcribed verbatim, and de-identified. For students, focus group discussions focused on: knowledge and understanding about HPV and HPV vaccination, HPV vaccine decision-making and HPV vaccination experience on the day. In addition, intervention groups were asked about the usefulness of HPV.edu education resources. Thematic analysis was used to code the data in NVivo9 (qualitative data computer software, QSR Ltd, Australia) and to analyse the data. Thematic analysis is a method for identifying, analysing and reporting patterns (themes) within data (Braun and Clarke 2006). Inductive (themes emerging from the data) and deductive (theoretical and analytical themes emerging from the research questions) were employed. Blinded analysis was undertaken across the cohorts to ensure objectivity; that is, the first author did not know which participants were from an intervention or control school during the process of coding and analysis.

Advisory Board

The study Advisory Board included representatives from the Government, Catholic and Independent education sectors and from health department and immunisation teams in both study jurisdictions. The Advisory Board provided input on all aspects of the study including resources (content and design), school recruitment, intervention implementation and dissemination of study findings.

Ethics and informed consent

We obtained ethical approval from all relevant bodies across our research sites. This included the Department of Health WA Human Research Ethics Committee (HREC), Women's and Children's Hospital (WCHN) HREC, relevant WA and SA government authorities and approval from the University of Sydney. WA and SA approved the conduct of the intervention in schools, without a requirement for parental consent. For student participation in the survey, parental/guardian opt-out consent was approved by all relevant SA authorities, while in WA we were required to obtain active parental/guardian consent, in addition to the requirement for student assent in all schools. Active parental/guardian consent and student assent was required for participation in student focus groups.

Education resources about HPV and HPV vaccination

The education intervention consisted of an educator guide and supplement with interactive lessons,[6] a DVD/film, a website[7] (http://takechargehpv.org), an app available on mobile devices across platforms, a magazine[8] and distraction/relaxation methods to be used prior to and during vaccination.[9] Further information on the development of the education intervention is detailed in a separate publication (Cooper et al. 2016). Briefly, the guide and supplement provided educators with background information regarding the development of the education resources, their relevance to the Australian curriculum and suggested lesson plans with 9 in-class activities linked to the DVD chapters. Five activities focused on HPV and vaccination,[10] two activities on the decision-making process,[11] one activity on the practical aspects of vaccination day[12] and one summary activity. The 18-min DVD consisted of seven chapters. Four of these chapters focused on HPV and vaccination,[13] one chapter covered the decision-making process,[14] one chapter addressed practical aspects of vaccination day[15] and the final chapter summarised key information. We designed the DVD to be screened in an interactive way during class time to promote discussion between students and their teacher/school nurse. The app also contained the DVD chapters, the text from the DVD chapters in summary form, an e-copy of the magazine, and distraction/relaxation methods. Schools were provided with the HPV.edu study website address and at least one hard copy of the magazine and decisional support tool per student.[16]

Relevance to Australian State and National Curricula

The education resources for study intervention schools were designed to meet the curriculum guide and outcomes for Physical Health and Education in South Australia and Western Australia. We supplied educators with a user guide and supplement. We also consulted with education professionals from The Australian Curriculum, Assessment and Reporting Authority (ACARA) to ensure that the resources were consistent with the outcomes of the National Curriculum. Our education intervention focused on developing health literacy, consistent with a strengths-based approach, recognising that schools are key settings for developing health-related knowledge and skills (ACARA 2012).[17]

In Western Australia, our educational resources addressed the 'Knowledge and Understandings' (includes promoting well-being), and 'Self-management Skills' (includes self-understanding and decision-making) phases of curriculum development in the Health and Physical Education Learning Area Statement (Curriculum Council 2005). Within the year 8 syllabus, HPV.edu was designed to meet the requirements of 'Contributing to Health and Active Communities', a strand focused on health promotion activities which target relevant health issues for young people and ways to prevent them (School Curriculum and Standards Authority 2016). In South Australia, the educator's guide and resources were designed to meet the South Australian Curriculum and SACSA Companion Document SERIES: R-10 Health and Physical Education Teaching Resource (DECS 2004), and the South Australian Curriculum, Standards and Accountability Framework—Strand: Health of Individuals and Communities (DECS 2001).

Implementation of the education intervention

Prior to the commencement of the intervention, study staff introduced the resources to educators in intervention schools, and provided advice about how they were intended to be used. Specific resources were used at the discretion of individual educators, who reported their selection via the educator logs. Overall 71 educator logs[18] were returned (at least 1 per school), which documented the implementation of the educational activities. The majority of schools reported that teachers taught the education sessions, however, at five schools in WA the school health nurse facilitated these sessions. Of 21 intervention schools, 15 reported the education sessions were conducted prior to students receiving their first school-based vaccinations (pre-HPV dose 1). Across all schools the average time spent teaching was 56 minutes (range 30 to 112 minutes). Individual schools were classified as low (utilising 0–6 resources), moderate (utilising 7–12 resources) or high (utilising 13–18 resources) implementers of the educational intervention. Five schools were high implementers, 13 schools were moderate implementers and 3 were low implementers. We understand that the number of resources used by intervention schools does not necessarily correspond to the *quality* of teaching and learning that took place in the classroom, but rather Table 1 below represents the level of implementation of the education resources.

Schools used an average of 10 resources (range 2 to 15). The DVD and the magazine were most used by educators. Each of the 21 intervention schools screened at least one chapter of the DVD, and 20 schools distributed the magazine to students. Fourteen schools used the HPV.edu study website and 16 schools used at least one in-class activity (averaging 2.7 activities per school, range 0 to 7). The crossword (12/21) and 'talk with your parents' (10/21) were the most used in-class activities.

Quantitative data findings

Students in intervention schools had, on average, 65% correct responses to the HAVIQ knowledge questions, which were administered pre-HPV dose 1 of vaccine. This compared to 33% of responses correct by students in control schools (Table 2). This meant that students in

Table 1. Number and type of education resources used by intervention schools.

Educational resource	Number of schools[a]
DVD chapter: What is HPV	21
DVD chapter: What is HPV vaccination	20
DVD chapter: Boys and HPV[b]	20
Magazine	20
DVD chapter: Vaccination on the Day	19
DVD chapter: HPV decision-making	18
DVD chapter: Vaccination in the Future	18
Website	14
In- class activity: Crossword puzzle	12
In- class activity: Talk with your parents	10
In-class activity: HPV Bingo	8
In- class activity: The decision-making process	6
In-class activity: The decision-making process	6
In- class activity: Meditation Exercise	4
In-class activity: Educate the Public	4
In-class activity: Summary	4
In- class activity: Matching Game	3
DVD chapter: Recap	3

[a]Each resource was used in at least one teaching session in each school.
[b]We developed a chapter for boys based on feedback from the study Advisory Board given that the vaccine became part of the SBIP from 2013 to clarify relevance of the HPV vaccine for this population. Information relevant to girls had already been incorporated into earlier DVD chapters.

GENDER AND SEXUALITY IN EDUCATION AND HEALTH

Table 2. Percent of knowledge questions answered correctly.

Time	Group	Number of schools	Number of students with valid knowledge scores	Mean percent answered correctly (%)	Difference (95% CI)[a]	P-value[a]
Pre dose 1	Intervention	21	1641	65	32% (27%, 36%)	<0.0001
	Control	19	1357	33		
Pre dose 3	Intervention	21	1677	53	20% (17%, 24%)	<0.0001
	Control	19	1479	32		

[a]Adjusted for year, state, sector, co-educational status and clustering of students within schools.

intervention schools had 32 percentage points more correct responses; this was highly statistically significant. Pre-dose 3 (6 months later) students in intervention schools had on average 53% correct responses to knowledge questions, compared to 32% of responses correct by students in control schools. Hence, at 6 months after the education, students in intervention schools had 20 percentage points more correct responses, on average, than students in control schools, again highly statistically significant.

Qualitative data findings

We now present our results for the student focus groups pertaining to knowledge and attitudes about HPV and HPV vaccination. Table 3 provides a snapshot of student knowledge about and attitudes towards HPV and HPV vaccination across control and intervention groups. There were marked differences in knowledge and understanding between control and intervention students. Table 4 provides demographic data from the case study schools that participated in the qualitative study. Most of the schools in our sample had higher than average Index of Community Socio-Educational Advantage (ICSEA) ranking.[19] We expected that schools with lower than average ICSEA rankings could also benefit from our education intervention as some control schools may have reduced agency to access high quality, research-based information about HPV and HPV vaccination to educate relevant students.

Facilitators and barriers to implementing the education intervention

The primary facilitators for educators teaching the intervention included having a comprehensive user guide, supplement and user-friendly, age-appropriate resources:

> I would definitely use the resources again. Um, I would definitely show the DVD, definitely. Um and I love the magazine so I would hope that we could give out the magazine again (School nurse, female, Year 8, Government co-educational school).

> I think in the classroom the actual programme, I found was really good. My girls although they were a bit giggly they really enjoyed it and I think they understood then why they are actually having it, otherwise they wouldn't have had any idea (Health and Physical Education teacher 1, female, Year 8, Independent School).

> Yeah, so I certainly enjoyed it, I was happy [that] I had a resource there to follow to give me some guidelines; I think that helped (Health and Physical Education, teacher 2, female, Year 8, Independent School).

GENDER AND SEXUALITY IN EDUCATION AND HEALTH

Table 3. Snapshot of student knowledge and understanding of HPV and HPV vaccination.

Topic	Control	Intervention
Knowledge about HPV	Limited /no knowledge: 'I'm not sure', 'Is it like one of those infectious kind of things?', 'Never heard it before', 'I have no idea'	Good knowledge: 'It causes cancer', 'Boys and girls can get it'
Diseases caused by HPV	Students were less confident: 'Is it like vaginal cancer?' [Is it something] 'to do with the reproductive system or something like that?'	Students were confident: 'It can cause cervical cancer', '[It can cause] genital warts', '[It can cause] genital cancer'
Transmission of HPV	Some students understood transmission through sexual contact. Others believed it was an 'airborne disease', or transmitted by sharing food and drinks, coughing and sneezing, or through saliva, or blood, or genetic	Most students understood that mode of transmission was through sexual contact
Doses required to complete quadrivalent HPV vaccine	Students had varied responses: some thought that 2 [sic.] doses were required	Students knew 3 doses were required
How the HPV vaccine works in the body	Students generally had limited/inconsistent/incorrect understanding	Students had good if not perfect understanding: the vaccine 'injects small doses of HPV into your body and then like it teaches your body how to like fight it off.'
Reason for getting HPV vaccine	Got vaccine because of trust in government/health professionals: 'I don't think there would be much of a risk with taking vaccinations because the people who made them know what they are doing.'	Got vaccine because of its benefits: 'One of the reasons I wanted to get it was just like I know in the future I am like protected by it.'
Attitudes to HPV vaccination and the SBIP	Generally positive, but had limited knowledge and therefore concerns: 'Like what if something happens'	Most were positive because of knowledge/understanding. Would encourage peers to get vaccine
Cervical screening	Did not mention cervical screening	Many girls knew that they still had to get Pap test: 'Oh I'm pretty sure it doesn't completely stop it [HPV] but if you keep going to get your Pap smear thingy that can tell you if you have it [HPV] or not.'
Where students learned about the HPV vaccine	Some said they learned about HPV vaccine at school, but also the Internet; friends; the news media; parents. Information was inconsistent: 'Yeah, we got told about it …' and '[…]I didn't get told anything.'	Learned about HPV vaccine from educators at school: 'we had a lot of lessons about it', and from their parents
Misinformation	Some thought it protected against HIV/AIDS: '…I am not sure if this is right, but it could also prevent AIDS maybe.'	Before intervention, some thought the vaccine protected against HIV/AIDS: '…about HPV I'm like, oh do you mean HIV? And they [the educator] go no, HPV'
Communication with parents/guardians about HPV vaccine	Many students did not discuss whether or not to have the vaccine with their parents/guardians	Some students discussed HPV vaccine with parents after education: 'I just told my parents and then they didn't want me to do it at first but I told them like what it does and that it could prevent'

I thought the DVD was really good, you know […] because it was informative and it did answer a lot of questions. It actually helped clear it up in my mind too a little, you know, and I felt more comfortable teaching it (Health and Physical Education teacher 1, Year 8, Independent School).

Educators also identified that experience and/or tertiary training teaching in health education was critical: 'I think it helps that we're PE [Physical Education] teachers and […] have taught a lot of health'. Other teachers commented that their background in science assisted

Table 4. HPV.edu school demographic data from qualitative study.

School No.	State	Group	Year	Sector	School type	ICSEA[a]	No. of focus groups	Participating students	Males %	Females %
201	WA	Control	2013	Independent	Boys	1191	1	3	100	0
202	WA	Intervention	2013	Independent	Boys	1191	2	15	100	0
218	WA	Intervention	2014	Government	Co-ed	1047	2	10	40	60
220	WA	Control	2014	Government	Co-ed	1047	3	20	35	65
223	WA	Control	2014	Catholic	Co-ed	994	3	18	33	67
224	WA	Intervention	2014	Catholic	Co-ed	1032	2	10	20	80
113	SA	Control	2014	Government	Co-ed	1074	1	11	55	45
110	SA	Intervention	2014	Government	Co-ed	1009	0	0[b]	0	0
115	SA	Intervention	2014	Independent	Co-ed	1068	1	9	56	44
107	SA	Control	2014	Independent	Co-ed	1162	0	0[b]	0	0
104	SA	Intervention	2013	Independent	Girls	1175	1	10	0	100
103	SA	Control	2013	Independent	Girls	1065	1	5	0	100

[a]ICSEA refers to Index of Community Socio-Educational Advantage. ICSEA is a scale, which allows for fair and reasonable comparisons among schools with similar students. ICSEA is set at an average of 1000, which can be used as a benchmark. The lower or higher the ICSEA value, the lower or higher the level of educational advantage of students who attend this school.
[b]Observations were conducted in these case study schools, but not focus groups as it was not convenient for the school.

them. Significantly, teachers/school nurses commented that the Teacher/school nurse user guide, supplement and resources would assist less experienced colleagues: 'I think inexperienced teachers would find that sort of framework helpful'. Most educators felt that, combined with their own knowledge and experience, the resources allowed them to effectively respond to student questions about HPV, HPV vaccination and related sexual health matters: 'I felt comfortable with and had the knowledge and was able to answer [students' questions] well'.

The main barriers for teachers and school nurses in implementing the education intervention in schools were 'time constraints'. In this study, schools were asked to teach students about HPV and HPV vaccination before the first dose of HPV vaccine was administered to students, which meant that some schools had a short lead in time to organise when and in what subject area the education was taught. While schools attempted to teach students the intervention during a Health class, or during another class period to keep class sizes to a minimum, some schools elected to teach the education intervention to large groups for logistical reasons, thus limiting the opportunities for a more interactive learning experience. While some teachers/ school nurses would have liked more lesson time to teach about HPV and HPV vaccination, all educators were able to use the resources provided to fit within the class lesson time provided. In addition, because the education intervention was compliant with the sexual health and relationships (SHR) Health curriculum, some teachers switched SHR education and a unit of study scheduled earlier in the year. The education intervention demonstrated that educators benefited from having access to training and to research-based, accurate information about HPV and HPV vaccination both for their own professional development, and to teach their students (Spratt et al. 2013).

Discussion and recommendations: implications for educators

This is a world-first RCT study to examine the impact of an educational intervention on knowledge about and attitudes towards HPV and HPV vaccination amongst young people in a mass SBIP (School Based Immunisation Program). We found that our education intervention was easy to implement, and was widely used by teachers and school nurses as part of the school curriculum during scheduled school time. Our education intervention, on average, resulted in students significantly increasing their knowledge and understanding of HPV and HPV vaccination. They also reported improved attitudes to the vaccination experience after education.

Our findings also have important implications for young people's understandings about future cervical cancer and HPV-related cancer prevention, improved knowledge, attitudes and skills around vaccination, improved knowledge and understanding of safe sex practices, and playing an active role in decisions about their own health and well-being. Study findings demonstrate that it is feasible for educators to teach students about HPV and HPV vaccination, at school, preferably as part of the Health curriculum (State and National), when they are supported by an educator user guide, supplement and user-friendly, age appropriate educational resources.

Our qualitative data provided a more nuanced understanding of how the education impacted on young people's understandings. Students in control groups had a limited understanding about HPV and HPV vaccination and in some cases students had misinformation about HPV and the HPV vaccine. Conversely, young people in intervention groups had good knowledge and understanding about HPV vaccination. Students in intervention groups demonstrated more comprehensive knowledge about HPV and HPV vaccination than students in control groups. While the questionnaire showed some attenuation of knowledge, although still a marked difference between intervention and control, it would be ideal to provide further education to support student knowledge and understanding about HPV and HPV vaccination and positively impact their attitudes and vaccination self-efficacy.

Many young people in the control group were not sure whether they had completed the HPV vaccine course, and some had no understanding of whether they had been vaccinated against HPV and the implications of this decision.[20] Students in the control group were primarily content to have the vaccine because of their trust in health professionals or the government, not because they had any knowledge or understanding about HPV and/or HPV vaccination nor its implications for them and herd immunity.[21] However, young people in the intervention group were primarily content to have the HPV vaccine because they had a sound knowledge and understanding about HPV and HPV vaccination. This knowledge and understanding appeared to promote positive student attitudes towards the HPV vaccine and self-efficacy on vaccination day more broadly.

With respect to the outcome of knowledge gain, intervention students' core beliefs were informed by improved knowledge and understanding, which led them to expectations[22] that they would be protected by the HPV vaccine, whereas in the control group, students' expectations about protection were simplistic, guided by pre-existing beliefs that authorities must be trusted. These findings illustrate the impact of the three guiding behavioural theories particularly regarding the concept of expectations (Cooper et al. 2016). In addition, observational learning[23] (Cooper et al. 2016), which occurred through students viewing the DVD and participating in class discussion, had a considerable impact on informing them and supported their beliefs about HPV and HPV vaccination. Many students in the intervention group used their knowledge and understanding to moderate their fear, anxiety or concerns about vaccination-related discomfort and pain. The education intervention positively impacted their attitudes and behaviour on vaccination day, therefore demonstrating both student behavioural capacity[24] and self-efficacy.[25]

Some students' participating in focus groups expressed limited knowledge about other HPV-related cancers (other than cervical cancer).[26] In future iterations of our education intervention, we recommend that all young people be taught about other HPV-related cancers, which will also help to assist in clarifying the relevance of the HPV vaccine for boys (including the effects of herd immunity and the reduction of disease burden). It is important that all young people be taught about all HPV-related diseases regardless of their sex. Denying students an opportunity to learn about HPV and HPV vaccination has implications for their human rights as well as future health behaviours. These include, but are not limited to, young people's role and attitudes in decision-making about their health and well-being and that of their future partners and family members, making informed decisions about immunisation, safe sex practices, and where relevant, participation in cervical screening in the future. Our findings indicate that young people's understandings in the control group were unlikely to promote these behaviours.

Our study showed that it is feasible to educate students in schools about HPV and HPV vaccination, preferably in health education classes, when using a research-based user guide, supplement and user-friendly educational resources to support educators. In our study, teachers and school nurses were restricted by time. However, in the future, educators could be informed about our educational package before the school year commences, allowing adequate preparation time. Educators found many of the resources useful, especially the DVD and student take-home magazine, in effectively communicating knowledge about, and promoting an understanding of, HPV and HPV vaccination to students. We recommend that HPV school-based vaccination programmes have access to our education package (updated as appropriate), or similar, so that educators can teach all students about HPV and HPV vaccination before they are invited to be vaccinated at school. This approach will promote informed young people who are better positioned to understand HPV and HPV vaccination, have positive attitudes towards vaccination and enhanced confidence on vaccination day (Figure 1).

Strengths and limitations

This comprehensive study, involving a random selection of 40 schools, allocated to control or intervention groups, employed a study design that reduced chance of systematic bias. It was conducted across two Australian states, and was broadly representative of the Australian population in our target group. Employing both quantitative and qualitative methods enabled us to gain greater insight about why and how the education intervention worked. Limitations included the fact that not all the HPV and HPV education was taught before HPV dose 1 was administered to students, which would have potentially reduced the knowledge gain in the intervention group pre-dose 1, but it may have assisted with persistence of knowledge, which was demonstrated. Since revision of unit content with students in an important part of any quality teaching and learning, it would have been ideal for teachers and/or school nurses to have provided revision, but this was not possible given time restrictions and an already full curriculum. Revision of this unit may have resulted in evidence of longer-term learning of HPV and HPV vaccination by students. While many of the 12 case study schools that participated in the qualitative study had higher than average ICSEA rankings, we expect that lower ranking ICSEA schools can also benefit from our education intervention for young people given the potential for reduced agency to access high quality, research based resources to educate students about HPV and HPV vaccination. School-based vaccination is a challenge for schools because it adds additional burden to educators. While not all schools could implement all resources, the intention of the education intervention was for schools to choose the most appropriate resources for their student cohort. Finally, the intervention was also designed to promote higher vaccination rates, primarily through the logistical components. Unfortunately this was not achieved, as the logistical intervention was not implemented as intended. At least one vaccine dose was given to 3277 (86.1%) students in intervention schools versus 2697 (85.4%) in control schools, difference 0.4% (95% CI: −2.6, 3.3). The complete findings from this part of the study, including vaccine course completion and detailed implementation and process evaluation have been presented[27] and will be published in a separate paper.

Conclusion

Study results showed that students in intervention schools demonstrated greater knowledge and understanding of HPV and HPV vaccination. Overall, greater knowledge and understanding of HPV and HPV vaccination appeared to promote positive attitudes towards vaccination and supported confidence with vaccination. The concepts of expectations, observational learning, behavioural capacity, and self-efficacy informed by the three guiding behavioural theories and as measured in our validated questionnaire, appeared to promote the outcomes observed in this study. HPV and HPV vaccination education for young people is useful to promote knowledge, understanding and healthy citizenship. Educators (teachers and school nurses), combined with their own knowledge and experience, found that an educator user guide, supplement and resources based on current research, made teaching students of vaccination age, about HPV and HPV vaccination in the school-setting feasible and achievable. Ideally education about HPV, HPV vaccination and vaccine preventable diseases more broadly, should be provided throughout schooling to assist in maintaining good levels of knowledge and understanding. This may also have an impact on vaccination attitudes and decision-making for students who parent or have guardianship of children in the future.

Notes

1. Prevalence increases in women with cervical pathology in proportion to the severity of the lesion reaching around 90% in women with grade 3 cervical intraepithelial neoplasia and invasive cancer (Forman et al. 2012).
2. Estimates for 2012–2016 (based on 2002–2011 incidence data) are presented.
3. There are about 40 HPV geno-types that infect the mucosal areas of the body, such as the cells lining the anus, genital or oral tract, of which 13–18 types have been identified as high risk, due to their association with malignancy. The HPV genotype most commonly responsible for HPV-related malignancy is 16, followed by 18, 45, 33 and 31. The proportion of malignancies due to each type varies slightly by geographical area, but these five types are responsible for 70–90% of all HPV related cancers, depending on geographical area and cancer type (please see Trottier and Burchell 2009).
4. Modelling suggests that HPV vaccination coverage rates need to be at target levels of 90% to reduce HPV disease burden.
5. Regression models with Generalised Estimating Equations (GEE) were used to account for clustering within schools.
6. The guide for educators is available as an attachment to download as part of our study protocol. See Skinner et al. 2015a.
7. The website includes information about HPV and HPV vaccination and is intended to reinforce the information taught in class. Adolescents can re-watch the film clips, sign up to receive reminders about vaccination, and share their stories about being vaccinated.
8. The magazine includes a range of practical information about HPV and HPV vaccination, and the school vaccination day, in an appealing format. The magazine is designed to be taken home by students to read in their own time.
9. iPads were available for student use on vaccination day to assist with relaxation and distraction and contained only the study app, which incorporated information from the website, the film chapters, the magazine, and relaxation exercises and distraction activities such as a painting tool.
10. 'HPV question panel,' 'Crossword puzzle,' 'Matching game,' 'Educate the public' and 'HPV Bingo'.
11. 'Talk with your parent' and 'the decision-making process'.
12. 'Meditation exercise'.
13. 'What is HPV,' 'What is HPV vaccination,'' Boys and HPV' and 'Vaccination in the Future'.
14. 'HPV decision-making'.
15. 'Vaccination on the day'.
16. Utilisation of the website and education resources are included in the section below: Implementation of the education intervention.
17. Specifically, we targeted area E in the broad learning sequence for years 7–8:

(E) Students investigate health issues relevant to young people to understand reasons for the choices people make about their health and wellbeing. They examine personal, environmental and social factors that can influence an individual's choices and explore and evaluate options, consequences and healthier and safer alternatives. (ACARA 2012 (August), 18)

18. Each educator (teacher and/or school nurse) was invited to complete a log documenting lesson type, student year group, number of students in attendance at the HPV.edu lesson, sex of students, lesson time spent educating student about HPV and HPV vaccination, educational resources used, No. of students that received the magazine, number of students that undertook the student questionnaire, kinds of questions asked by students about HPV and HPV vaccination, educator confidence with responding to student questions, educator comments and suggestions regarding the education resources.

19. The ICSEA ranking was determined by consulting the My School website: <https://www. myschool.edu.au> viewed 10 September 2016.

20. The qualitative findings are supported by the findings in the quantitative survey. Forty-two per cent of students in the control group that participated in the HAVIQ student survey said they did not know whether they had completed the HPV vaccine course compared to 32% of students in the intervention group. These percentages exclude students that did not respond to this question.

21. When a high percentage of the population is vaccinated, it is difficult for infectious diseases that are contagious to spread, because there are not many people who can be infected. Herd immunity only works if most people in the population are vaccinated. See Vaccine Knowledge Project, University of Oxford: http://vk.ovg.ox.ac.uk/herd-immunity, accessed 1 July 2016.

22. Expectations refer to an individual's belief about the probable results from their actions.

23. Observational learning refers to individuals learning from one another through watching each other's behaviour, attitudes and outcomes of those behaviours.

24. Behavioural capacity refers to the knowledge and skills that are necessary to effect or change behaviour.

25. Self-efficacy refers to an individual's confidence of their ability to overcome perceived barriers.

26. Please note that these are the results for the qualitative findings. We did not ask a specific question in the HAVIQ student survey about other HPV related cancers, and therefore cannot provide the percentage of students who lacked knowledge about other HPV-related cancers.

27. Please see: LB1.1 Randomised controlled trial of a complex intervention to improve school-based hpv vaccination for adolescents: the hpv. edu study http://sti.bmj.com/content/91/Suppl_2/A77.1.abstract?sid=953e0699-b984-42e3-a59c-5b8620425003

Acknowledgements

We would like to acknowledge the contributions to this study by members of the HPV.edu Study Group, including: Annette Braunack-Mayer: School of Population Health, University of Adelaide, Adelaide, SA, Australia; Julia Brotherton: National HPV Vaccination Program Register, VCS, and School of Population and Global Health, University of Melbourne, Melbourne, Victoria, Australia; Suzanne M. Garland: Women's Centre for Infectious Diseases, The Royal Women's Hospital, Melbourne, VIC, Australia; Melissa Kang: Faculty of Health, Australian Centre for Public and Population Health Research, University of Technology Sydney; John Kaldor: The Kirby Institute for Infection and Immunity in Society, Faculty of Medicine, UNSW Sydney, NSW, Australia; Julie Leask; School of Public Health, University of Sydney, Sydney, NSW, Australia; Kirsten McCaffrey; David G. Regan: The Kirby Institute for Infection and Immunity in Society, Faculty of Medicine, UNSW Sydney, NSW, Australia; Peter Richmond: Vaccine Trials Group, Telethon Kids Institute, Perth, WA, Australia, and School of Paediatrics and Child Health, University of Western Australia, Perth, WA, Australia; Patti Whyte, Deakin University, SRC Population Health, Deakin Health Economics, Melbourne, VIC, Australia. We thank our study Advisory Boards in Western Australia and South Australia for their cooperation and their invaluable advice and feedback, and we also acknowledge the support of WA Health and SA Health. We wish to acknowledge the

GENDER AND SEXUALITY IN EDUCATION AND HEALTH

invaluable input of the research participants: the students, teachers, school nurses, parents/guardians and immunisation team members that allowed the research to be undertaken across schools in Western Australia and South Australia. We would like to acknowledge GSK for an investigator initiated educational grant (to fund educational materials); the BUPA Foundation (funded the decisional support tool); and Seqirus (BioCSL) for providing an investigator initiated research grant to assist in collection of data from boy. We also wish to acknowledge Gemma Abraham and Harrison Lindsay Odgers for their contribution to coding the qualitative data in NVivo. Gemma's contribution was enabled by the Sydney Medical School Summer Scholars Program, University of Sydney, Australia, and Harrison kindly donated his time to the HPV.edu study while completing his MPH.

Disclosure statement

No potential conflict of interest was reported by the authors.

Funding

This work was supported by the Australian National Health and Medical Research Council [grant application number 1026765]; Helen Marshall was supported by a NHMRC CDF 2 Fellowship [APP1084951]. GSK Australia [4806] provided an investigator initiated educational grant for the development of HPV educational materials, which were used in this study. Trial registration: Australian and New Zealand Clinical Trials Registry [ACTRN12614000404628], 14.04.2014; and Seqirus (BioCSL).

References

ACARA. 2012. *The Shape of the Australian Curriculum: Health and Physical Education*. Sydney: Australian Curriculum, Assessment and Reporting Authority.

Agius, P. A. 2010. "Human Papillomavirus and Cervical Cancer: Gardasil® Vaccination Status and Knowledge amongst a Nationally Representative Sample of Australian Secondary School Students." *Vaccine* 28 (27): 4416–4422.

AIHW. 2014. "Head and Neck Cancers in Australia". *Cancer Series*. Canberra: Australian Instititue of Health and Welfare. http://www.aihw.gov.au/publication-detail/?id=60129547291

AIHW. 2016. "Incidence and Mortality of Anal Cancer." Australian Institute of Health and Welfare. Accessed April 28, 2016. http://www.aihw.gov.au/cancer/cancer-in-australia-overview-2014/appendixb/-t3

Ajzen, Icek. 2012. "The Theory of Planned Behavior." In *The Handbook of Theories of Social Psychology*, edited by P. A. M. Van Lange, A. W. Kruglanski and E. T. Higgins, 438–459. London: SAGE.

Bowyer, H. L., L. A. Marlow, S. Hibbitts, K. G. Pollock, and J. Waller. 2013. "Knowledge and Awareness of HPV and the HPV Vaccine among Young Women in the First Routinely Vaccinated Cohort in England." *Vaccine* 31 (7): 1051–1056.

Braun, V., and V. Clarke. 2006. "Using Thematic Analysis in Psychology." *Qualitative Research in Psychology* 3 (2): 77–101.

Burns, K., and C. Davies. 2015. "Constructions of Young Women's Health and Wellbeing in Neoliberal times: A Case Study of the HPV Vaccination Program in Australia." In *Rethinking Youth Wellbeing: Critical Perspectives*, edited by K. Wright and J. McLeod, 71–90. New York, NY: Springer.

Children's Hospitals Australasia. 2011. *Charter on the Rights of Children and Young People in Healthcare Services in Australia*. Association of the wellbeing of children in Healthcare. http://www.awch.org.au/pdfs/Charter-Children-Young%20People-Healthcare-Au-version-FINAL-210911b-web.pdf

Cooper Robbins, C., D. Bernard, K. McCaffery, J. M. Brotherton, and S. R. Skinner. 2011. "'I Just Signed': Factors Influencing Decision-making for School-based HPV Vaccination of Adolescent Girls." *Health Psychology* 29 (6): 618–625.

Cooper Robbins, C., D. Bernard, K. McCaffery, S. M. Garland, and S. R. Skinner. 2010. "'Is Cancer Contagious?' Australian Adolescent Girls and their Parents: Making the Most of Limited Information about HPV and HPV Vaccination." *Vaccine* 28 (19): 3398–3408.

GENDER AND SEXUALITY IN EDUCATION AND HEALTH

Cooper Robbins, S., D. Bernard, K. McCaffery, and S. R. Skinner. 2010. "'It's a Logistical Nightmare!' Recommendations for Optimising Human Papillomavirus School-based Vaccination Experiences." *Sexual Health* 7 (3): 271–278.

Cooper, S. C., C. Davies, K. Mahendran, J. Blades, T. Stoney, H. Marshall, and S. R. Skinner. 2016. "Development of an HPV Vaccination Intervention for Australian Adolescents." *Health Education Journal* 75 (5): 610–620.

Curriculum Council. 2005. *Curriculum Framework Curriculum Guide – Health and Physical Education*. Western Australia: Curriculum Council.

Davies, C., and K. Burns. 2014. "Mediating Healthy Citizenship in the HPV Vaccination Campaigns." *Feminist Media Studies* 14 (5): 711–726.

Davies, C., and K. Robinson. 2010. "Hatching Babies and Stork Deliveries: Risk and Regulation in the Construction of Children's Sexual Knowledge." *Contemporary Issues in Early Childhood* 11 (3): 249–262.

DECS. 2001. "South Australian Curriculum, Standards and Accountability Framework – Health of Individuals and Communities. Department of Education and Children's Services". Accessed June 28. http://www.sacsa.sa.edu.au/index_fsrc.asp?t=CB

DECS. 2004. "R–10 Health and Physical Education Teaching Resource: R-10 Health and Physical Education." In *SACSA Companion Document Series: South Australian Curriculum Standards and Accountability Framework*. DECS Publishing: Department of Education and Children's Services. http://www.sacsa.sa.edu.au/ATT/%7BF51C47E3-B6F3-4765-83C3-0E27FF5DD952%7D/R-10_H&PE.pdf

Drolet, M., É. Bénard, M. C. Boily, H. Ali, L. Baandrup, H. Bauer, S. Beddows, et al. 2015. "Population-level Impact and Herd Effects following Human Papillomavirus Vaccination Programmes: A Systematic Review and Meta-analysis." *Lancet Infectious Diseases* 15 (5): 565–580.

Forman, D., C. de Martel, C. J. Lacey, I. Soerjomataram, J. Lortet-Tieulent, L. Bruni, J. Vignat, et al. 2012. "Global Burden of Human Papillomavirus and Related Diseases." *Vaccine* 30 (5): F12–F23.

Garland, S. M., Mauricio Hernandez-Avila, Cosette M. Wheeler, Gonzalo Perez, Diane M. Harper, Sepp Leodolter, Grace W. K. Tang, et al. 2007. "Quadrivalent Vaccine against Human Papillomavirus to Prevent Anogenital Diseases." *The New England Journal of Medicine* 356 (19): 1928–1943.

Grulich, A. E., F. Jin, E. L. Conway, A. N. Stein, and Jane Hocking. 2010. "Cancers Attributable to Human Papillomavirus Infection." *Sexual Health* 7 (3): 242–252.

Illes, J. 2012. "Young Sexual Citizens: Reimagining Sex Education as an Essential Form of Civic Engagement." *Sex Education* 12 (5): 613–625.

Kelly-Hanku, A., S. Ase, V. Fiya, P. Toliman, H. Aeno, G. M. Mola, J. M. Kaldor, L. M. Vallely, and A. J. Vallely. 2017. "Ambiguous Bodies, Uncertain Diseases: Knowledge of Cervical Cancer in Papua New Guinea." *Ethnicity & Health*. Published Online First. doi:10.1080/13557858.2017.1283393, http://www.tandfonline.com/eprint/AcDkqQNnX2snA4n6tMFw/full

Luszczynska, A., and R. Schwarzer. 2005. "Social Cognitive Theory: Research and Practice with Social Cognition Models." In *Predicting Health Behviour*, edited by M. Conner and P. Norman, 127–169. Maidenhead: Open University Press.

Markowitz, L. E., V. Tsu, S. L. Deeks, H. Cubie, S. A. Wang, A. S. Vicari, and J. M. Brotherton. 2012. "Human Papillomavirus Vaccine Introduction – The First Five Years." *Vaccine* 30 (10): F139–F148.

Marshall, H. S., P. Ryan, D. Roberton, and P. Baghurst. 2007. "A Cross-sectional Survey to Assess Community Attitudes to Introduction of Human Papillomavirus Vaccine." *Australian and New Zealand Journal of Public Health* 31 (3): 235–242.

Marshall, H. S., J. Collins, T. Sullivan, R. Tooher, M. O'Keefe, S. R. Skinner, M. Watson, T. Burgess, H. Ashmeade, and A. Braunack-Mayer. 2013. "Parental and Societal Support for Adolescent Immunization through School Based Immunization Programs." *Vaccine* 31 (30): 3059–3064.

National HPV Vaccination Program Register. 2016. "Coverage Data". Accessed January 18, 2017. http://www.hpvregister.org.au/research/coverage-data

Regan, D. G., D. J. Philp, J. S. Hocking, and M. G. Law. 2007. "Modelling the Population-level Impact of Vaccination on the Transmission of Human Papillomavirus Type 16 in Australia." *Sexual Health* 4 (3): 147–163.

Robinson, K. H., and C. Davies. 2017. "Sexuality Education in Early Childhood." In *Handbook of Sexuality Education*, edited by L. Allen and M. Rasmussen, 217–242. London: Palgrave.

Robinson, K. H. 2013. *Innocence, Knowledge and the Construction of Childhood: The Contradictory Nature of Sexuality and Censorship in Children's Contemporary Lives*. London: Routledge.

Robinson, K. H., and C. Davies. 2014. "Doing Sexuality Research with Children: Ethics, Theory, Methods and Practice." *Global Studies of Childhood* 4 (4): 250–263.

de Sanjosé, S., L. Alemany, J. Ordi, S. Tous, M. Alejo, S. M. Bigby, E. A. Joura, et al. 2013. "Worldwide Human Papillomavirus Genotype Attribution in over 2000 Cases of Intraepithelial and Invasive Lesions of the Vulva." *European Journal of Cancer* 49 (16): 3450–3461.

School Curriculum and Standards Authority. 2016. "Health and Physical Education: Year 8 Syllabus. School Curriculum and Standards Authority." Government of Western Australia. Accessed June 28. http://k10outline.scsa.wa.edu.au/home/p-10-curriculum/curriculum-browser/health-and-physical-education

Sibbald, B., and M. Roland. 1998. "Understanding Controlled Trials: Why Are Randomised Controlled Trials Important?" *British Medical Journal* 316: 201.

Skinner, S. R., C. Davies, S. Cooper, T. Stoney, H. Marshall, G. Zimet, D. Regan, et al. 2015a. "HPV.edu Study Protocol: A Cluster Randomised Controlled Evaluation of Education, Decisional Support and Logistical Strategies in School-based Human Papillomavirus (HPV) Vaccination of Adolescents." *BMC Public Health* 15 (1): 896.

Skinner, S. R., C. Davies, S. Cooper, T. Stoney, H. Marshall, J. Jones, J. Collins, et al. 2015b. "LB1.1 Randomised Controlled Trial of a Complex Intervention to Improve School-based HPV Vaccination for Adolescents: The HPV.edu Study." *Sexually Transmitted Infections* 91: A77. http://sti.bmj.com/content/91/Suppl_2/A77.1.abstract?sid=953e0699-b984-42e3-a59c-5b8620425003

Spratt, J., J. Shucksmith, K. Philip, and R. McNaughton. 2013. "Active Agents of Health Promotion? The School's Role in Supporting the HPV Vaccination Programme." *Sex Education* 13 (1): 82–95.

Strecher, V. J., and I. Rosenstock. 1997. "The Health Belief Model." In *Cambridge Handbook of Psychology, Health and Medicine*, edited by Andrew Baum, Stanton Newman, John Weinman, Robert West and Chris McManus, 113–116. Cambridge: Cambridge University Press.

Tabrizi, S., J. M. Brotherton, J. M. Kaldor, S. R. Skinner, E. Cummins, B. Liu, D. Bateson, K. McNamee, M. Garefalakis, and S. M. Garland. 2012. "Fall in Human Papillomavirus Prevalence following a National Vaccination Program." *Journal of Infectious Diseases* 206 (11): 1645–1651.

Trottier, H., and A. N. Burchell. 2009. "Epidemiology of mucosal human papillomavirus infection and associated diseases." *Public Health Genomics* 12 (5–6): 291–307.

Wight, D., C. Abraham, and S. Scott. 1998. "Towards a Psycho-social Theoretical Framework for Sexual Health Promotion." *Health Education Research* 13 (3): 317–330.

Wigle, J., Holly B. Fontenot, and G. D. Zimet. 2016. "Global Delivery of Human Papillomavirus Vaccines." *Pediatric Clinics of North America* 63: 81–95.

Teacher positivity towards gender diversity: exploring relationships and school outcomes for transgender and gender-diverse students

Jacqueline Ullman [iD]

ABSTRACT
Transgender and gender diverse secondary students report routine social and curricular marginalisation at school, factors which have been linked to negative social and academic outcomes. This paper examines data from the *Free2Be?* project, which surveyed 704 same-sex attracted and gender-diverse Australian teenagers (aged 14–18), to examine school gender climate as a potential stressor for the 51 (7%) students who identified as gender diverse. The paper focuses on these students' reports of their teachers' positivity regarding diverse gender expression, as a critical element of school gender climate. Multiple regression analyses revealed the significant predictive impact of teachers' positivity on gender diverse students' sense of connection to their school environment, highlighting the need for educators to be knowledgeable and affirming of gender diversity.

Introduction

During the months preceding the writing of this manuscript, the media uproar surrounding both a New South Wales secondary school's decision to screen *Gayby Baby*,[1] an Australian documentary depicting same-sex headed families and the *Safe Schools Coalition Australia* (*SSCA*),[2] an opt-in national programme containing lessons promoting awareness and acceptance of sexuality and gender diversity,[3] has driven home a critical message: Australian schools include such content at their peril. Most noteworthy, the negative media discourse surrounding the Safe Schools Coalition Australia positions lesson content designed to promote affirmation and inclusivity of gender diverse students as particularly 'radical' (Brown 2016; Donnelly 2016), driven by 'out there academic theory' rather than community or practical need, and positioned squarely in contrast to 'vanilla' (e.g. inoffensive, non-controversial) lessons on anti-homophobia (Brown 2016). When combined with a national curriculum which falls painfully short of articulating spaces for such inclusivity (Ferfolja and Ullman 2014; Ullman and Ferfolja 2015), it is no wonder that Australian teachers express concerns about whether, when and how to discuss sexuality and gender diversity with their students (Cumming-Potvin and Martino 2014; Smith et al. 2011). In consequence, many classrooms remain woefully silent on such topics (Mitchell et al. 2014). As might be suspected, inclusive content specifically related to gender diversity and the lived experiences of gender diverse individuals is the least likely to be included in the Australian classroom (Robinson et al. 2014; Ullman 2015a).

National trend data from across Australia shows that the reported experience of schooling for sexuality and gender diverse students has become worse rather than better over the last decade, with data from the *Writing Themselves In* series of studies (Hillier et al. 2010) as well as from my own series of two national studies (Ullman 2015a, 2015b) showing increased rates of school-based harassment for sexuality and gender diverse students. While the visibility of such students may be on the rise (Hillier et al. 2010), Australian gender diverse secondary students appear to experience a more marginalising secondary schooling environment, reporting higher levels of school-based harassment when compared to their same-sex attracted, cisgender peers (Jones and Hillier 2013). Much has been written about the ways in which a negative school climate[4] towards sexuality and gender diversity impacts the social and academic outcomes for sexuality and gender diverse students (Kosciw et al. 2013; Ullman 2015b); however, much remains unknown about the mechanisms by which these various environmental stressors and supports translate into school-based well-being, attitudes and identities for this cohort and the best means by which compassionate educators and school leaders might transform their school climate.

Research has consistently shown that the presence of a supportive school-based adult serves as a protective factor for broad-based populations of adolescents and children, and this element of school climate has been found to be positively associated with motivational and academic outcomes (Wentzel 2009). These findings have been further replicated with populations of sexuality and gender diverse students (Goodenow, Szalacha, and Westheimer 2006; Kosciw et al. 2013; Ullman 2015b), underscoring the importance of school staff members who are viewed as inclusive and affirming of sexuality and gender diversity. While formal curricular and content restrictions may present challenges to the manner by which such inclusivity is expressed during classroom lessons in some schooling environments, teachers' overt communication of their support via positivity toward their sexuality and gender diverse students, and to related topics more generally, is an element of school climate less subject to external regulation.

Given Australian media framing which positions fluidity of gender expression and transgender topics as too radical and inappropriate for the K-12 schooling context, and a dearth of content addressing gender diversity, fluidity and non-binary gender expression within the Australian national curriculum, this paper seeks to explore the schooling experiences of a small cohort of 51 gender diverse students (14–18 years old) from across Australia to investigate their reported school climate with regard to sexuality and gender diversity. Of specific interest are reports of teachers' positivity regarding gender diversity and the relationship between this element of perceived teacher emotional support – viewed here as especially poignant for gender diverse students – and these students' school well-being.

Background

Australian sexuality and gender diverse students report routine social isolation and marginalisation in the secondary school setting, perpetrated by both peers and school staff (Hillier et al. 2010; Robinson et al. 2014; Ullman 2015b). An examination of relevant research from both Australian and US contexts highlights that these experiences are not only linked to a lowered sense of school belonging and connection to school (Pearson, Muller, and Wilkinson 2007), but also to diminished educational outcomes, including safety fears (Hillier, Turner, and Mitchell 2005), higher rates of absenteeism (Poteat and Espelage 2007), difficulty concentrating at school (Blackburn 2012), lower academic self-concept (Ullman 2015b) and lower academic achievement (Kosciw et al. 2013).

School climate concerns appear to be compounded for gender diverse young people. In their 2013 National School Climate Survey of students across the USA, Kosciw et al. (2014) found that, compared to same-sex attracted, cisgender students, those students who identified as transgender, genderqueer or 'another gender', faced the most hostile school climates. These young people were more likely to report having experienced harassment or physical assault related to their gender expression or (perceived) sexual orientation and less likely to report feeling safe at school (Kosciw et al. 2014).

In the Australian context, findings from the latest iteration of the *Writing Themselves In* series of studies (Jones and Hillier 2013) found that, for students who had disclosed their sexuality and/or gender diversity to one of their teachers (*n* = 1141), gender diverse young people were significantly more likely to report being rejected by that teacher than same-sex attracted, cisgender young people (38% vs. 10% reporting subsequent rejection). Furthermore, across every measure of school outcomes (e.g. impact on grades, attendance, concentration, etc.) gender diverse young people reported significantly higher proportions of negative impact of school-based victimisation than their same-sex attracted, cisgender peers (Jones and Hillier 2013). Such findings echo these authors' earlier findings, wherein gender diverse young people were more likely than their same-sex attracted, cisgender peers to report feeling unsafe at school, experience difficulties concentrating in class, report lower marks, missing or dropping out of school, and hiding from classmates (Hillier et al. 2010).

School climate and connection to teachers and school

While historically, research into the lived experiences of sexuality and gender-diverse young people tended to focus on the frequency of various negative behavioural or mental health outcomes (e.g. drug/alcohol abuse, suicide ideation) (D'Augelli, Pilkington, and Hershberger 2002; Schwartzkoff et al. 2003), more current explorations have turned their focus to an examination of the schooling environments themselves. Such research has sought a better understanding of how elements of school climate towards sexuality and gender diversity function as protective factors and/or as social and psychological stressors for sexuality and gender diverse students as they navigate through their K-12 schooling experiences. Inherent in such explorations is the desire to understand how school staff, curriculum designers and state/federal education policy-makers might be held accountable for their role in sexuality and gender diverse students' outcomes and how curricular, policy and pedagogical changes might positively impact the schooling experience.

Numerous recent studies have explored the relationship of a positive school climate which is inclusive and affirming of sexuality and gender diversity to sexuality and gender diverse students' sense of school safety. An overview of this work has highlighted the positive impact of a supportive peer group (D'Augelli 2003), an inclusive curriculum (Kosciw et al. 2012; Snapp et al. 2015) and a visible, active gay–straight alliance (Toomey et al. 2011), on sexuality and gender diverse students' sense of safety and a reduction in bias-based victimisation.

However, feeling safe at school is, perhaps, the bare minimum of what sexuality and gender diverse students should be able to expect from the adults entrusted with their care. We might imagine that most educators strive to promote their students' sense of connection and school belonging in efforts to enhance their students' learning motivation. This sense of caring and effort that teachers invest to connect with their students, a concept referred to by Wentzel (2009, 304) as 'perceptions of positive emotional support from teachers', has been the subject of a great deal of research within the field of educational psychology. Numerous studies have highlighted the impact of perceived teacher emotional support, empathy and connection – the perception that teachers and other school staff members are invested in one's well-being and academic outcomes – on students' sense of connection to school, their learning motivation and, ultimately, their academic success (Goodenow and Grady 1993; Roeser, Eccles, and Sameroff 2000; Wentzel 2009).

In the light of school climate research which has specifically implicated teachers in the construction of marginalising schooling environments for sexuality and gender diverse youth, through the avoidance of inclusive content, failure to intervene during homophobic/transphobic incidents at school – or worse, active participation in these instances (Sausa 2005; Ullman 2014), recent research has sought to isolate and explore perceived teacher emotional support as a critical element of school climate. In a landmark study, Murdock and Bolch's (2005) investigation of the schooling experiences of 101 lesbian-, gay- and bisexual-identifying students reported perceived teacher support to be positively, significantly correlated with students' sense of school belonging as well as their academic outcomes. Furthermore, their cluster analysis highlighted the protective impact of perceived teacher support finding that, even in schools with high levels of reported victimisation of same-sex attracted students, students with a sense of teacher support remained connected to the schooling environment and reported higher academic outcomes. Such findings were echoed in work by Goodenow, Szalacha, and Westheimer (2006), who found that lesbian-, gay- and bisexual-identifying students who were able to distinguish a school staff member whom they could talk to were 'about one third as likely as those without such perceived support to report being threatened' (580).

More recently, in their regression model predicting school engagement – measured as students' sense of belonging, productivity and educational aspiration – Seelman et al. (2015) found that the presence of 'safe adults' (e.g. school staff members with whom students might discuss their sexuality and/or gender diversity) predicted sexuality and gender diverse students' reported school engagement. They concluded:

> Such a finding reflects how personal relationships *matter* for LGBTQ [lesbian, gay, bisexual, transgender and queer] students – adults who communicate an openness, rather than hostility, about LGBTQ students contribute to the overall high school climate for this population. Having access to a safe adult is not just about increasing a students' comfort; since school engagement is theorised to play an important role in mediating the connection between school context and academic outcomes, safe adults could help contribute to the pathway between school engagement and stronger school performance for these students … .(26)

Connection to teachers and school for gender diverse students

Given what is known about the reported school climate for gender diverse students, particularly regarding the silences and misinformation that surround gender diversity and non-binary gender expression, it stands to reason that these students' sense of teacher care and connection plays an equally critical role in their overall school well-being. In recent years, we have begun to see such cohort-specific analyses. In their examination of 295 transgender-identified young people who participated in GLSEN's 2007 *National School Climate Survey*, Greytak, Kosciw, and Diaz (2009) noted that transgender students reported both higher levels of school-based victimisation and lower reported school belonging than same-sex attracted, cisgender students in their sample. Critically, transgender students in their sample who reported that they were able to talk about sexuality and/or gender diversity at school, either through raising such topics in class with an accepting teacher or speaking about them with a school staff member, were more likely to feel a sense of connection and belonging at school (Greytak, Kosciw, and Diaz 2009).

Likewise, when compared to a general population of cisgender students ($n = 2192$) in their sample of California secondary students, transgender students ($n = 68$) reported a significantly poorer school climate across multiple measures including classmates' use of transphobic comments and LGBT-inclusive curriculum (McGuire et al. 2010). Most notably, when a measure of transgender students' sense of personal connection to an adult at their school was added to the authors' regression model predicting students' reported school safety, not only was the variable a significant predictor, its addition rendered other protective school factors insignificant. A subsequent structural model confirmed the mediating impact of this key element of school climate for their sample; in other words, school protective factors were related to students' feelings of safety but only indirectly, through students' reported sense of connection to their teachers and other school staff members (McGuire et al. 2010).

Research with Australian cohorts of gender diverse young people has produced similar findings. In a recent survey of 189 gender diverse and transgender-identifying young people aged 14–25, young people who reported receiving no support from their teachers were over four times as likely to leave school (Jones et al. 2016). Furthermore, young people reporting that their teachers' use of pronouns or names was 'mostly inappropriate', likely straining the teacher/student relationship, were less able to concentrate during classes and more likely to report a drop in grades or leaving school entirely (Jones et al. 2016).

While research from the Australian context has investigated the schooling experiences of gender diverse young people using an array of methodological approaches, to date no quantitative research has interrogated the predictive value of gender diverse students' perceptions of their teachers' positivity toward diversity of gender expression on their sense of school connection more broadly. Given what is known about the teacher/student relationship and its relevance to students' identification with the school domain, coupled with the various ways this relationship might be challenged for gender diverse students as a result of their teachers' framing of gender, such an investigation would aid in efforts to improve the schooling environment for this cohort of young people.

Theoretical framework

This work sits at a point of convergence of social constructionism and poststructuralism; it acknowledges the ways in which the institutional structure of schooling, replete with myriad social interactions and power differentials, constructs masculinities/femininities while also recognising gender as performative and the critical influence of discourse, particularly in the schooling environment. Accordingly, this paper begins from the premise that schools participate as active sociocultural agents in the marginalisation of sexuality and gender diverse young people, in line with Kehily (2002) who views schools as 'sites for the *production* of gendered/sexualised identities' (50, emphasis in original) through peer culture, formal and informal curricula and associated pedagogical practices.

For many children and young adults, an unwillingness or inability to perform one's gender 'correctly' results in social stigma and associated victimisation, as gender is governed by 'clearly punitive and regulatory social conventions' (Butler 1988, 527). Nowhere is this more obvious than in the school setting, where schools systemically enforce this 'gender regime' through their formal and informal dress codes, the defining of certain curriculum areas as masculine and feminine (Connell 1996), the social regulation of acceptable gender performance (Martino 2000), and a 'cultural script' (Robinson 2005, 27) based on 'compulsory heterosexuality' (Rich 1980/1993) – the enactment of which lies at the heart of school-based marginalisation of sexuality and gender diverse young people (Ullman 2014; Youdell 2004).

While, historically, the concept of school climate has been used to investigate the ways in which schools both affirm and marginalise lesbian, gay and bisexual subjectivities, the use of school *gender climate,* as a both a theoretical concept and measurable construct, seeks to explicitly acknowledge the norms and values communicated to students about the boundaries of acceptable gender expression and is viewed as the essence of school-based homophobia and transphobia. Gender climate encompasses the official (e.g. organisationally enforced) and unofficial (e.g. socially enforced) policing of students' physical appearance, contingent on their assumed biological sex; the hidden curriculum of 'gendered' areas of study; and both the academic and social rewards and punishments linked to students' gender expression (Ullman 2014).

For gender diverse students, the cisnormative policing that characterises gender climate in many schooling environments can take the form of teachers' use of birth names and/or birth gender rather than students' preferred/affirmed names, gender and pronouns (Grossman and D'augelli 2006; Jones et al. 2016) as well as the overt victim-blaming of gender diverse youth who have been subjected to school-based harassment (Sausa 2005; Ullman 2015b). For instance, in a recent survey of 189 gender diverse young people (14–19) in Australia, one quarter of participants (and half of all participants who had attended Christian schools) avoided school because they could not 'conform to the gender stereotypes dominant within those contexts' (Jones et al. 2016, 163).

Thus, while a focus on anti-homophobia education within Australian national curriculum (ACARA 2014) is perhaps a move in the right direction with regard to school climate, schools' failure to acknowledge gender climate as a critical element of homophobic marginalisation, to recognise and examine of the social construction of gender norms, or to problematise the institutionalised boundaries of acceptable gender presentation in the schooling environment stands as a tacit endorsement of a heteronormative, cisnormative *'natural* order of gender appropriate behaviour' (Harry 1992, 166; with emphasis added).

Methods

In order to better understand how the Australian school climate might impact school wellbeing for gender diverse young people, this paper draws on findings from the *Free2Be?* national survey of sexuality and gender diverse students from across Australia ($N = 704$; see Ullman 2015b for the full report and explanation of the research design). The online questionnaire sought students' accounts of their teachers' and classmates' treatment of sexuality and gender diversity, in terms of curricular and social inclusivity and/or marginalisation. Measures included original items investigating the construct of gender climate; specifically, a three-item subscale (Cronbach's alpha = 0.78; 0.84 for the full sample) of this construct examined perceived teacher positivity with regard to diversity of gender expression and sexuality (Table 1).

Furthermore, participants were asked to report on their sense of school well-being, connection, safety and select academic outcomes using scale measures from the previously validated *Attitudes Towards School Survey* (DEECD Victoria 2006) employed in secondary schools across the Australian state of Victoria (see Table 2). As academic self-concept has been shown to have a reciprocal relationship with students' actual academic achievement (Valentine, DuBois, and Cooper 2004) and has been previously linked to reported school climate for sexuality and gender diverse students (Ullman 2015a), a well-established measure of this construct was also included. The 8-item general academic self-concept scale from the *Academic Self-Description Questionnaire II* (Marsh 1990) was used as an additional measure

Table 1. Three-item gender climate subscale reliability: teacher positivity.

Item	Cronbach's alpha (α) if item deleted	Scale Cronbach's alpha (α)
'My teachers say that it's ok for people to express their gender in different ways'.	$\alpha = 0.722$	$\alpha = 0.779$
'In my school, if someone made fun of me about the way I express my gender, the teachers would defend me'.	$\alpha = 0.708$	
'In my school, teachers talk about same-sex attraction (lesbian, gay or bisexual people or topics) in a positive way'.	$\alpha = 0.672$	

Notes: NB: Items measured on a 9-point Likert scale, ranging from 'definitely true' (9) to 'definitely false' (1). Scale Mean = 4.78; SD = 2.25, N = 51.

Table 2. Descriptive statistics and Pearson's product moment correlations for teacher positivity scale with selected student well-being and academic outcome measures.

		Teacher positivity scale
Scales from the *ATSS* (DEECD Victoria 2006); $n = 51$		
School Morale, 5-item scale[a]	$M = 3.39$	$r = 0.62$***
Sample item: 'I feel happy at school'	$SD = 1.39$	
School Distress, 6-item scale[a]	$M = 4.86$	$r = -0.56$***
Sample item: 'I feel tense at school'	$SD = 1.45$	
Teacher Empathy, 7-item scale[b]	$M = 3.30$	$r = 0.52$***
Sample item: 'My teachers listen to what I have to say'	$SD = 0.86$	
School Connection, 5-item scale[b]	$M = 2.80$	$r = 0.58$***
Sample item: 'I feel I belong at this school'	$SD = 1.16$	
Student Safety, 5-item scale[b]	$M = 2.90$	$r = -0.36$**
Sample item: 'I have been bullied recently at this school'	$SD = 1.09$	
Learning Confidence, 4-item scale[b]	$M = 3.56$	$r = 0.45$***
Sample item: 'I find it easy to learn new things'	$SD = 0.78$	
Student Motivation, 4-item scale[b]	$M = 3.81$;	$r = 0.35$**
Sample item: 'I try very hard in school'	$SD = 1.01$	
Scale from the *ASDQII* (Marsh 1990); $n = 46$		
Academic Self-Concept, 8-item scale[c]	$M = 4.51$;	$r = 0.41$*
Sample item: 'I have always done well in most school subjects'	$SD = 1.47$	

Notes: Negatively worded scales [e.g. School Distress & Student Safety] show a negative correlation with teacher positivity.
[a]Measured on 7-point Likert scale. [b]Measured on 5-point Likert scale. [c]Measured on 8-point Likert scale. *$p \leq 0.05$; **$p \leq 0.01$; ***$p \leq 0.001$.

of academic outcomes.[5] All analysis was conducted using the Statistical Package for the Social Sciences (SPSS).

Participants

Participants were recruited using targeted advertising on social media (Facebook), where the recruitment post was specifically shown to Australian teens between the ages of 14–18 years who had either (a) indicated that they were 'interested in' people of the same reported biological sex or (b) indicated interest in lesbian, gay, bisexual, transgender or intersex-related topics, as evidenced by page 'likes' on Facebook. According to Facebook tracking, the recruitment statement was posted on 37,568 individual Facebook pages with 1292 young people clicking through to commence the survey (3.4% response rate). Of these, final numbers were reduced to 704 usable survey participants. Gender diverse participants ($n = 51$; 7% of the sample) were identified using their response to a single item ('What is your gender?') which included a 'genderqueer or transgender' response category. This participant group ranged in age from 14 to 18, as per the larger sample, with the majority of these young people aged 15 ($n = 15$), 16 ($n = 12$) and 17 ($n = 15$). Outcomes for this participant cohort were examined using bivariate analyses (e.g. t-tests, correlations, chi-squares) and multivariate analysis (linear regression).

Participants in this group identified with a range of gender identities, including transgender female-to-male ($n = 16$); transgender male-to-female ($n = 7$) and an array of participant-identified identities including, genderqueer ($n = 6$); agender ($n = 4$); genderneutral ($n = 3$); and gender-fluid ($n = 2$). The majority (61%, $n = 31$) expressed physical attraction to members of both sexes and identified as pansexual (41%, $n = 21$). Participants came from every Australian state/territory except the Northern Territory, with a postcode analysis showing the majority as being from major urban centres (75%, $n = 38$). Eighty-tow per cent of participants' ($n = 42$) first language was English with 80% ($n = 41$) of participants born in Australia. Two participants identified as Aboriginal or Torres Strait Islander.

Results

Transphobia and teacher positivity

Transphobic language was defined in the survey as: 'negative phrases or terms to describe people who are genderqueer, gender ambiguous or identify as transgender', with examples provided such as calling someone 'it' or forcing someone to define/demonstrate their biological sex. Gender diverse students in the sample were significantly more likely than same-sex attracted, cisgender students to report having heard transphobic language at school from their peers ($x^2_{(1, 669)} = 19.49, p < 0.001$); 88% of gender diverse students had heard transphobic language at school, compared to 57% of their cisgender peers. Students who had heard transphobic language at school were also asked to report on its frequency in the month preceding the survey, with gender diverse students reporting a significantly higher frequency of such language ($t_{(413)} = 2.11, p = 0.04$; mean difference 0.35 on a 4-point Likert scale). Of those students who reported hearing transphobic language at school, nearly 67% of the gender diverse student cohort reported such language on a weekly basis[6] compared to 43.8% of the same-sex attracted, cisgender sample.

Gender diverse students were significantly less likely than same-sex attracted, cisgender students to report that their teachers were 'openly positive about gender a-typicality or supportive of genderqueer or transgender people' in a single, standalone item ($t_{(702)} = 1.98$, $p = 0.05$; mean difference 0.34 on a 5-point Likert scale), with 43% of gender diverse students reporting that their teachers were 'never' positive, compared to 28% of their peers. Furthermore, an examination of the teacher positivity subscale as reported in Table 1 showed that gender diverse students were somewhat less likely to describe their teachers as inclusive or positive ($M = 4.78$; SD = 2.30 for cisgender students compared to $M = 4.20$; SD = 2.13 for gender diverse students), although this difference was not large enough so as to be statistically significant. Collapsing this scale further into measures of high, medium and low reports of teacher positivity revealed that, while same-sex attracted, cisgender students reported an array of experiences, with near-equal proportions indicating high/low positivity, gender diverse students' responses were negatively skewed, with almost double the number of students reporting low levels of teacher positivity than high.

Teacher positivity and student outcomes

Given gender diverse students' lower reports of teacher positivity regarding diversity of gender, correlational analyses were conducted to understand the degree to which this element of the teacher/student relationship might be related to measures of school well-being and academic outcomes. Analysis revealed teachers' reported positivity regarding diversity of gender and sexuality, as measured by the 3-item *teacher positivity* subscale, to be significantly associated with each of these measures, as shown in Table 2. The strength of these correlations is of interest, particularly for measures of students' personal school well-being and belonging (e.g. morale, distress, school connection).

In order to further investigate the role of teacher positivity with regard to diverse gender expression and sexuality, a multiple regression analysis of gender diverse students' sense of school connection was conducted, with the 3-item teacher positivity scale included as a key predictor of interest. Students' sense of school connection was positioned as the dependent variable of interest given its previously recognised links to sexuality and gender diverse students' academic outcomes (Pearson, Muller, and Wilkinson 2007; Ullman 2015a). Furthermore, as this outcome variable is also clearly linked to student reports of their school safety as a key indicator of school-climate (Kosciw et al. 2013), it was deemed important to include school safety as an independent variable in order to determine the predictive abilities of teachers' positivity on school connection above and beyond the influence of school safety. Age, location of school (urban vs. regional/rural), school type (public school; private-Catholic; and private-independent[7]) and SES, as measured by parents' education as a proxy indicator (Lim and Gemici 2011) were included as Step 1 of the regression model as control variables, but are not depicted below for simplicity of reporting.

Table 3 summarises the results of the hierarchical regression analyses for each of the two key independent variables. Predictors were included in the model using the Enter method, and diagnostic tests concluded that all relevant measurement assumptions related to multicollinearity, homoscedasticity and independence were met. Step 2 shows that school safety was indeed a significant predictor of gender diverse students' reported school connection, above and beyond their location, school type, SES or age, explaining 31% of the total adjusted variance. In line with results reported above, the addition of the 3-item measure of gender

GENDER AND SEXUALITY IN EDUCATION AND HEALTH

Table 3. Regression of school-climate variables on reported school connection for gender diverse students.

School-climate predictors		School connection (5-item scale)			
		B	SE_B	Beta (β)	p-value
Step 2	Adj. $\Delta R^2 = 0.17$**				
	$F(5, 30) = 4.14$				
School safety		−0.52	0.18	−0.48	$p = 0.006$
Step 3	Adj. $\Delta R^2 = 0.22$***				
	$F(6, 29) = 7.54$				
School safety		−0.38	0.15	−0.35	$p = 0.018$
Teacher positivity		0.28	0.07	0.53	$p = 0.001$

Notes: $N = 51$; Controls for participants' age, location (urban/regional/rural), school type (government/Catholic/independent), SES were included in the analysis as Step 1 but are not depicted here.
Adj. $R^2 = 0.31$ for Step 2, Adj. $R^2 = 0.53$ for Step 3.
**$p < 0.01$; ***$p < 0.001$.

diverse students' reported teacher positivity in Step 3 explained another 22% of the total variance in their sense of school connection.

Discussion

The findings presented here provide critical insights into the schooling experience of gender diverse students in Australia. Comparisons between gender diverse participants and their same-sex attracted, cisgender peers point to gender diverse students' heightened awareness of transphobic language and their sense of a more hostile school climate with regard to diversity of gender. It stands to reason that gender diverse students' higher reported frequency of transphobic language may be related to their being positioned as the target of such language and/or such language being used specifically in their presence. Gender diverse students' more discerning sense of their teachers' inclusivity and/or reinforcement of a traditional gender binary are noteworthy here, pointing to their attentiveness to the portrayal of transgender and gender diverse individuals more generally and likely reflective of their personal investment in a positive depiction of such topics and subjectivities.

Findings further highlight the relationship of perceived teacher positivity regarding diversity of gender expression and an array of school well-being outcomes for gender diverse students. It is noteworthy, and consistent with previous literature (Ullman 2015a), that sexuality and gender diverse students who report having teachers who are positive and supportive of such diversity also report higher academic self-concept and being more confident and motivated learners, with the opposite relationship also apparent. Of greatest interest is the strength of the correlation between gender diverse students' reports of teacher positivity and their sense of school-based morale and distress; given that nearly 70% of young people reported that their teachers were 'never' or 'hardly ever' positive about gender diversity on the stand-alone item, this relationship appears to depict a culture of classroom invisibility and social stressors for gender diverse students. Most worrisome, given the high percentage of total variance of students' reported school connection explained by teacher positivity regarding diversity of gender expression and sexuality, this research underscores the criticality of gender diverse students having access to school staff members who are trained, knowledgeable, administratively supported, and unafraid to normalise diversity of gender expression and discuss the ways that gender performance is learned and socially constructed.

This work highlights the need for a better understanding of the ways in which teachers are implicated in gender diverse students' sense of school connection and what can be done to strengthen the teacher/student relationship. Findings echo current Australian research pointing to the need for additional teacher training to support their intervention during instances of homophobic and transphobic verbal and physical harassment (Hillier et al. 2010; Robinson et al. 2014); however such a focus does not appear to be sufficient. While it is long known that gender stereotypes are damaging to mainstream populations of young people (Watt and Eccles 2008), comparatively little empirical work has sought to understand the social and psychological mechanisms by which teachers' attitudes toward gender expression – notions of gender essentialism and/or gender construction and fluidity – effect the school-based well-being of gender diverse and sexuality diverse young people. The work presented here is but a small contribution to a field which requires significantly more attention to safeguard the educational trajectories of all students.

Limitations

It is important to note that, as with most other research focusing on sexuality and gender diverse young people, this study relied on a self-selecting, convenience sample. This, combined with the cross-sectional nature of the data, means that the true causality of the relationships depicted here cannot be established. Furthermore, the small sample size of gender diverse participants imposed some restrictions on multivariate analyses, making further statistical modelling of direct and indirect effects of teacher positivity unreliable.

Notes

1. http://thegaybyproject.com/.
2. http://www.safeschoolscoalition.org.au/.
3. The term 'sexuality and gender diversity' is used throughout to denote individuals (and, in the context of school-based learning, associated topics) who may be sometimes referred to as lesbian, gay, bisexual, transgender, queer and intersex (LGBTQI). Additionally, and most importantly, this term also foregrounds movements, particularly in the youth sector, away from naming or labelling one's sexuality and/or gender diversity while simultaneously seeking to capture those identities not represented by the LGBTQI acronym (e.g. pansexual, genderfluid, agender, demisexual, bigender, etc.).
4. The term *school climate*, in general, refers to the 'quality and character of school life as it relates to norms and values, interpersonal relations and social interactions, and organisational processes and structures and … is predictive of students' ability to learn and develop in healthy ways' (http://www.schoolclimate.org/climate/faq.php). The phrase *school climate with regards to sexuality and gender diversity* captures this same concept as specifically related to school-based norms and values related to gender expression and sexual orientation.
5. See Ullman (2015b) for a full-description of these scales, including reliability scores for the full participant cohort.
6. Frequencies for the following three Likert-scale responses were collapsed to indicate an overall weekly reported frequency: 'Almost every day', 'Several times per week', 'Once or twice per week'.
7. These categories are aligned with the major typologies of Australian secondary schools.

Acknowledgements

I would like to acknowledge Hua Zhong who served this project as a Research Assistant. I would also like to acknowledge Jawed Gabriel, Research Officer with the Centre for Educational Research (Western Sydney University), who assisted with the preparation of the manuscript.

Disclosure statement

No potential conflict of interest was reported by the author.

Funding

This work was generously funded by a grant from Western Sydney University.

ORCID

Jacqueline Ullman (iD) http://orcid.org/0000-0002-6999-423X

References

ACARA (Australian Curriculum, Assessment and Reporting Authority). 2014. *The Australian Curriculum: Health and Physical Education, Foundation to Year 10.* http://www.australiancurriculum.edu.au/healthandphysicaleducation/Curriculum/F-10

Blackburn, Mollie. 2012. *Interrupting Hate: Homophobia in Schools and What Literacy Can Do about It.* New York: Teachers College Press.

Brown, Greg. 2016. "Safe Schools Program Hijacked, Says Gay Activist." *The Australian*, June 2. http://www.theaustralian.com.au/national-affairs/state-politics/safe-schools-program-hijacked-says-gay-activist/news-story/596ffa70bf88afb8756e8dae3c894430

Butler, Judith. 1988. "Performative Acts and Gender Constitution." *Theatre Journal* 40 (4): 519–531.

Connell, R. W. 1996. "Teaching the Boys: New Research on Masculinity and Gender Strategies for Schools." *Teachers College Record* 98 (2): 206–235.

Cumming-Potvin, Wendy, and Wayne Martino. 2014. "Teaching about Queer Families: Surveillance, Censorship, and the Schooling of Sexualities." *Teaching Education* 25 (3): 309–333.

D'Augelli, Anthony R. 2003. "Lesbian and Bisexual Female Youths Aged 14 to 21: Developmental Challenges and Victimization Experiences." *Journal of Lesbian Studies* 7: 9–29.

D'Augelli, Anthony R., Neil W. Pilkington, and Scott L. Hershberger. 2002. "Incidence and Mental Health Impact of Sexual Orientation Victimization of Lesbian, Gay, and Bisexual Youths in High School." *School Psychology Quarterly* 17 (2): 148–167.

DEECD Victoria (Department of Education and Early Childhood Development). 2006. *Attitudes towards School Survey*. Melbourne: DEECD Victoria.

Donnelly, Kevin. 2016. "Safe Schools Coalition is More about LGBTI Advocacy than Making Schools Safer." *The Age*, February 11. http://www.theage.com.au/comment/government-and-teacher-union-hypocrisy-as-lgbti-agenda-plugged-in-schools-20160208-gmp18 h.html

Ferfolja, Tania, and Jacqueline Ullman. 2014. "Opportunity Lost or (Re) Written out: LGBTI Content in Australia's New National Health and Physical Education Curriculum." In *Contemporary Issues of Equity in Education*, edited by Margaret Somerville and Susanne Gannon, 69–87. London: Cambridge Scholars.

Goodenow, Carol, and Kathleen E. Grady. 1993. "The Relationship of School Belonging and Friends' Values to Academic Motivation among Urban Adolescent Students." *Journal of Experimental Education* 62 (1): 60–71.

Goodenow, Carol, Laura Szalacha, and Kim Westheimer. 2006. "School Support Groups, Other School Factors, and the Safety of Sexual Minority Adolescents." *Psychology in the Schools* 43 (5): 573–589.

Greytak, Emily A., Joseph G. Kosciw, and Elizabeth M. Diaz. 2009. *Harsh Realities: The Experiences of Transgender Youth in Our Nation's Schools*. New York: GLSEN.

Grossman, Arnold H., and Anthony R. D'augelli. 2006. "Transgender Youth: Invisible and Vulnerable." *Journal of Homosexuality* 51: 111–128.

Harry, Joseph. 1992. "Conceptualising Anti-gay Violence." In *Hate Crimes: Confronting Violence against Lesbians and Gay Men*, edited by Gregory M. Herek and Kevin T. Berrill, 113–122. Newbury Park, CA: SAGE.

Hillier, Lynne, Tiffany Jones, Marisa Monagle, Naomi Overton, Luke Gahan, Jennifer Blackman, and Anne Mitchell. 2010. *Writing Themselves in 3 (WTi3): The Third National Study on the Sexual Health and Wellbeing of Same Sex Attracted and Gender Questioning Young People*. Melbourne: Australian Research Centre in Sex, Health and Society, La Trobe University.

Hillier, Lyne, Alina Turner, and Anne Mitchell. 2005. *Writing Themselves in Again: 6 Years on: The Second National Report on the Sexuality, Health and Well-being of Same Sex Attracted Young People in Australia*, Monograph Series No. 50. Melbourne: Australian Research Centre in Sex, Health and Society, La Trobe University.

Jones, Tiffany, and Lynne Hillier. 2013. "Comparing Trans-spectrum and Samesex- Attracted Youth in Australia: Increased Risks, Increased Activisms." *Journal of LGBT Youth* 10 (4): 287–307.

Jones, Tiffany, Elizabeth Smith, Roz Ward, Jennifer Dixon, Lynne Hillier, and Anne Mitchell. 2016. "School Experiences of Transgender and Gender Diverse Students in Australia." *Sex Education* 16 (2): 156–171.

Kehily, Mary. 2002. *Sexuality, Gender and Schooling: Shifting Agendas in Social Learning*. London: Routledge.

Kosciw, Joseph G., Emily A. Greytak, Mark J. Bartkiewicz, Madelyn J. Boesen, and Neal A. Palmer. 2012. *The 2011 National School Climate Survey: The Experiences of Lesbian, Gay, Bisexual and Transgender Youth in Our Nation's Schools*. New York: GLSEN.

Kosciw, Joseph G., Emily A. Greytak, Neal A. Palmer, and Madelyn J. Boesen. 2014. *The 2013 National School Climate Survey: The Experiences of Lesbian, Gay, Bisexual and Transgender Youth in Our Nation's Schools*. New York: GLSEN.

Kosciw, Joseph G., Neal A. Palmer, Ryan M. Kull, and Emily A. Greytak. 2013. "The Effect of Negative School Climate on Academic Outcomes for LGBT Youth and the Role of In-school Supports." *Journal of School Violence* 12 (1): 45–63.

Lim, Patrick, and Sinan Gemici. 2011. *Measuring the Socioeconomic Status of Australian Youth*. Adelaide: National Centre for Vocational Education Research.

Marsh, Herbert W. 1990. "The Structure of Academic Self-concept: The Marsh/Shavelson Model." *Journal of Educational Psychology* 82 (4): 623–636.

Martino, Wayne. 2000. "Policing Masculinities: Investigating the Role of Homophobia and Heteronormativity in the Lives of Adolescent School Boys." *The Journal of Men's Studies* 8 (2): 213–236.

McGuire, Jenifer K., Charles R. Anderson, Russell B. Toomey, and Stephen T. Russell. 2010. "School Climate for Transgender Youth: A Mixed Method Investigation of Student Experiences and School Responses." *Journal of Youth and Adolescence* 39: 1175–1188.

Mitchell, Anne, Kent Patrick, Wendy Heywood, Pamela Blackman, and Marian Pitts. 2014. *5th National Survey of Australian Secondary Students and Sexual Health 2013*, ARCSHS Monograph Series No. 97. Melbourne: Australian Research Centre in Sex, Health and Society, La Trobe University.

Murdock, Tamera B., and Megan B. Bolch. 2005. "Risk and Protective Factors for Poor School Adjustment in Lesbian, Gay, and Bisexual (LGB) High School Youth: Variable and Person-centered Analyses." *Psychology in the Schools* 42 (2): 159–172.

Pearson, Jennifer, Chandra Muller, and Lindsey Wilkinson. 2007. "Adolescent Same-sex Attraction and Academic Outcomes: The Role of School Attachment and Engagement." *Social Problems* 54 (4): 523–542.

Poteat, V. Paul, and Dorothy L. Espelage. 2007. "Predicting Psychosocial Consequences of Homophobic Victimization in Middle School Students." *Journal of Early Adolescence* 27: 175–191.

Rich, Adrienne. 1980/1993. "Compulsory Heterosexuality and Lesbian Existence." In *The Lesbian and Gay Studies Reader*, edited by Henry Abelove, Michele Aina Barale, and David M. Halperin, 227–254. New York: Routledge.

Robinson, Kerry H. 2005. "Reinforcing Hegemonic Masculinities through Sexual Harassment: Issues of Identity, Power and Popularity in Secondary Schools." *Gender and Education* 17 (1): 19–37.

Robinson, Kerry H., Peter Bansel, Nida Denson, Georgia Ovenden, and Cristyn Davies. 2014. *Growing up Queer: Issues Facing Young Australians Who Are Gender Variant and Sexuality Diverse*. Melbourne: Young and Well Cooperative Research Centre.

Roeser, Robert W., Jacquelynne S. Eccles, and Arnold J. Sameroff. 2000. "School as a Context of Early Adolescents' Development: A Summary of Research Findings." *Elementary School Journal* 100: 443–471.

Sausa, Lydia A. 2005. "Translating Research into Practice: Trans Youth Recommendations for Improving School Systems." *Journal of LGBT Youth* 3 (1): 15–29.

Schwartzkoff, J., A. Wilczynski, S. Ross, J. Smith, G. Mason, D. Thomas, and B. Nicholson. 2003. " 'You Shouldn't Have to Hide to Be Safe': Homophobic Hostilities and Violence against Gay Men and Lesbians in New South Wales." Report Prepared by Urbis Keys Young for the Crime Prevention Division. Sydney: New South Wales Attorney General's Department.

Seelman, Kristie, N. Nicholas Forge, Eugene Walls, and Nadine Bridges. 2015. "School Engagement among LGBTQ High School Students: The Roles of Safe Adults and Gay-Straight Alliance Characteristics." *Children and Youth Services Review* 57: 19–29.

Smith, Anthony, Marisa Schlichthorst, Anne Mitchell, Jenny Walsh, Anthony Lyons, Pam Blackman, and Marian Pitts. 2011. *Sexuality Education in Australian Secondary Schools 2010* [Monograph Series No. 80]. Melbourne: La Trobe University, The Australian Research Centre in Sex, Health & Society.

Snapp, Shannon D., Jenifer K. McGuire, Katarina O. Sinclair, Karlee Gabrion, and Stephen T. Russell. 2015. "LGBTQ-inclusive Curricula: Why Supportive Curricula Matter." *Sex Education* 15 (6): 580–596.

Toomey, Russell B., Caitlin Ryan, Rafael M. Diaz, and Stephen T. Russell. 2011. "High School Gay-straight Alliances (GSAs) and Young Adult Well-being: An Examination of GSA Presence, Participations, and Perceived Effectiveness." *Applied Developmental Science* 15: 175–185.

Ullman, Jacqueline. 2014. "Ladylike/Butch, Sporty/Dapper: Exploring 'Gender Climate' with Australian LGBTQ Students Using Stage-environment Fit Theory." *Sex Education* 14 (4): 430–443.

Ullman, Jacqueline. 2015a. "'At-risk' or School-based Risk? Testing a Model of School-Based Stressors, Coping Responses, and Academic Self-concept for Same-sex Attracted Youth." *Journal of Youth Studies* 18 (4): 417–433.

Ullman, Jacqueline. 2015b. *Free to Be? Exploring the Schooling Experiences of Australia's Sexuality and Gender Diverse Secondary School Students*. Penrith: Centre for Educational Research, School of Education, Western Sydney University.

Ullman, Jacqueline, and Tania Ferfolja. 2015. "Bureaucratic Constructions of Sexual Diversity: 'Sensitive', 'Controversial' and Silencing." *Teaching Education* 26 (2): 145–159.

Valentine, Jeffrey C., David L. DuBois, and Harris Cooper. 2004. "The Relationship between Self-beliefs and Academic Achievement: A Meta-analytic Review." *Educational Psychologist* 39 (2): 111–133.

Watt, Helen M. G., and Jacqueline Eccles. 2008. *Gender and Occupational Outcomes: Longitudinal Assessment of Individual, Social, and Cultural Influences*. Washington, DC: American Psychological Association.

Wentzel, Kathryn R. 2009. "Students' Relationships with Teachers as Motivational Contexts." In *Handbook of Motivation at School*, edited by Kathryn Wentzel and Allan Wigfield, 301–322. Mahwah, NJ: LEA.

Youdell, Deborah. 2004. "Wounds and Reinscriptions: Schools, Sexualities and Performative Subjects." *Discourse: Studies in the Cultural Politics of Education* 25 (4): 477–493.

That's so homophobic? Australian young people's perspectives on homophobic language use in secondary schools

Karyn Fulcher

ABSTRACT

It is generally accepted that hearing homophobic language can be detrimental to the well-being of same-sex attracted young people. *Writing Themselves In 3*, a survey of Australian same-sex attracted young people, found that almost half of the respondents reported hearing such language on a regular basis, and considered it offensive. Less is known however about heterosexual young people's experiences. Homophobic language use is often assumed to be motivated by prejudice, but this topic has not been well studied. Using interviews and an online discussion with young people aged 16–21 years, this study explored heterosexual young people's perspectives on homophobic language use at school. Contrary to the framing often used in anti-homophobia education, the meaning of this form of language was seen to largely depend on the context in which it was employed, frequently functioning to reinforce masculine gender norms, particularly for popular male students. Furthermore, while many heterosexual participants in this study used homophobic language regularly, they did not see themselves as homophobic and viewed school policies against the use of homophobic language as largely ineffective. Findings suggest that heterosexual young people may respond more favourably to anti-homophobia education if these programmes acknowledge the variety of meanings and functions of language commonly understood to be homophobic in character.

Introduction

Over the last decade, educators and policy-makers in Australia have recognised and attempted to rectify the difficulties often faced by same-sex attracted young people at school, difficulties that are now known to be linked to experiencing homophobia, including peers' use of homophobic language. In Australia, rates of depression and anxiety are higher among people who identify as homosexual or bisexual, compared to those who identify as heterosexual (Lyons 2015), and young people are no exception to this. The results of the third national survey of Australian same-sex attracted and gender diverse young people, *Writing Themselves In 3*, indicated that experiencing homophobia in the form of verbal or physical abuse was 'associated with feeling less safe, excessive drug use, self-harm and suicide' (Hillier et al. 2010, 49). Of the 61% of respondents who reported experiencing homophobic abuse, 80% indicated the abuse took place at school, and these results are consistent with findings from research conducted in the UK, Canada, and the USA (Adams, Cox, and Dunstan 2004; Chesir-Teran and Hughes 2009; DesRoches and Sweet 2008; Rivers 2011; Rivers and Cowie 2006).

While there is less information available concerning the effects of homophobic language specifically on same-sex attracted young people, it does appear to be potentially detrimental. One finding of *Writing Themselves In 3* (Hillier et al. 2010) was that nearly half of respondents heard homophobic language from their peers on a regular basis, and considered the use of this kind of language a form of homophobia. In response to this research, a number of policies have been implemented in Australia to ensure school is a safe space for same-sex attracted students, and education programmes have been developed with the goal of raising students' awareness of the potential harms of homophobia, including homophobic language such as 'that's so gay' (Ferfolja 2013; Jones 2012).

Despite the implementation of anti-homophobia initiatives, it has proven difficult to reduce students' use of homophobic language. Five years after *Writing Themselves In 3*, another study of Australian same-sex attracted young people's school experiences found that nearly all participants in the study reported hearing homophobic language at school at least once a week, and these young people overwhelmingly viewed it as a form of homophobia (Ullman 2015). However, in contrast to the views of educators, policy-makers and same-sex attracted students themselves, it seems that students who use this kind of language may not always use it to express prejudice, but rather as a joke (Warwick and Aggleton 2014).

There is a large body of literature documenting the link between homophobia and masculinity, including in school environments (Kimmel 1994; McCormack 2011; Nayak and Kehily 1997; Pascoe 2007). McCann, Plummer, and Minichiello (2010) have suggested that homophobic behaviour and language serve to reinforce the kinds of gendered behaviours that are considered acceptable, particularly for men. Psychological research has linked homophobic beliefs to an investment in traditional gender roles (Lehavot and Lambert 2007; Mohipp and Morry 2004). Homophobic language use is frequently motivated by gender norms, but the social situations in which homophobic language is used, the various meanings young people assign to it and their understanding of its relation to gender are not well understood.

This paper explores the functions of homophobic language in the school social interactions of heterosexual Australian young people, and considers the implications for the development and implementation of anti-homophobia education programmes and policies. The overall aim of the study was to better understand homophobic language within its social context, guided by the research question: What role(s) does homophobic language play in the everyday social interactions of young people at school?

It should be noted that throughout this paper, the term 'homophobic language' is used not to indicate any assumed motivations in its use, but simply because it is the most practical and commonly used way to refer to language that has the potential to be interpreted as homophobic. Similarly, the use of terms such as same-sex attracted and heterosexual to refer to young people's sexual orientations is done in order to accurately represent the

Homophobic language in Australian education policy and practice

In order to contextualise the findings of this study, it is necessary to understand the current framing of homophobia and homophobic language in Australian educational policies and learning materials. Many current anti-homophobia initiatives were developed in response to the findings from the *Writing Themselves In* studies (Hillier et al. 1998, 2010; Hillier, Turner, and Mitchell 2005) including the resources designed by the Safe Schools Coalition Victoria, which was founded in 2010 to assist schools in the state of Victoria to create safer environments for same-sex attracted and gender-diverse students and which has since been expanded to a national scale. Along with Safe Schools Coalition Victoria, a number of federal, state and school policies have been implemented with the goal of reducing homophobic harassment and bullying (Jones and Hillier 2012; Leonard et al. 2010).

A report by Leonard et al. (2010) which sought to analyse homophobia in schools and other institutions defined homophobia as the 'fear and hatred of lesbians and gay men' (ii). The Australian Education Union (2003) uses a similar definition in their GLBT (gay, lesbian, bisexual and transgender) policy outline, stating that homophobia is the 'fear and hatred … of homosexuality, which in turn motivates the bullying of young GLBT people' (1). These are but two of many examples of policies and guidelines that have shaped the ways in which schools in Australia endeavour to protect same-sex attracted students from harm, and their definitions of homophobia are similar to those used in other documentation (Dankmeijer 2011; UNESCO 2012; Witthaus 2010; Women's Health in the North and Reidy 2011).

Australian state departments of education also provide guidelines for dealing with homophobia in schools. The Department of Education and Training in the State of Victoria, for example, states that homophobic language, including homophobic jokes, should be considered a type of bullying (Rigby and Victorian Department of Education 2013). This view is echoed in Safe Schools Coalition Victoria materials; one such resource states that homophobia is most commonly encountered as homophobic language use and name calling (Smith, Ward, and Mitchell 2011). These resources arguably assume that the use of homophobic language is motivated by prejudice; the classification of all homophobic language use as bullying implies that the goal of such language use is always to do harm. However, in his work on the use of racist language in everyday conversations, Guerin (2005) has posited that the expression of prejudice is not the only motivation for this kind of language use, and suggests that interventions for addressing racist talk are based on the assumption that it stems from an inherent characteristic of people called racism. He argues that these interventions aim to 'change the understanding that people have of their racism or racist behaviour, or raise the general "awareness" of other cultures and races, with the idea that this will change those people's actions' (47). Warwick and Aggleton's (2014) finding that some students in London schools may view homophobic language use as joking or teasing, in addition to the studies previously mentioned that document the use of this language to reinforce masculine gender norms (Kimmel 1994; McCann, Plummer, and Minichiello 2010; McCormack 2010; Pascoe 2007; Plummer 2001), point to the possibility that Guerin's framework could be applied to better understand homophobic language, and to strengthen interventions aimed at reducing students' use of this language.

Methods

Participants were recruited through a Facebook page and a series of Facebook advertisements. The young people who took part in the study were located in different parts of Australia, with the majority residing in Victoria, and most attended large public schools, although a few attended religious private schools. While not all participants were heterosexual, this paper is concerned only with the perspectives of those who did identify as such due to a lack of information on the perspectives of heterosexual young people relative to those of their same-sex attracted peers.

Data collection took place in two phases between September 2012 and March 2014. The first phase consisted of semi-structured interviews (Adams 2010; DiCicco-Bloom and Crabtree 2006; Hunt and Fazio 2011) in person or via Skype with 16 young people between the ages of 16 and 21. The interview topics were developed based on the literature on homophobic language, as well as the literature concerning social hierarchies in secondary school environments. Interviews explored the social organisation of participants' schools as well as their experiences using or hearing homophobic language at school. Prompts about social organisation included asking participants to describe the various social groups, interactions between groups and possible connections between sexual orientation, gender expression and social status. Interview prompts about homophobic language explored the specific words or phrases used, the context in which it was used and its possible meanings, as well as any differences (gender or social status) in who used it most often.

The second phase of the study took the form of a three-week-long asynchronous online discussion (De Wever et al. 2006; Remmers de Vries and Valadez 2008; Stewart and Williams 2005) conducted with another six young people, using the open-source software phpBB3.[1] The discussion focused on four topics, drawn from the themes identified in the preliminary analysis of the interview data: social organisation of participants' schools, links between sexual orientation and social status, the kinds of behaviour that were considered 'gay' or gender-nonconforming and the use of homophobic language.

Data were analysed according to the guidelines for inductive thematic analysis (Braun and Clarke 2006). Interviews were audio recorded and transcribed. Each transcript was then read twice through, and notes were made on a hard copy before coding began to identify possible themes (Green et al. 2007; Tuckett 2005). Preliminary analysis was undertaken concurrently with interviews, as recommended in the literature on thematic analysis (Braun and Clarke 2006; Guest, MacQueen, and Namey 2012). For analytic purposes, the data from the online discussion were dealt with as if they were one interview transcript. Analysis did not begin on these data until after the online discussion had concluded.

Analysis was aided by QSR NVivo 10 software. Initial coding involved assigning a code to each segment of text while remaining close to the data and avoiding the use of a priori codes, as suggested in the literature (Braun and Clarke 2006; Green et al. 2007; Ryan and Bernard 2003; Tuckett 2005). When initial coding was complete, the codes were examined for potential connections, and those that appeared related were grouped together as a theme. These groups of codes were then reviewed to ensure that they formed a coherent pattern (Braun and Clarke 2006). Once themes had been identified and reviewed, they were checked against the data by looking through the interview and discussion transcripts for examples of each theme to ensure that the themes accurately represented the data. Finally, each theme was assigned a short phrase descriptor to describe the core idea within it theme (Fereday and Muir-Cochrane 2006).

Findings

Three key themes were identified in participants' views on homophobic language use. The first was the importance of social context in helping decipher meaning, and the value of homophobic language use in maintaining social relationships. The second theme concerned the use of homophobic language to indicate that a (generally popular) male student was not conforming to masculine gender norms, and therefore putting their social status at risk. Finally, heterosexual participants did not interpret the use of homophobic language as evidence of the speaker's homophobic beliefs, and they did not view the everyday use of phraseology such as 'that's so gay' as a form of homophobia.

The role of context in determining meaning

In their examination of the use of 'gay' in Australian English, Lalor and Rendle-Short (2007) suggest that the word has three distinct meanings. The first meaning defines 'gay' as synonymous with 'happy'. The second meaning equates gay with 'homosexual' and the third and newest meaning is the one in which gay is used to indicate that something is stupid or weird. The young people in this study described themselves and their peers using 'gay' according to meanings two and three, and noted that 'that's so gay', 'fag' and 'faggot' were also used.

Regardless of word choice, one clear pattern in the data was the way that young people relied on context (including the relationship between speaker and listener) in interpreting meaning and intent, and, relatedly, the use of this kind of language to maintain or solidify social relationships. The young people in this study, like those in Warwick and Aggleton's (2014) work, differentiated between homophobic language used as a joke, an insult or as an expression of disapproval, and indicated that its use could have social benefits.

When I asked one participant, Matt, about the connection between context and meaning, he responded:

> Like with all of these sort of slightly derogatory sort of words, like using them in public and using them in private is sort of a different matter … if you were like making a speech in front of your year level … you're going to steer clear of all of those sort of words. But if you're among a close-knit friendship group or something like that, you can call someone gay and they don't take offence to it. It's almost a way of building solidarity between [*sic*] a group. If you're with your friends or someone who you've met and you've got along pretty well, and then you start swearing mildly around them, then that can be a sign that you're comfortable … you don't feel like you're being judged or something. (Matt, M, 17)[2]

His explanation illustrates some of the factors that he felt need to be taken into account when interpreting homophobic language. Any potentially offensive language was inappropriate in a formal setting, but the same language could be viewed positively among a group of friends. Matt's description of meeting someone new and demonstrating his comfort with them through his choice of language illustrates the role that such language can play in developing new relationships or maintaining existing ones. In such situations, putatively homophobic language communicates far more information than the words alone might suggest.

Harry (M, 17), concurred and explained that homophobic language could additionally be used to demonstrate membership in a social group: 'Yeah, that term is also not super derogatory, because I mean friends use it among themselves, and … it's sort of like a way to exclude other people, like grownups and all that'.

In these examples, in addition to the role that social context played in helping to determine the meaning of homophobic language, it appears that the use of this language could be socially beneficial for students. Rather than expressing prejudice, superficially homophobic language could be employed to show membership of a group or to facilitate the development of a friendship with a new acquaintance, both of which may seem as positive outcomes.

Homophobic language use, masculinity and popularity

In discussing the use of homophobic language, participants were all of the opinion that this type of language was used almost exclusively by male students at their schools. As noted earlier, homophobic language may be used to reinforce masculine gender norms, and participants' experiences were no exception. However, participants indicated that these this type of language was employed most frequently by the most popular male students at their schools, in interaction with other male students of similar status.

When I asked Rebecca (F, 19) about the worst things that students could have said to one another at her school, she stated that for boys, 'I guess being gay. If some of them didn't play sport or something people would be like oh why aren't you playing sport'. Lily (F, 16) described the same use of this language at her school:

> I hear the guys calling each other … like 'you're such a faggot' or 'oh you're so gay' but it's more … I think they just think it's funny, like it's a joke, or you did something that's not very manly.

Notably, in Lily's example, there is no mention of the target of these comments being perceived as gay, rather they are called faggot or gay because they have apparently failed – if only momentarily – to adhere to their peers' idea of masculinity.

In addition, Lily remarked it was the most popular male group at her school that used this language: 'Yeah, particularly with the more popular guys, you know they're really sporty and if you're not very manly and very strong, you're a faggot or you're gay'. Theo (M, 18) concurred that at his school, it was 'definitely more males, especially popular males' who used homophobic language most frequently, and this appeared to be because these students' social status depended in part on their adherence to masculine norms, including athletic ability, as he explained: 'if you're very good at [sport] or if you play it … and you're above average say, you'll be popular'.

The literature on social status in secondary school indicates that conformity to gender norms is a key factor in achieving and maintaining popularity, especially for boys, and that popular adolescents in particular place high value on their social status (Adler, Kless, and Adler 1992; Borch, Hyde, and Cillessen 2011; Dijkstra et al. 2009; Govender 2011; Horn 2006, 2007; Martino 1999; Poteat, Espelage, and Green 2007). Comments by participants in this study support this: they described the popular male students at their school as those who conformed to norms of masculinity most closely, and indicated that gender conformity was an important contributor to social status. The frequent use of homophobic language by such students suggests that not only is homophobic language use one way of stressing the importance of masculinity, but also that it is a means of maintaining status in a social hierarchy that privileges gender conformity.

This use of homophobic language to reinforce gender norms and popularity simultaneously was particularly clear in the case of one participant in the online discussion, William. Although he did not specify the status of the social group he belonged to, some of his comments indicate it was, if not the most popular group, still of relatively high status. He stated at one point that he and his friends used homophobic language more than any other group.

> ... we generally use it when talking to our straight friends to let them know that whatever they're doing might give the wrong impression of their sexuality ... So that's usually why we'd call each other gay for doing something or the other. (William, M, 16)

Although William talked about impressions of sexuality in this example, not gender, his comment concerns behaviour that is considered unacceptable, and one interpretation of this statement is that he and his friends were attempting to ensure none of them behaved in a way that could be seen as feminine. Failing to conform to gendered expectations is often interpreted as an indication of same-sex attraction, particularly for men (Blashill and Powlishta 2009) and it is likely that William and his friends' use of the term 'gay' in this context was a result of their concern over potentially being seen by their peers as not masculine, which in turn could lead to a loss of social status.

Is homophobic language a form of homophobia?

In addition to there being a range of meanings participants assigned to homophobic language, participants views regarding if and when it ought to be considered offensive varied, with many stating that this was entirely dependent on the social context. As William remarked, 'I wouldn't say using gay as a slur is the end of the world as long as you know the people around you won't be offended'. Young people, while they described some language use as offensive or insensitive, felt that there was a difference between using homophobic language and actually being homophobic. William's explanation of homophobia was one such example of this; he repeatedly explained that he and his friends were 'not homophobic in any sense' but at the same time,

> ... we're still pretty insensitive about how we use the term gay to make fun of each other, I make sure they're careful about who they say it around and we'd never say it around anyone we believe to be gay, just keep it within the group. (William, M, 16)

In his opinion, being homophobic involved expressing clearly negative beliefs about same-sex attraction:

> At my school there aren't really any people that are homophobic, I know one or two girls that don't agree with it and say that it's not natural ... but they're both a Christian and a Muslim, and they realised not to voice that opinion because they got ripped into for even saying they disagree. (William, M, 16)

The distinction that William made here, between being insensitive and being homophobic, summarised not only his interpretation of the concept of homophobia, but also that other heterosexual participants' perspectives as well. Becky (F, 16) offered a similar description in her understanding of homophobia as it occurred at her school: 'there are some people that are very openly against homosexual activity ... one friend who is in a homosexual relationship has been isolated and excluded from other circles'.

GENDER AND SEXUALITY IN EDUCATION AND HEALTH

In William's case, he acknowledged that his group could be insensitive while emphasising that this should not be taken as evidence of any negative beliefs about same-sex attraction, unlike the two students he *did* consider to be homophobic. In contrast to some of the same-sex attracted online discussion participants who stated that they found homophobic language use in *any* context offensive, William described his use as a 'bad habit' but maintained that this did not make him homophobic.

Matt was another participant who distinguished between the use of homophobic language and holding homophobic attitudes:

> I think it's [that's so gay] completely dependent on who you're saying it around … among just a casual group of friends, like everyone straight or whatever, then I don't really see it as being that offensive … But if you have a friend who's homosexual, then that certainly can cause a bit of tension, maybe. And it wouldn't be received as well. So it can fluctuate. (Matt, 17, straight)

His views were similar to William's: he appeared to view homophobia and the use of homophobic language as largely unrelated, referring to homophobic language as 'offensive' instead. This perspective was somewhat unexpected: the literature on homophobia suggests that individuals who are personally acquainted with someone who identifies as gay or lesbian – as Matt was – are less likely to hold homophobic attitudes and as a result to feel that homophobia of any kind is unacceptable (Worthen 2014).

Discussion

According to heterosexual study participants, homophobic language had several context-dependent functions, supporting Guerin's (2005) suggestion that prejudiced language may have social value. In this study, it was employed to convey the second and third meanings noted by Lalor and Rendle-Short (2007); to demonstrate membership in a social group or comfort with new acquaintances; or to indicate that the target was not conforming to masculine norms and therefore jeopardising their own social status and the status of their group. Additionally, participants distinguished between homophobic language use and behaviour they considered to be homophobic, indicating that classifying all use of this type of language as motivated by prejudice is not an accurate reflection of many young people's social realities.

This perspective of participants in this study contradicts the notion that homophobic language is only used by individuals who are prejudiced and whose goal is to express their prejudice, the framework implied in policy and educational materials. According to this assumption and the idea that awareness of the challenges faced by same-sex attracted students leads to a decrease in homophobic behaviour and language use, Matt's relationship with his friend should have prompted him to feel more strongly that homophobic language was unacceptable in any context, but this was not the case.

The complexity of heterosexual participants' views on homophobic language use and its multiple functions in everyday conversation have significant implications for educators and policy-makers. Most obvious are the implications for the implementation of anti-homophobia education programmes. Such initiatives are valuable for raising awareness of sexual and gender diversity; but in framing homophobic language use as homophobia, these interventions likely do not reflect students' everyday experiences, potentially making them less relatable to and less relevant from these young people's perspectives. The question then is: How effective such programmes can ultimately be at prompting long-term behaviour change and reduction in the use of this language, if the suggestions made are not ones that students view as applicable to their lives?

One possible strategy to remedy this may be to incorporate discussions into anti-homophobia initiatives in which students have the opportunity to consider the full range of uses of homophobic language in their social lives in order to illustrate its potential effects on *all* students regardless of their sexual orientation. This has the benefit of avoiding labelling certain terms or people homophobic regardless of context – a label many young people may not see as applicable to themselves – while at the same time making the issue personally relevant.

Similarly, it may be helpful to incorporate discussions and classroom activities on gender and social groups into anti-homophobia education to provide students with a space in which to consider not only how language is used to reinforce gender norms, but also how these norms play out in their social interactions. Participants' descriptions of the use of homophobic language to reinforce ideas about masculinity, as documented in the literature (Carnaghi, Maass, and Fasoli 2011; Fair 2011; Kimmel 1994; McCormack and Anderson 2014; Tharinger 2008; Theodore and Basow 2000), clearly demonstrates the entanglement and conflation of sexuality and gender in students' lives, and the intersection of these two concepts must be addressed with students in order to provide them with opportunities to discuss and question *why* and *how* gender presentation is often taken to indicate sexual preference, and allow them to consider how this may effect everyone regardless of their sexuality.

Anti-homophobia initiatives could be further strengthened by taking into account the role of homophobic language in maintaining social hierarchies among secondary school students. The use of homophobic language by the most popular male students not only to reinforce norms of masculinity but also to protect their social status further supports the necessity of addressing homophobic language not only as a form of homophobia, but within broader conversations about social norms, particularly in the light of the increasing popularity of student-led gay–straight alliances (Collins 2004; Curran 2002; Walls, Kane, and Wisneski 2009; Zammitt, Pepperell, and Coe 2015). The connection between homophobic language use, popularity and masculinity found in this study suggests that the social status of specific individuals involved in these groups may make a difference, and this is a potentially valuable area of future research. Given the significant social influence and visibility of popular students in secondary school environments, and the considerable value that young people place on the opinions of their peers (Adler, Kless, and Adler 1992; de Bruyn and Cillessen 2006; Cillessen and Rose 2005; Parkhurst and Hopmeyer 1998), it may be useful for teachers or school staff members who supervise such groups to make attempts to work closely with some of these popular students: their presence may highlight the value of these groups in the eyes of their peers. An examination of how best to go about implementing these changes, and how anti-homophobia initiatives could be connected to other strategies to create safe school environments for all students would be another worthwhile subject for future research.

Notes

1. This software creates an online space in which users can create their own topics for discussion and respond to the topics created by others.
2. Participants are referred to throughout by a pseudonym as well as M for male or F for female, and their age. Matt was a male participant, 17 years of age.

Disclosure statement

No potential conflict of interest was reported by the author.

References

Adams, Eike. 2010. "The Joys and Challenges of Semi-Structured Interviewing." *Community Practitioner* 83 (7): 18–21.

Adams, Natasha, Tamsin Cox, and Laura Dunstan. 2004. "'I Am the Hate That Dare Not Speak Its Name': Dealing with Homophobia in Secondary Schools." *Educational Psychology in Practice* 20 (3): 259–269.

Adler, Patricia A., Steven J. Kless, and Peter Adler. 1992. "Socialization to Gender Roles: Popularity among Elementary School Boys and Girls." *Sociology of Education* 65 (3): 169–87.

Australian Education Union. 2003. *Policy on Gay, Lesbian, Bisexual and Transgender People*. Hobart: Australian Education Union.

Blashill, Aaron J., and Kimberly K. Powlishta. 2009. "Gay Stereotypes: The Use of Sexual Orientation as a Cue for Gender-related Attributes." *Sex Roles* 61 (11–12): 783–793.

Borch, Casey, Allen Hyde, and Antonius H. N. Cillessen. 2011. "The Role of Attractiveness and Aggression in High School Popularity." *Social Psychology of Education* 14 (1): 23–39.

Braun, Virginia, and Victoria Clarke. 2006. "Using Thematic Analysis in Psychology." *Qualitative Research in Psychology* 3 (2): 77–101.

de Bruyn, E. H., and A. H. N. Cillessen. 2006. "Popularity in Early Adolescence: Prosocial and Antisocial Subtypes." *Journal of Adolescent Research* 21 (6): 607–627.

Carnaghi, Andrea, Anne Maass, and Fabio Fasoli. 2011. "Enhancing Masculinity by Slandering Homosexuals: The Role of Homophobic Epithets in Heterosexual Gender Identity." *Personality & Social Psychology Bulletin* 37 (12): 1655–1665.

Chesir-Teran, Daniel, and Diane Hughes. 2009. "Heterosexism in High School and Victimization among Lesbian, Gay, Bisexual, and Questioning Students." *Journal of Youth and Adolescence* 38 (7): 963–975.

Cillessen, Antonius H. N., and Amanda J. Rose. 2005. "Understanding Popularity in the Peer System." *Current Directions in Psychological Science* 14 (2): 102–105.

Collins, Anthony. 2004. "Reflections on Experiences in Peer-based Anti-homophobia Education." *Teaching Education* 15 (1): 107–112.

Curran, Greg. 2002. *Young Queers Getting Together: Moving beyond Isolation and Loneliness*. Melbourne: University of Melbourne.

Dankmeijer, Peter. 2011. *GALE Toolkit Working with Schools 1.0. Tools for School Consultants, Principals, Teachers, Students and Parents to Integrate Adequate Attention of Lesbian, Gay, Bisexual and Transgender Topics in Curricula and School Policies*. Amsterdam: GALE The Global Alliance for LGBT Education.

De Wever, B., T. Schellens, M. Valcke, and H. Van Keer. 2006. "Content Analysis Schemes to Analyze Transcripts of Online Asynchronous Discussion Groups: A Review." *Computers & Education* 46 (1): 6–28.

DesRoches, Sarah, and Michael Ernest Sweet. 2008. "Citizenship for Some: Heteronormativity as Cloaked Bullying." *Journal of Gay & Lesbian Social Services* 19 (3–4): 173–87.

DiCicco-Bloom, Barbara, and Benjamin F. Crabtree. 2006. "The Qualitative Research Interview." *Medical Education* 40 (4): 314–321.

Dijkstra, J. K., A. H. N. Cillessen, S. Lindenberg, and R. Veenstra. 2009. "Same-gender and Cross-gender Likeability: Associations with Popularity and Status Enhancement: The TRAILS Study." *The Journal of Early Adolescence* 30 (6): 773–802.

Fair, B. 2011. "Constructing Masculinity through Penetration Discourse: The Intersection of Misogyny and Homophobia in High School Wrestling." *Men and Masculinities* 14 (4): 491–504.

Fereday, Jennifer, and Eimear Muir-Cochrane. 2006. "Demonstrating Rigor Using Thematic Analysis: A Hybrid Approach of Inductive and Deductive Coding and Theme Development." *International Journal of Qualitative Methods* 5 (1): 80–92.

Ferfolja, Tania. 2013. "Sexual Diversity, Discrimination and 'Homosexuality Policy' in New South Wales' Government Schools." *Sex Education* 13 (2): 159–171.

Govender, K. 2011. "The Cool, the Bad, the Ugly, and the Powerful: Identity Struggles in Schoolboy Peer Culture." *Culture, Health & Sexuality* 13 (8): 887–901.

Green, Julie, Karen Willis, Emma Hughes, Rhonda Small, Nicky Welch, Lisa Gibbs, and Jeanne Daly. 2007. "Generating Best Evidence from Qualitative Research: The Role of Data Analysis." *Australian and New Zealand Journal of Public Health* 31 (6): 545–550.

Guerin, Bernard. 2005. "Combating Everyday Racial Discrimination without Assuming Racists or Racism: New Intervention Ideas from a Contextual Analysis." *Behavior and Social Issues* 14 (1): 46–70.

Guest, Greg, Kathleen M. MacQueen, and Emily E. Namey. 2012. *Applied Thematic Analysis*. Thousand Oaks, CA: Sage.

Hillier, Lynne, Deborah Dempsey, Lyn Harrison, Lisa Beale, Lesley Matthews, and Doreen Rosenthal. 1998. "Writing Themselves." In *Report on the Sexuality, Health and Well-being of Same-sex Attracted Young People*. Melbourne: Australian Research Centre in Sex, Health & Society, La Trobe University.

Hillier, Lynne, Tiffany Jones, Marisa Monagle, Naomi Overton, Luke Gahan, Jennifer Blackman, and Anne Mitchell. 2010. *Writing Themselves in 3: The Third National Study on the Sexual Health and Wellbeing of Same Sex Attracted and Gender Questioning Young People*. Melbourne: Australian Research Centre in Sex, Health & Society, La Trobe University.

Hillier, Lynne, Alina Turner, and Anne Mitchell. 2005. *Writing Themselves in Again: 6 Years on: The 2nd National Report on the Sexual Health & Well-being of Same-sex Attracted Young People in Australia*. Melbourne: Australian Research Centre in Sex, Health & Society, La Trobe University.

Horn, Stacey S. 2006. "Group Status, Group Bias, and Adolescents' Reasoning about the Treatment of Others in School Contexts." *International Journal of Behavioral Development* 30 (3): 208–218.

Horn, Stacey S. 2007. "Adolescents' Acceptance of Same-sex Peers Based on Sexual Orientation and Gender Expression." *Journal of Youth and Adolescence* 36 (3): 302–28.

Hunt, Geoffrey, and Adam Fazio. 2011. "Embarking on Large-scale Qualitative Research: Reaping the Benefits of Mixed Methods in Studying Youth, Clubs and Drugs." *Nordisk Alkohol- & Narkotikatidskrift* 28 (5–6): 1–17.

Jones, Tiffany. 2012. *Discrimination and Bullying on the Grounds of Sexual Orientation and Gender Identity in Western Australian Education*. Perth: Western Australian Equal Opportunity Commission.

Jones, Tiffany Mary, and Lynne Hillier. 2012. "Sexuality Education School Policy for Australian GLBTIQ Students." *Sex Education* 12 (4): 437–454.

Kimmel, Michael S. 1994. "Masculinity as Homophobia: Fear, Shame, and Silence in the Construction of Gender Identity." In *Theorizing Masculinities*, edited by Harry Brod and Michael Kaufman, 119–141. Thousand Oaks, CA: Sage.

Lalor, Therese, and Johanna Rendle-Short. 2007. "'That's So Gay': A Contemporary Use of Gay in Australian English." *Australian Journal of Linguistics* 27 (2): 147–173.

Lehavot, Keren, and Alan J. Lambert. 2007. "Toward a Greater Understanding of Antigay Prejudice: On the Role of Sexual Orientation and Gender Role Violation." *Basic and Applied Social Psychology* 29 (3): 279–292.

Leonard, William, Daniel Marshall, Lynne Hillier, Anne Mitchell, and Roz Ward. 2010. *Beyond Homophobia: Meeting the Needs of Same-sex Attracted and Gender Questioning (SSAGQ) Young People in Victoria. A Policy Blueprint*. Melbourne: Australian Research Centre in Sex, Health & Society, La Trobe University.

Lyons, Anthony. 2015. "Resilience in Lesbians and Gay Men: A Review and Key Findings from a Nationwide Australian Survey." *International Review of Psychiatry* 27 (5): 435–443.

Martino, Wayne. 1999. "'Cool Boys', 'Party Animals', 'Squids' and 'Poofters': Interrogating the Dynamics and Politics of Adolescent Masculinities in School." *British Journal of Sociology of Education* 20 (2): 239–263.

McCann, P. D., D. Plummer, and V. Minichiello. 2010. "Being the Butt of the Joke: Homophobic Humour, Male Identity, and Its Connection to Emotional and Physical Violence for Men." *Health Sociology Review* 19 (4): 505–521.

McCormack, Mark. 2010. "The Declining Significance of Homohysteria for Male Students in Three Sixth Forms in the South of England." *British Educational Research Journal* 37 (2): 337–53.

McCormack, Mark. 2011. "Mapping the Terrain of Homosexually-themed Language." *Journal of Homosexuality* 58 (5): 664–679.

McCormack, Mark, and Eric Anderson. 2014. "The Influence of Declining Homophobia on Men's Gender in the United States: An Argument for the Study of Homohysteria." *Sex Roles* 71 (3–4): 109–120.

Mohipp, Charmaine, and Marian M. Morry. 2004. "The Relationship of Symbolic Beliefs and Prior Contact to Heterosexuals' Attitudes toward Gay Men and Lesbian Women." *Canadian Journal of Behavioural Science* 36 (1): 36–44.

Nayak, Anoop, and Mary Jane Kehily. 1997. "Playing It Straight: Masculinities, Homophobias and Schooling." *Journal of Gender Studies* 5 (2): 211–30.

Parkhurst, J. T., and A. Hopmeyer. 1998. "Sociometric Popularity and Peer-perceived Popularity: Two Distinct Dimensions of Peer Status." *The Journal of Early Adolescence* 18 (2): 125–144.

Pascoe, C. J. 2007. *"Dude, You're a Fag": Masculinity and Sexuality in High School*. Berkeley: University of California Press.

Plummer, D. 2001. "The Quest for Modern Manhood: Masculine Stereotypes, Peer Culture and the Social Significance of Homophobia." *Journal of Adolescence* 24 (1): 15–23.

Poteat, V. Paul, Dorothy L. Espelage, and Harold D. Green Jr. 2007. "The Socialization of Dominance: Peer Group Contextual Effects on Homophobic and Dominance Attitudes." *Journal of Personality & Social Psychology* 92 (6): 1040–1050.

Remmers de Vries, Sabina, and Albert A. Valadez. 2008. "Let Our Voices Be Heard: Qualitative Analysis of an Internet Discussion Board." *Journal of Creativity in Mental Health* 3 (4): 383–400.

Rigby, Ken, and Victorian Department of Education. 2013. *Challenging Homophobic Behaviour*. Melbourne: State Government of Victoria.

Rivers, Ian. 2011. "Narratives of Marginalisation: The Legacy of Homophobia at School." *International Journal of Adolescence and Youth* 16 (2): 157–177.

Rivers, Ian, and Helen Cowie. 2006. "Bullying and Homophobia in UK Schools: A Perspective on Factors Affecting Resilience and Recovery." *Journal of Gay & Lesbian Issues in Education* 3 (4): 11–43.

Ryan, Gery W., and H. Bernard. 2003. "Techniques to Identify Themes." *Field Methods* 15 (1): 85–109.

Smith, Bec, Roz Ward, and Anne Mitchell. 2011. *Challenging Homophobia in Schools*. Melbourne: Safe Schools Coalition Victoria.

Stewart, Kate, and Matthew Williams. 2005. "Researching Online Populations: The Use of Online Focus Groups for Social Research." *Qualitative Research* 5 (4): 395–416.

Tharinger, Deborah J. 2008. "Maintaining the Hegemonic Masculinity through Selective Attachment, Homophobia, and Gay-baiting in Schools: Challenges to Intervention." *School Psychology Review* 37 (2): 221–27.

Theodore, P. S., and S. A. Basow. 2000. "Heterosexual Masculinity and Homophobia." *Journal of Homosexuality* 40 (2): 31–48.

Tuckett, Anthony G. 2005. "Applying Thematic Analysis Theory to Practice: A Researcher's Experience." *Contemporary Nurse* 19 (1–2): 75–87.

Ullman, Jacqueline. 2015. *Free2Be? Exploring the Schooling Experiences of Australia's Sexuality and Gender Diverse Secondary School Students*. Penrith: Western Sydney University.

UNESCO. 2012. *Education Sector Responses to Homophobic Bullying 8*. Paris: United Nations Educational, Scientific and Cultural Organization.

Walls, N. E., S. B. Kane, and H. Wisneski. 2009. "Gay-straight Alliances and School Experiences of Sexual Minority Youth." *Youth & Society* 41 (3): 307–32.

Warwick, Ian, and Peter Aggleton. 2014. "Bullying, 'Cussing' and 'Mucking About': Complexities in Tackling Homophobia in Three Secondary Schools in South London, UK." *Sex Education* 14 (2): 159–173.

Witthaus, D. 2010. *Pride and Prejudice*. Moorabin: Hawker Brownlow Education.

Women's Health in the North, and Catherine Reidy. 2011. *Pridentity*. Thornbury: Women's Health in the North.

Worthen, Meredith G. F. 2014. "The Interactive Impacts of High School Gay-Straight Alliances (GSAs) on College Student Attitudes toward LGBT Individuals: An Investigation of High School Characteristics." *Journal of Homosexuality* 61 (2): 217–250.

Zammitt, Kimberly A., Jennifer Pepperell, and Megan Coe. 2015. "Implementing an Ally Development Model to Promote Safer Schools for LGB Youth: A Trans-disciplinary Approach." *Journal of Homosexuality* 62 (6): 687–700.

Knowing, performing and holding queerness: LGBTIQ+ student experiences in Australian tertiary education

Andrea Waling ⓘ and James A. Roffee ⓘ

ABSTRACT

This paper explores LGBTIQ+ students' experiences of knowing, performing and holding queerness in a tertiary educational environment. Through interviews conducted with LGBTIQ+ students at a large Australian metropolitan university, we examine the students' engagement with other LGBTIQ+ students in the tertiary educational space. Although originally intending to explore LGBTIQ+ students' experience of violence, harassment and abuse on campus, the study identified a number of themes concerning the normalisation of a set of beliefs, practices, presentations and performances. Drawing on frameworks of hetero/homo and trans-normativity, we explore how LGBTIQ+ students articulated concerns in knowing, performing and holding 'authentic' queerness. We find LGBTIQ students experienced barred access to knowledge, hostility and dismissal by other LGBTIQ+ students when they were either perceived as too queer, or not queer enough. Behind these interactions and at the heart of these tensions is the notion of an authentic queer identity in a post-gay era and the continuous challenges all LGBTIQ+ students face within a heteronormative society. New insights into how LGBTIQ+ students negotiate, manage and shape their interactions in a higher educational settings are provided, and the implications for tertiary educational institutions, in particular the need to support a diverse LGBTIQ+ community, are discussed.

Introduction

LGBTIQ+ communities and social movements have been herald as sites of progressive social ideas concerning social equality and issues concerning gender and sexuality. However, there is a persistent myth of LGBTIQ+ togetherness and the existence of a single community, where internalised homophobia/biphobia/transphobia is utilised to support a particular narrative of queerness; reliant on achieving normality within a heterosexist discourse (Weeks 1991; Weiss 2003). Community tensions based on factors such as race and ethnicity, gender identity, and 'deviant' sexuality are often rendered invisible in mainstream LGBTIQ+ narratives (Ridge, Hee, and Minichielle 1999). While queerness is 'theoretically based around inclusion and diversity', it has been argued that the concept can tend to become embroiled in the very culture it seeks to critique (Ridge, Hee, and Minichielle 1999, 45). Thus, the notion of an 'authentic' queer can, in many cases, be based in exclusion and conformity (Weeks 1991; Ridge, Hee, and Minichielle 1999). Such notions are enveloped in ideas concerning what scholars term 'cultural knowledge' defined as knowledge of a culture's norms, ideals and practices, where access to such knowledge may be hindered, barred, expected, and/or embedded in identity politics, resulting in the exclusion and maltreatment of those who lack it (Wane, Kempf, and Simmons 2011; Lareau 2015). Furthermore, such processes can be normalised, such as in the form of hetero/homo/trans-normativity. In educational settings experiences of exclusion can be amplified; in schools and colleges there is diversity of participants bringing a mixture of knowledge, and students learn not only subject content, but also skills and ways of thinking and behaving.

While much has been written about LGBTIQ+ experiences in educational settings, in particular around themes of harassment and violence (Jayakumar 2009), and experiences of heterosexism in the classroom, (Ferfolja 2007), there is little that explores the engagement of LGBTIQ+ young people with learning what it is to be a member of an LGBTIQ+ community in a tertiary setting.[1] Our approach to the study of knowledge encompasses individuals having access to facts, information, skills, and familiarity with the social processes belonging to the group they are seeking to engage with (Lareau 2015). Those with access to knowledge are more likely to succeed than those who do not (Lareau 2015). Within the contemporary further and higher education context, where it is assumed by many that knowledge is widely accessible (see DiMaggio et al. 2004), we ask, what processes and concepts of normalisation and beliefs concerning 'authentic' LGBTIQ+ identities are prevalent?

Through qualitative interviews with 16 students who identified as LGBTIQ+, we examined the role a tertiary space can have in influencing how students engage with other LGBTIQ+ students. While the study originally intended to explore LGBTIQ+ students' experience of violence, harassment and bullying on campus, we found several emerging themes concerning what it meant to participants to be queer, and 'non-inclusion' experienced by those who did not conform to a set of expectations, experiences, labels, or demonstrate appropriate knowledge. We argue that these experiences highlight tensions concerning identity; in not being perceived as 'queer enough'; in subscribing to rather than rejecting homonormativity; and in some cases, being 'too queer', where those with gender-diverse identities such as genderqueer and non-binary transgender do not adhere to practices of transnormativity. The result of such experiences led some students to avoid LGBTIQ+ spaces and the broader LGBTIQ+ community in the tertiary setting. We approach the term 'queer' as an umbrella term for sexual and gender minorities that are not heterosexual or cisgender, but recognise that 'queer' as a term also carries a variety of meanings and socio-historical/political connotations, such as its use to reject essentialist and/or traditional LGBTIQ identities (see Gamson 1995). However, our aim here is not to theorise 'queerness' itself, but rather, to explore how perceptions as to what it means to be 'too queer' or 'not queer enough' are presented in the tertiary education landscape.

We begin by reviewing two major areas of enquiry. The first, concerns research into LGBTIQ+ experiences in education, and in particular within tertiary settings. Following this, we detail relevant research concerning issues of internal community marginalisation, isolation and exclusion. We then discuss our theoretical framework concerning sociological accounts of the concept of authenticity and its relationship to hetero/homo and transnormativity. We then outline our methodological approach, followed by a discussion of our results around themes of *knowing*, *performing*, and *holding* queerness. We conclude with a discussion of some implications for tertiary educational institutions, noting that universities should invest in supporting their LGBTIQ+ population.

LGBTIQ+ in educational settings

Renn (2010) notes that research concerning LGBTIQ+ communities and tertiary education has followed a distinct thematic path. Beginning with research that explored homosexuality and deviance, Renn outlines the trajectory of LGBTIQ+ studies, from work concerning normalcy and civil rights, the visibility of LGBTIQ+ people, to issues concerning campus climates, and changing constructions of identities. Homophobic violence and subsequent impacts has seen an increase in research activity, and it has been found that those perceived to be part of the LGBTIQ+ community experience harassment and physical violence (Oswalt and Wyatt 2011; Tetreault et al. 2013). Such experiences have significant negative impacts on mental health and well-being (Woodford et al. 2014; Seelman 2016), and lead to poorer academic outcomes (Robinson and Espelage 2011). There is also research on perceptions of discrimination as opposed to actual experiences (Almeida et al. 2009) and it is known community members avoid spaces perceived to be unsafe (Kosciw et al. 2012).

There have been numerous studies on campus climates exploring quality of life, including while residing, studying or working on campus (Evans and Broido 2002; Garber 2002; Brown et al. 2004; Rankin 2005, 2006; Vaccaro 2012), experiences of violence on campus climate (Waldo, Hesson-McInnis, and D'Augelli 1998), and evaluations of LGBTIQ+ inclusive practice programmes (Draughn, Elkins, and Roy 2002; Little and Marx 2002; Yep 2002). Other research has concerned explorations of the relationship between queer identities and access to career prospects (Tomlison and Fassinger 2003; Abes and Jones 2004), the intersections between leadership, student identity and queer identity development (Renn and Bilodeau 2005a, 2005b; Mayberry 2006; Renn 2007), and identity issues and the intersections of race and class (Poynter and Washington 2005).

However, there is a paucity of research exploring how LGBTIQ+ students interact with each other. Meyer's (2004) study is an exception, documenting the 'imagined tensions' arising from LGBTIQ+ student organisations when attempting to engage in student activism are explained.

LBGTIQ+ marginalisation, exclusion, and isolation

Lichterman (1999) contends that different forms of togetherness allow for and shape a range of opportunities concerning how individuals connect themselves to, and interact with each other. For Lichterman (1999), these forms of togetherness are cultural, whereby different solidarities enable people to understand and define different responsibilities towards each other. In such a framework, the LGBTIQ+ community has been understood as working towards assimilating some segments of sexual minorities into mainstream heteronormative culture and attempting to achieve cultural sameness (Ghaziani 2008, 2011, 2014). However, in what Ghaziani (2014) terms a 'post-gay' era, there are greater possibilities for individuals to move away from singular narratives of cultural sameness to determine the place their sexual and gender identities have in their lives and their interactions with others within the wider community. This can cause tensions, as noted by a number of researchers, concerning emerging sexual and gender identities and practices that do not conform to stereotypical LGBTIQ+ experiences (see Ghaziani 2008, 2011, 2014; McLean 2008; Stone 2009).

It is well recognised that the latter half of the community acronym, i.e. those who identify as −BTIQ+; bisexual, transgender, intersex and queer, as well as those regarded as 'deviant' (including but not limited to genderqueer, pansexual and other emerging identity categories) are often excluded from recognition within the LGBTIQ+ community, and have their narratives of marginalisation disregarded (see Weiss 2003; Hayfield, Clarke, and Halliwell 2014). For example, Ghaziani (2008) and Valentine (2007) note that trans-exclusion is situated within the premise that trans-individuals undermine the promotion of sexual minority rights. In doing so, transgender and genderqueer people are understood as invading community spaces, and are rendered deviant by virtue of their lack of adherence to the gender dichotomy (Stone 2009). Bisexuals are also often excluded from LGBTIQ+ spaces (Hartman 2005), and their narratives of sexuality considered deviant and unacceptable by a 'progressive' gay and lesbian rights movement (Diamond 2005; McLean 2008).

While some gay men and lesbian women support the inclusion of other queer identities, a number feel threatened by the presence of identities that do not adhere to normative ideas of gender and view alternative relationships as detrimental to broader acceptance in a heteronormative society (Weiss 2003; Stryker 2008). Heteronormative values of monogamy and same-generation pairings become favoured, while identities outside normative practice such promiscuous, same-sex and cross-generational relationships become considered to be deviant or bad. Adherence to a modified heteronormative approach allows many gays and lesbians to render their identities as legitimate and normalised in a society that seeks to disempower them.

Authenticity and hetero/homo/trans-normativity

In thinking through processes of normalisation and experiences of exclusion, it may be useful to consider what it means to have authenticity as an LGBTIQ+ identifying person. Authenticity may be understood as an 'inherent quality of some object, person or process' and cannot 'be stripped away, nor can it be appropriated' (Vannini and Williams 2009, 2). However, it is perhaps better understood as an evaluative concept, whereby it is 'the objectification of the process of representation… [referring] to a set of qualities that people in a particular time and place have come to agree represent an ideal or exemplar' (Vannini and Williams 2009, 3). Notions of an authentic identity can be articulated in a number of ways, through media representations, language, and everyday performances of the self.

For example, Foucault's ([1976] 1978) work on language and sexuality highlights how notions of 'authentic' and the 'inauthentic' may be naturalised and legitimated in everyday society. For Foucault ([1976] 1978), language works to normalise certain ideologies surrounding cultural bodies and reproduces these ideologies of the 'real' and the 'fake'. The real (or authentic) is organic and believed to be a 'natural' occurrence, and the fake (or inauthentic) is understood to be the mechanic or the created, conceptualised as artificial and fake and afforded less value.

Notions of authenticity are also found in the performance of the self. Butler's (1988) work on the performativity of gender argues that 'the body becomes its gender through a series of acts which are renewed, revised and consolidated through time' (Butler 1988, 523). Such acts are produced and reproduced, and are then seen as 'normal' and 'natural' (Butler 1988,

525). Failure to replicate such acts will result in often severe social consequences, whereby 'those who fail to do their gender right are regularly punished' (Butler 1988, 522). These ideas of authenticity are also complicated where 'the mechanics of authenticity are always in danger of constructing, and then "naturalising," new authenticities as a part of an essential, hallowed identity' (Cheng 2004, 174, 175). This naturalisation is based in 'an unarticulated anxiety of losing the subject' where the perceived loss of identity and subjectivity require a continuous 'construction and maintenance of difference and superiority' (Cheng 2004, 32). This leads us to the concepts of hetero/homo and trans-normativity when considering authenticity and LGBTIQ+ identities.

Heteronormativity refers to the belief that there is a distinct separation of genders with 'natural roles' in life and daily conduct, including the notion that heterosexuality is the only normal sexual orientation (Warner 1991) and that certain biological bodies assigned particular genders (i.e. penis, testes and scrotum result in a male-sexed body and with gender presentation as masculine) are the only natural or authentic ones (Serano 2007). Such a belief system is responsible for the social organisation of contemporary Western culture and subsequent social institutions such as the nuclear family (Ingraham 2005). Those with identities and experiences considered to be non-normative, often members of the LGBTIQ+ community, are often pathologised, stigmatised, and experience violence (Grossman and Augelli 2007), barred access to services (Jackson, Johnson, and Roberts 2008), and exclusion from everyday life (Serano 2007).

Homonormativity may be understood as the perceived assimilation of heteronormative ideals and constructs into LGBTIQ+ culture and identity, in which LGBTIQ+ communities are divided into hierarchies of worthiness; where those who can mimic heteronormative values (i.e. marriage) are more worthy of receiving rights than others (Duggan 2003). It can be understood as the practice of upholding heteronormative beliefs within queer culture, and is premised on the support of assimilating heteronormative lifestyles (Griffin 2007). Additionally, homonormativity values the norms of certain groups, such as gays and lesbians over the concerns of marginalised groups, such as transgender and gender diverse, whereby such individuals are chastised and excluded for not behaving in accordance with the valued norms (Stryker 2008; Robinson 2012).

Similar to hetero and homonormativity, transnormativity is an emerging concept which describes the legitimisation of some experiences of being transgender, and the marginalisation of others (Stryker 2008; Johnson 2016). Transnormativity is understood as promoting a medicalised model of transgender life (i.e. seeking medical intervention including hormone replacement therapy and sex reassignment surgery), adopting a binary model of sex and gender transition (i.e. transition from male to female and thus, man to woman), and a narrative in which individuals 'always knew' they were assigned the wrong gender and or were in the wrong body (Johnson 2016). Experiences marginalised in transgender terms often come from those who identify as non-binary transgender and/or genderqueer (i.e. not identifying as either a man or a woman); those who reject medicalised intervention; and those who do not subscribe to the standard 'wrong body' narrative. All forms of normativity (hetero/homo/trans-) speak to anxieties around authenticity and legitimate subjectivities, where certain LGBTIQ+ identities are rendered in a hierarchy as more legitimate than others, while all are seeking recognition in a heteronormative society that seeks to oppress them.

Methods and methodology

This qualitative study was developed within a social constructivist paradigm, in which human development seen as socially situated, knowledge is constructed through the process of interaction with others, and people work together to create social artefacts (Creswell 2009). The focus is on the development of individual LGBTIQ students and their identities through their experiences interacting with the LGBTIQ/queer community on campus, and their situation and identification as part of the LGBTIQ/queer community. Feminist and queer theoretical orientations informed the design and conduct of the project (see Roffee and Waling 2017 for details).

The data come from 16 pilot study interviews undertaken by both authors with participants who met eligibility criteria which included being enrolled as an undergraduate student, over the age of 18, and identifying as LGBTIQ, questioning, or of non-binary gender. Postgraduate students were not included to delimit the focus of the pilot study. Participants were recruited using posters on campus, advertising in classes and lectures, and online through social media; and participants could select an interviewer or state no-preference. At the onset of the interview, the project was explained along with a statement of reporting relating to any disclosure of information that might involve questioning of university processes and legislation. This statement indicated that the researchers would not report incidents spoken about to the university (see Roffee and Waling 2017). Participants were also provided with information on how to access counselling and other LGBTIQ+ friendly services.

Prior to the interview, participants were asked to complete a brief demographic survey. The purpose of this survey was to collect demographic information to allow the researchers to understand language and terminology used by participants to denote their lived experiences of sexed bodies, sexuality and gender expression, and identity.

Table 1 highlights the demographic breakdown of the participants. The majority (10) of participants indicated having female sexed bodies. Gender identity was varied and included woman (8), man (4), non-binary transgender (2) and agender (1), participants were aged between 20 and 25 years and stated having a range of gender presentations including 'masculine', 'feminine', 'non-binary', 'fluctuating', 'androgynous' and 'complex'. Sexual orientation was also varied; students identified as gay, lesbian, bisexual, pansexual, queer, queer/bisexual, pansexual/queer, and bi-curious. Participants were recruited from a large, international university based in an outer suburban area of Victoria, Australia, close to Melbourne.

Interviews were conducted using progressive-focusing, a method utilising an interview guide as a loose structural tool to allow for the development of organic conversation; open space is provided to explore unexpected discussions, and reach data saturation (Strauss and Corbin 1994; Guest, Bunce, and Johnson 2006). Interviews lasted between 36 and 82 min, and were transcribed and read by both researchers. The interviews were recorded and contemporaneous notes were taken.

The project utilised phenomenological analysis to make sense of the data (Polit and Beck 2009). A descriptive approach was favoured, where focus was on describing the phenomena and everyday experiences discussed within the interviews (Reiners 2012). This method of analysis was chosen as it focuses on the identification of individual experiences. In the case of this study, this was based on the experience of identifying as LGBTIQ+ and its impact on experiences in tertiary education settings.

GENDER AND SEXUALITY IN EDUCATION AND HEALTH

Table 1. Demographic characteristics of participants.

Age		Ethnicity		Gender identity	
20	4	Australian	2	Agender	1
21	2	Australian/Nigerian	1	Non-binary transgender	2
22	2	Australian/Caucasian	1	Woman	8
23	5	Italian/Australian	1	Man	4
24	1	White (or Caucasian)	7	Other	1
25	2	Jewish/White	1		
		Chinese	1		
		South East Asian	1		
		Eurasian	1		
Gender expression		**Sexed body**		**Sexual orientation**	
Masculine	3	Female	10	Gay	3
Feminine	6	Male	4	Lesbian	2
Androgynous	2	Non-binary	1	Bisexual	3
Masculine/occ. androgynous	1	Not Answered	1	Pansexual	2
Feminine/occ. androgynous	1			Queer	3
Non-binary	1			Queer/Bisexual	1
Fluctuating/Off the Scale	1			Pansexual/Queer	1
Complex	1			Bi-curious	1
Faculty		**Degree**		**Degree major**	
Arts	7	B. Arts/Science	1	Chemistry/Spanish	1
Law	2	B. Medicine	2	Sociology	2
Medicine, Nursing & Health Sciences	3	B. Arts	6	Psychology/Film	1
Arts/Medicine	1	B. Arts/Social Work	2	Psychology/Sociology	1
Arts/Education	1	B. Arts/Education	1	Criminology	1
Science	2	B. Science	2	Sociology/Primary Education	1
		B. Arts/Law	1	Medicine	2
		B. Medicine Hons	1	History/Law	1
				Sociology/History	1
				Film/Screen	1
				Social Work	2
				Law/Sociology	1
				Immunology/Sociology	1
Time at university		**Study status**		**Belong to clubs/ societies**	
1 year	2	Full-time	13	Yes	6
1.5 years	2	Part-time	3	No	10
2 years	2				
2.5 years	5				
3 years	3				
4.5 years	2				

Note: Sample $N = 16$.

The process of analysis occurred in four stages, beginning with a preliminary journal reflection on the authors' opinions about LGBTIQ+ student experiences and then, a journal reflection after each interview. Once transcribed the researchers read the transcripts to undertake an analysis of emergent themes and to gain an overall sense of the material collected. This was then discussed by the authors. In the second stage, each researcher coded two transcripts to generate and compare codes and the emerging salient themes using an open-coding process (see Strauss and Corbin 1994). Major themes included broad categories such as university, space, politics, identity and the LGBT community. The authors then discussed sub-headings within these categories which allowed for the further exploration of sub-themes emerging from this major categories. The researchers then agreed upon and assigned a coding schedule and coded the transcripts for the themes identified, using NVIVO software. This coding was assessed to ensure validity and consistency through biweekly meetings. The third stage of coding tracked the emerging patterns from the data and clustered together to create a preliminary narrative regarding the data. The final stage of analysis involved researchers exploring how the categories corresponded with each other.

Findings

In reviewing the interview data, it became clear participants gestured towards the normalisation of a set of beliefs, practices, gender presentation, performance, and use of language regarding what it meant to be a 'good' or 'authentic' queer person. Within this tertiary community it included adopting and using a set of language and beliefs; performing queerness in a particular way through gender identity and narratives of coming out; and the questioning of identity and authenticity by others who 'know better'.

Knowing queerness

As acknowledged above, both accessing and having knowledge can function as a form of power and result in either the inclusion or exclusion of individuals in a society (see Foucault [1976] 1978). Such power can thus privilege those who may have access to experiences or social factors, such as technology, environmental and political upbringing and, ethnic/racial and class status amongst others. This can allow them access to a particular space or community, and thus be rendered as legitimate and authentic. Those who may not have access to one or more of these factors, such as perhaps, those brought up in a conservative environment or of a certain cultural background, may be predisposed to lack such knowledge and as such, have less access to types of social power within that community.

A dominant narrative for participants concerned the presence of an expectation placed on queer youth to have knowledge of and utilise appropriate language; and for participants to have adopted a set of political and intellectual beliefs concerning the LGBTIQ+ community prior to engagement with other community members; and participants being ostracised should they make mistakes when engaging with other LGBTIQ+ students. Many students spoke of difficulties regarding their lack of knowledge about topics pertaining to a queer identity, as well as sexual practices, or on the emerging recognition of gender and sexual identities not within the LGBTIQ+ acronym. This resulted in students feeling excluded and or feeling inferior in terms of their queer identities:

> [Discussing sexual practices with queer friends] And they were just like 'I love to snu-snu [practice of sitting on someone's face] when I, I don't know like when I'm at my friend's house' and I'm just like 'What I don't even know what that means' and then all these people are talking about it and the ironic thing is that the space is for people to sort of explore these things but in the way there was almost the cliquishness about it, like 'if you identify as a different sexuality you would obviously know about this stuff because you're different.' When really I'm just like actually I just really like sex and I'm interested in it both personally and like intellectually and I want to know more but I didn't feel like I could ask that question because there was kind of this arrogance within the space of 'Oh yeah, people would know about that.' Bridget (cisgender woman, bi-curious)

Bridget highlights here that when engaging with other queer students, others held an expectation that she already had knowledge of, and was aware of sexual practices engaged in by some community members. Her comments highlight the frustration in having to balance her desire to know more about such sexual practices and the responses received, leaving her unable and unwilling to ask further questions. A number of other participants noted facing difficulties concerning their asking questions about queer identities, and noted they encountered others who assumed that as members of the LGBTIQ community they already held such knowledge by virtue of community membership:

> [When asked about the queer lounge.] That is not a place for them [people questioning their sexuality/gender] if they want to find stuff out. I know it's a safe place, but it's not … If people who are straight and want to figure out their sexuality, or wanted just talk about it, you can't go there … I'd get yelled at or told off…or like passive-aggressively, no, condescendingly told. I feel like the community can sometimes be a little bit condescending when talking to people who don't know stuff. Kyle (cisgender man, gay)

Kyle discusses his experience of attending the queer lounge, and felt that only those who were already confident in their sexual and gender identities, and those with knowledge of LGBTIQ+ politics could engage with other LGBTIQ+ students within the space. Kyle noted that students who may have been questioning their identities, or seeking further information could be treated poorly. Others who asked questions faced hostility as a result:

> I find that when I encounter a term, like when I first encountered genderqueer when I wasn't sure what it was, I asked somebody and they told me it wasn't their job to educate me. Jordan (cisgender woman, bisexual)

Jordan reflected on a desire learn about other identities and experiences, and attempted to do so when frequenting the queer space. However, she asked questions that were not in line with expectations (i.e. already knowing), and thus encountered resistance and hostility. A recurrent theme therefore was, that students were expected have already accessed and hold relevant knowledge by virtue of their identification with a non-heterosexual identity.

Alongside the expectation to hold a knowledge set concerning LGBTIQ identities, language and sexual practices, participants also noted that the failure to support certain viewpoints as a barrier to engagement with other members of the queer community, as illustrated by Carly:

> I feel like if you put forward a viewpoint that's … maybe not consistent with the mainstream of the gay rights movement or whatever, the sexual liberation movement … that viewpoint, just of itself, does not make you conservative or homophobic or whatever. Even if it's really not different, if it's just a way of saying, 'I view this issue differently from you, I am not against whatever good. I just don't have the same understanding of sexuality or gender that you do.' Carly (does not identify with any gender identification, pansexual)

While there are multiple perspectives concerning sex and gender, by demonstrating and airing alternative viewpoints and when attempting to engage others in debate, students can find themselves ostracised. As highlighted above, Carly had to navigate being regarded as homophobic when presenting an alternative understanding of sexuality and gender. All four experiences, feeling able to ask questions, asking questions and experiencing hostility, and the expectation to conform to a set of beliefs, as well as the risk of being seen as homophobic when presenting alternative viewpoints, underline the expectation of a consistent narrative of queerness (see Ghaziani 2014). In this case, this idea of having a set of knowledge privileges a particular set of experiences and access that others within the community do not have. As students felt they lacked that knowledge, they were unable to hold a position as legitimate or authentic within the tertiary LGBTIQ space and felt excluded or marginalised as a result.

Performing queerness

The performance of queerness shares similarities with Butler's (1988) assertions regarding the performance of gender, whereby to be queer is produced and reproduced in a number of ways that are naturalised as authentic and legitimate. These include language and expressions, behaviour, as well as physical appearance and clothing. Participants articulated expectations to 'perform' their queerness by adopting behaviours and practices speaking to an authentic queer identity. We found such practices did not always subscribe to homonormativity but rather in some cases, rejected them. As such, those students perceived as subscribing to homonormativity, or appearing too 'mainstream' were often challenged about their perceived lack of queerness:

> I think certain communities would probably see me as a conformist to the sort of the heterosexual feminine ideal. I think certain people would criticise that ... as being like ... manufactured. Carly (cisgender woman, queer)

> I think because my presentation is ... I mean not significantly different from the way that a lot of straight women present ... I don't think I'm registered to other people as being part of the queer community ... and even when I'm in a queer space I think sometimes it's sort of like oh yeah but you're also sort of like the lowest scale type of queer person ... like I feel like there are almost degrees [of being LGBTIQ+] ... it's like hierarchies of queerness. Carrie (cisgender woman, bisexual/queer)

Participants here recognise that because they present in ways associated with heterosexual, cisgender women, they are not seen by others as being part of the community, or regarded as holding an LGBTIQ+ identity. This echoes Davis's (2015) recent work on queer clothing and sexuality, where her research found that participants made strategic clothing choices to illustrate their sexual identities and preferences. Although the participants did not indicate they changed clothing to be seen as more authentic, it was clear that they knew they would be seen as more authentic if they conformed. Thus, participants reported feelings of exclusion even when frequenting labelled LGBTIQ+ spaces, as result of their gender expression through clothing choice. They did not feel as though they were 'queer enough' and perceived to be considered to be conforming to homonormative expectations.

Performance of queerness through markers and self presentation is contrasted against those who are not seen to be performing queerness correctly.

> I don't feel queer enough sometimes like probably related to that. Like not having had the queer struggle ... not being really vocal about it. Also like I haven't dated anyone ... not until sort of this year ... I just feel like a little bit illegitimate in my claiming of any queer space or queer identity. Jennifer (cisgender woman, queer)

> I am 90% certain that I identify as purely cisgender so I think that people within the LGBT community are kind of sick of that. I think that more of the minority you become the more you dislike the majority and I think people just see me as the majority and they just shut me off a little bit. Ryan (cisgender man, gay)

The failure to hold a homogenised narrative of struggle and difficulty leaves students such as Jennifer feeling unable to claim a queer identity or engage with LGBTIQ+ designated spaces. For example, Jennifer reported a positive coming-out experience that included support from family and friends, and because of narratives she heard in the tertiary education space, she felt unable claim a queer identity without having had a negative experience. Ryan felt as though his identification was not queer enough to be accepted within the LGBTIQ tertiary community, feeling excluded and isolated as a result. Students highlighted that due to their alignment with what can be perceived as homonormative performances, or what they referred to as 'mainstream' visual representations of queer identity, they were seen as inauthentic. Such claims came from some students who articulated these feelings often without having first hand experiences to validate or corroborate such concerns. As such, the perceptions of authenticity and performance are important even if the students have not had direct experiences of others dictating, explaining or suggesting particular ways of performing.

Holding queerness

Bennett (2014) notes that the 'born this way' rhetoric of queerness is a biological apparatus of knowledge, which can be used to legitimise non-normative genders and sexualities within a heterosexist society. However, Bennett (2014) cautions against its use, arguing it cannot account for all variations and fluidities of sexuality or for those who are still struggling to determine their gender or sexuality. This essentialism was noted by participants who identified a sense of having or *holding* queerness, or an innate identity, that could be discovered or found, and that such identities could be contested by others who were more knowledgeable. Holding queerness is significant, as it allows individuals, who are perceived to hold appropriate embodiments, access to community and experience solidarity and inclusion, while those who venture outside are made to feel marginalised or dismissed as a result:

> Do I need to completely justify it? I don't know like when my gay friend was saying to me 'oh you're definitely bisexual' I thought I felt the need to defend myself like no I'm not or maybe I am. Bridget (cisgender woman, bi-curious)

> I have had someone ask if I'm pansexual. And, I said, No. Like. I'm bisexual. They are like, 'Mhm. But, you're probably pansexual.' I was like. No. No. I'm just like. I'm quite aware of what that is. They are like, 'No. It's not that... It's like, you know... you're not bisexual.' I was like. No. I have said I'm bisexual. I'm quite happy with that. So, I have had a lot of people dance around the bisexual category...that gets hurtful because being perceived as an illegitimate sexual minority isn't the best. Sarah (cisgender woman, bisexual)

As the above examples illustrate, students have their identities questioned and contested by others. In Bridget's case, it is a form of forced labelling, in which her friend deems her to be bisexual due to her interest in both men and women. Bridget said that this form of labelling caused her to feel defensive and that she had to justify her position. In Sarah's case, her bisexual identity was dismissed and she was 're-educated' by a community member that she is pansexual despite her protests. Such labelling in the latter case was perhaps undertaken to realign Sarah with what could be deemed a more progressive sexual identity (for example pansexuality), while in the former case, it acted to censor sexuality and those who identify as questioning, curious or in a state of flux.

While some students articulated holding an identity that other LGBTIQ+ students were attempting to alter or correct their claims of sexuality, others experienced complete dismissal of the identities they hold:

GENDER AND SEXUALITY IN EDUCATION AND HEALTH

> There's just a lot of nastiness within trans communities. I've experienced, personally, even here at [university], a lot of people who are binary and trans and who are like 'you are not really trans because you're not like a binary trans person...' I just find that really bad. James (non-gender binary transgender, queer/pansexual)

> To be non-binary if you were assigned female but you must be masculine, presenting to be trans-masculine or something and then having to deal with liking feminine clothing or things in general. And pink and stuff like that [it] immediately pushes your gender back into what you are [assigned at birth as], as in people are like, why not just be a woman, because if you like all those things then you are a woman. And it is like the [non-gender binary transgender] identity does not exist. And it really sucks existing in the queer world as well. Leslie (non-binary transgender, queer)

> Even within gay communities are people who are like 'You're not really this or that.' They presume to know for you, like they know what goes on in my head, or something. Eric (agender, pansexual)

James who identified as non-binary transgender, noted they (James' preferred pronoun) are presumed by others to be inauthentic, on the basis that they chose not to identify with the opposite gender. Leslie argued that their identity is rendered invisible because they identify as non-binary transgender and demonstrate both masculine and feminine presentation as opposed to conforming to a binary notion of gender (i.e. being female-bodied and choosing to only present as trans-masculine). Both James and Leslie experienced marginalisation as the result of this transnormativity, and can be understood as being, what we term *too queer*. Eric highlighted the perception that those already identifying with the community are able to tell others outside the community about a third party's identity. While all three participants did not subscribe to a binary model of gender, and in the case of two of the participants, a medicalised model of transgender identity, their identity and experiences were dismissed and deemed invalid.

These experiences illustrate the significance of language as holding power. Firstly, as both James and Leslie identified outside a standard trans narrative, they were stripped by other transgender students, of any sense of solidarity or community through being told that they 'really' trans. Others dictated that their performances of identity did not subscribe to appropriate norms and behaviours, and as such, were rendered illegitimate. Beyond this, forced labelling, through which members of the community hold power over how much an individual (such as James) can claim a queer identity, served to dismiss alternative understandings of performance of gender and sexuality. Other participants including Bridget and Sarah (and those who were questioning) were labelled by a community members who claimed to hold greater knowledge regarding LGBTIQ+ identities and thus the power to confer concomitant benefits (i.e. community belonging). In these cases, the act of holding an appropriate queerness is dictated by those who are perceived to be performing and embodying appropriate queer identities with access to relevant language and knowledge.

Discussion and conclusion

While we originally sought in this study to explore students experiences of bullying, harassment and violence, we instead found participants wishing to speak about their experiences of exclusion and marginalisation when attempting to access and engage with LGBTIQ+ spaces and community. Many of the experiences described here resonate with Lichterman's (1999, 110) suggestion that 'to speak as queer, then [is] to relate to a sexual identity-to carry it-in a certain way'. This identity talk becomes embedded within cultural constraints and expectations regarding what it means to be queer in a contemporary Australian tertiary education setting.

In this study, students perceived as subscribing to homonormativity, or problematically being too mainstream and conformist, felt excluded and unwelcome in the tertiary LGBTIQ+ community. In essence, they were not *queer enough*. As Butler (1988) contends, the performance of an appropriate role or identity leads to acceptance within society, while an inappropriate performance or one that transgresses the set rules leads to the performers' ostracisation and marginalisation. Similar experiences of exclusion were reported by those who were perceived as rejecting transnormativity, but instead of not being *queer enough* they were situated at other end of the spectrum and were seen as *too queer*.

Students were reflective on their own comfort in presenting in what was perceived as a more homonormative way, but they also recognised that this was insufficiently transgressive to enable them to engage with the wider LGBTIQ+ community. As their performance of gender, and by extension their sexuality (see Butler 1988), did not seek to reject these homonormative ideas, they felt unwelcome and excluded. Perhaps in consequence, a number of students indicated that they have been deterred from increasing their knowledge or from 'knowing', in a place designed to enhance learning and facilitate education.

It is important to reiterate that our findings are not reflective of pathological dysfunction within LGBTIQ+ communities. Rather, they are suggestive of Ghaziani's (2014) notion that in a post-gay era there are new and emerging ways of being an LGBTIQ+ person, triggering reconsideration of what it means to be queer in relation to broader hetero/homo/transnormative structures, politics and discourses. Furthermore, all of the experiences detailed by students in this study were framed within broader heteronormative discourses and structures through which many, if not all, members of the LGBTIQ+ community must navigate. While participants noted difficulties in engaging with the others within the tertiary LGBTIQ+ community, specifically by not being queer enough (in relation to homonormative discourse) and by being too queer (in relation to transnormative discourse), it is important to note that their practices developed out of the collective desire to be valued and recognised within a heteronormative society. However, a tension emerges between wanting to belong and wanting to reject and redefine, premised on beliefs concerning what and how an authentic queer should behave and dress, and the appropriate knowledge a queer person holds. Adherence to, or the rejection of these notions seriously affected LGBTIQ+ students' experiences on campus.

There may be value in tertiary educational institutions increasing their awareness of the impact of LGBTIQ+ community groups on learning. Many students joining such institutions may be ill equipped to navigate the tertiary education space by virtue of not knowing, performing or holding queerness in ways similar to other more visible queer tertiary community members. While not the intended aim of this project, it is clear that some students felt excluded and barred from accessing education and knowledge regarding LGBTIQ+ identity, as well as from participation in the wider LGBTIQ+ community. In consequence, students may not access resources that could be helpful for them, such as support for issues including mental health (see Grant et al. 2014) or gaining knowledge about the diversity of the LGBTIQ+ community in a positive and encouraging manner. It is important therefore to consider how tertiary educational institutions can best support the diversity of LGBTIQ+ communities within the student population so as to address these issues.

GENDER AND SEXUALITY IN EDUCATION AND HEALTH

There are limitations to this work. The findings are not intended to be generalisable for application to all Australian tertiary populations due to the small-scale and unrepresentative sample size. Because of this, we recommend further research exploring LGBTIQ+ experiences and interactions between LGBTIQ+ persons within the tertiary education space. While students may be engaging with tertiary education community and gaining new knowledge about LGBTIQ+ identities and practices, further research is required into how practices of normalisation may impact upon them, and the educational opportunities available in the tertiary education space.

Note

1. Tertiary here refers to post-secondary education, including university or further-education technical college.

Disclosure statement

No potential conflict of interest was reported by the authors.

Funding

This work was supported by the School of Social Sciences at Monash University.

ORCID

Andrea Waling ⓘD http://orcid.org/0000-0003-1370-5600
James A. Roffee ⓘD http://orcid.org/0000-0002-2099-3789

References

Abes, Elisa S., and Susan R. Jones. 2004. "Meaning-making Capacity and the Dynamics of Lesbian College Students' Multiple Dimensions of Identity." *Journal of College Student Development* 45 (6): 612–632.

Almeida, Joanna, Renee M. Johnson, Heather Corliss, Beth E. Molnar, and Deborah Azreal. 2009. "Emotional Distress among LGBT Youth: The Influence of Perceived Discrimination Based on Sexual Orientation." *Journal of Youth Adolescence* 38 (7): 1001–1004.

Bennett, J. 2014. "'Born This Way': Queer Vernacular and the Politics of Origins." *Communication and Critical/Cultural Studies* 11: 211–230.

Brown, Robert, Brandy Clarke, Valerie Gortmaker, and Rachel Robinson-Keilig. 2004. "Assessing the Campus Climate for Gay, Lesbian, Bisexual and Transgender (LGBT) Students Using a Multiple Perspectives Approach." *Journal of College Student Development* 45 (1): 8–26.

Butler, Judith. 1988. "Performative Acts and Gender Constitution: An Essay in Phenomenology and Feminist Theory." *Theatre Journal* 40 (4): 519–531.

Cheng, Vincent J. 2004. *Inauthentic: The Anxiety over Culture and Identity*. New Brunswick: Rutgers University Press.

Creswell, John W. 2009. *Research Design: Qualitative, Quantitative, and Mixed Methods Approaches*. Thousand Oaks, CA: SAGE.

Davis, Alexander K. 2015. "Epiphenomenology of the Closet: Feeling and Fashioning Sexuality in Everyday Life." *Sexualities* 18 (8): 959–979.

Diamond, Lisa M. 2005. "'I'm Straight, but I Kissed a Girl': The Trouble with American Media Representations of Female-female Sexuality." *Feminism & Psychology* 15 (1): 104–110.

DiMaggio, Paul, Eszter Hargittai, Coral Celeste, and Steven Shafer. 2004. "From Unequal Access to Differentiated Use: A Literature Review and Agenda for Research on Digital Inequality." In *Social Inequality*, edited by Kathryn Neckerman, 355–400. New York: Routledge.

Draughn, Tricia, Becki Elkins, and Rakhi Roy. 2002. "Allies in the Struggle: Eradicating Homophobia and Heterosexism on Campus." *Journal of Lesbian Studies* 6 (3–4): 9–20.

Duggan, Lisa. 2003. *The Twilight of Equality? Neoliberalism, Cultural Politics, and the Attack on Democracy*. Boston, MA: Beacon Press.

Evans, Nancy J., and Ellen M. Broido. 2002. "The Experiences of Lesbian and Bisexual Women in College Residence Halls: Implications for Addressing Homophobia and Heterosexism." *Journal of Lesbian Studies* 6 (3–4): 29–40.

Ferfolja, Tania. 2007. "Schooling Cultures: Institutionalising Heteronormativity and Heterosexism." *International Journal of Inclusive Education* 11 (2): 147–162.

Foucault, Michel. [1976] 1978. *The History of Sexuality, Vol 1: An Introduction*. New York: Random House.

Gamson, Joshua. 1995. "Must Identity Movements Self-destruct? A Queer Dilemma." *Social Problems* 42 (3): 390–407.

Garber, Linda. 2002. "Weaving a Wide Net: The Benefits of Integrating Campus Projects to Combat Homophobia." *Journal of Lesbian Studies* 6 (3–4): 21–28.

Ghaziani, Amin. 2008. *The Dividends of Dissent: How Conflict and Culture Work in Lesbian and Gay Marches on Washington*. Chicago, IL: University of Chicago Press.

Ghaziani, Amin. 2011. "Post-gay Collective Identity Construction." *Social Problems* 58 (1): 99–125.

Ghaziani, Amin. 2014. *There Goes the Gayborhood?* Princeton, NJ: Princeton University Press.

Grant, Jon E., Brian L. Odlaug, Katherine Derbyshire, Liana R. N. Schreiber, Katherine Lust, and Gary Christenson. 2014. "Mental Health and Clinical Correlates in Lesbian, Gay, Bisexual, and Queer Young Adults." *Journal of American College Health* 62 (1): 75–78.

Griffin, Penny. 2007. "Sexing the Economy in a Neo-liberal World Order: Neo-liberal Discourse and the (Re)Production of Heteronormative Heterosexuality." *British Journal of Politics and International Relations* 9 (2): 220–238.

Grossman, Arnold, and Anthony R. Augelli. 2007. "Transgender Youth and Life-threatening Behaviours." *Suicide and Life-Threatening Behaviour* 37 (5): 527–537.

Guest, Greg, Arwen Bunce, and Laura Johnson. 2006. "How Many Interviews Are Enough?: An Experiment with Data Saturation and Variability Field Methods." *Methods* 18 (1): 59–82.

Hartman, Julie E. 2005. "Another Kind of 'Chilly Climate': The Effects of Lesbian Separatism on Bisexual Women's Identity and Community." *Journal of Bisexuality* 5 (4): 63–76.

Hayfield, Nikki, Victoria Clarke, and Emma Halliwell. 2014. "Bisexual Women's Understandings of Social Marginalisation: 'The Heterosexuals Don't Understand Us but Nor Do the Lesbians.'" *Feminism & Psychology* 24 (3): 352–372.

Ingraham, Chrys. 2005. "Introduction: Thinking Straight." In *Thinking Straight: The Power, the Promise and the Paradox of Heterosexuality*, edited by Chrys Ingraham, 1–14. New York: Routledge.

Jackson, Nick C., Michael Johnson, and Roe Ann Roberts. 2008. "The Potential Impact of Discrimination Fears of Older Gays, Lesbians, Bisexuals and Transgender Individuals Living in Small- to Moderate-sized Cities on Long-term Health Care." *Journal of Homosexuality* 54 (3): 325–339.

Jayakumar, Uma M. 2009. "The Invisible Rainbow in Diversity: Factors Influencing Sexual Prejudice among College Students." *Journal of Homosexuality* 56 (6): 675–700.

Johnson, Austin J. 2016. "Transnormativity: A New Concept and Its Validation through Documentary Film about Transgender Men." *Sociological Inquiry* 86 (4): 465–491.

Kosciw, Joseph G., Emily A. Greytak, Mark J. Bartkiewicz, Madelyn J. Boesen, and Neal A. Palmer. 2012. *The 2011 National School Climate Survey: The Experiences of Lesbian, Gay, Bisexual and Transgender Youth in Our Nation's Schools*. New York: GLSEN.

Lareau, Annette. 2015. "Cultural Knowledge and Social Inequality." *American Sociological Review* 80 (1): 1–27.

Lichterman, Paul. 1999. "Talking Identity in the Public Sphere: Broad Visions and Small Spaces in Sexual Identity Politics." *Theory and Society* 28 (1): 101–141.

Little, Patricia, and Marcia Marx. 2002. "Teaching about Heterosexism and Creating an Empathic Experience of Homophobia." *Journal of Lesbian Studies* 6 (3–4): 205–218.

GENDER AND SEXUALITY IN EDUCATION AND HEALTH

Mayberry, Maralee. 2006. "The Story of a Salt-Lake City Gay-straight Alliance: Identity Work and LGBT Youth." *Journal of Gay and Lesbian Issues in Education* 4 (1): 13–31.

McLean, Kirsten. 2008. "Inside, Outside, Nowhere: Bisexual Men and Women in the Gay and Lesbian Community." *Journal of Bisexuality* 8 (1–2): 63–80.

Meyer, Michaela D. E. 2004. "'We're Too Afraid of These Imaginary Tensions': Student Organising in Lesbian, Gay, Bisexual and Transgender Campus Communities." *Communication Studies* 55 (4): 499–514.

Oswalt, Sara B., and Tammy J. Wyatt. 2011. "Sexual Orientation and Differences in Mental Health, Stress, and Academic Performance in a National Sample of U.S. College Students." *Journal of Homosexuality* 58 (9): 1255–1280.

Polit, Denise F., and Cheryl T. Beck. 2009. *Essentials of Nursing Research: Appraising Evidence for Nursing Practice.* 7th ed. Philadelphia, PA: Wolters Kluwer Health.

Poynter, Kerry John, and Jamie Washington. 2005. "Multiple Identities: Creating Community on Campus for LGBT Students." *New Directions for Student Services* 111: 41–47.

Rankin, Susan R. 2005. "Campus Climates for Sexual Minorities." *New Directions for Student Services* 111: 17–23.

Rankin, Susan R. 2006. "LGBTQA Students on Campus: Is Higher Education Making the Grade?" *Journal of Gay and Lesbian Issues in Education* 3 (2–3): 111–117.

Reiners, Gina M. 2012. "Understanding the Differences between Husserl's (Descriptive) and Heidegger's (Interpretive) Phenomenological Research." *Journal of Nursing & Care* 1 (5): 1–3.

Renn, Kristen A. 2007. "LGBT Student Leaders and Queer Activists: Identities of Lesbian, Gay, Bisexual, Transgender, and Queer-identified College Student Leaders and Activists." *Journal of College Student Development* 48 (3): 311–330.

Renn, Kristen A. 2010. "LGBT and Queer Research in Higher Education: The State and Status of the Field." *Educational Researcher* 39 (2): 132–141.

Renn, Kristen A., and Brent L. Bilodeau. 2005a. "Leadership Identity Development among Lesbian, Gay, Bisexual, and Transgender Student Leaders." *Journal of Student Affairs Research and Practice* 42 (3): 342–367.

Renn, Kristen A., and Brent L. Bilodeau. 2005b. "Queer Student Leaders: An Exploratory Case Study of Identity Development and LGBT Student Involvement at a Midwestern Research University." *Journal of Gay and Lesbian Issues in Education* 2 (4): 49–71.

Ridge, Damien, Amos Hee, and Victor Minichielle. 1999. "'Asian' Men on the Scene." *Journal of Homosexuality* 36 (3–4): 43–68.

Robinson, Brandon A. 2012. "Is This What Equality Looks like?: How Assimilation Marginalises the Dutch LGBT Community." *Sexuality Research & Social Policy* 9 (4): 327–336.

Robinson, Joseph P., and Dorothy L. Espelage. 2011. "Inequities in Educational and Psychological Outcomes between LGBTQ and Straight Students in Middle and High School." *Educational Researcher* 40 (7): 315–330.

Roffee, James A., and Andrea Waling. 2017. "Resolving Ethical Challenges When Researching with Minority and Vulnerable Populations: LGBTIQ Victims of Violence, Harassment and Bullying." *Research Ethics* 13 (1): 4–22.

Seelman, Kristie. 2016. "Transgender Adults' Access to College Bathrooms and Housing and the Relationship to Suicidality." *Journal of Homosexuality* 63 (10): 1378–1399.

Serano, Julie. 2007. *Whipping Girl: A Transsexual Woman on Sexism and the Scapegoating of Femininity.* New York: Seal Press.

Stone, Amy L. 2009. "More than Adding a T: American Lesbian and Gay Activists' Attitudes towards Transgender Inclusion." *Sexualities* 12 (3): 334–354.

Strauss, Anslem, and Juliet M. Corbin. 1994. "Grounded Theory Methodology." In *The Handbook of Qualitative Research*, edited by Norman K. Denzin and Yvonna S. Lincoln, 1st ed, 217–285. Thousand Oaks, CA: SAGE.

Stryker, Susan. 2008. *A Transgender History.* New York: Seal Press.

Tetreault, Patricia A., Ryan Fette, Peter C. Meidlinger, and Debra Hope. 2013. "Perceptions of Campus Climate by Sexual Minorities." *Journal of Homosexuality* 60 (7): 947–964.

Tomlison, Merideth J., and Ruth E. Fassinger. 2003. "Career Development, Lesbian Identity Development, and Campus Climate among Lesbian College Students." *Journal of College Student Development* 44 (6): 845–860.

Vaccaro, Annemarie. 2012. "Campus Microclimates for LGBT Faculty, Staff, and Students: An Exploration of the Intersections of Social Identity and Campus Roles." *Journal of Student Affairs Research and Practice* 49 (4): 429–446.

Valentine, David. 2007. *Imagining Transgender: An Ethnography of a Category*. New York: The Feminist Press.

Vannini, Phillip, and J. Patrick Williams, eds. 2009. *Authenticity in Culture, Self and Society*. Farnham: Ashgate Publishing.

Waldo, Craig R., Matthew S. Hesson-McInnis, and Anthony R. D'Augelli. 1998. "Antecedents and Consequences of Victimisation of Lesbian, Gay and Bisexual Young People: A Structural Model Comparing Rural University and Urban Samples." *American Journal of Community* 26 (2): 307–334.

Wane, Njoki, Arlo Kempf, and Marlon Simmons, eds. 2011. *Introduction: The Politics of Cultural Knowledge*. Boston, MA: Sense Publishers.

Warner, Michael. 1991. "Introduction: Fear of a Queer Planet." *Social Text* 29: 3–17.

Weeks, Jeffrey. 1991. *Against Nature: Essays on History, Sexuality and Identity*. London: Rivers Oram Press.

Weiss, Jillian T. 2003. "GL vs. BT: The Archaeology of Biphobia and Transphobia within the US Gay and Lesbian Community." *Journal of Bisexuality* 3 (3–4): 25–55.

Woodford, Michael R., Yoosun Han, Shelley Craig, Colin Lim, and Malinda M. Matney. 2014. "Discrimination and Mental Health among Sexual Minority College Students: The Type and Form of Discrimination Does Matter." *Journal of Gay & Lesbian Mental Health* 18 (2): 142–163.

Yep, Gust A. 2002. "From Homophobia and Heterosexism to Heteronormativity: Toward the Development of a Model of Queer Interventions in the University Classroom." *Journal of Lesbian Studies* 6 (3–4): 163–176.

'That happened to me too': young people's informal knowledge of diverse genders and sexualities

Paul Byron and Jessie Hunt

ABSTRACT

This paper explores how young people of diverse genders and sexualities share information about sex, sexualities and genders. Formal approaches to education often fail to consider young people's communication and information exchange practices, including the circulation of peer knowledge through social media. In the wake of recent Australian backlash against the Safe Schools Coalition, we can observe how homophobia and queerphobia in the broader community can impact upon young peoples' ability to learn about themselves and their bodies through formal education. Yet young people of diverse genders and sexualities can be observed to support each other in peer spaces, utilising their knowledge networks. This paper explores young people's informal learning practices, the capacity of peer networks to support and educate young people, and the challenges of recognising such networks in a culture in which health and education discourses present them as 'risk subjects' rather than 'health agents'. These issues are discussed in relation to our own experiences in research and health promotion, including one author's role as a youth peer educator. Drawing on our workplace experiences, we provide a number of anecdotal examples which highlight the complexities of informal knowledge practice and information circulation, and the ways these can challenge and reform professional health, education, and research approaches.

Introduction

This paper explores informal knowledge networks of young people with diverse genders and sexualities through reflections on research and drawing upon our engagements with young people in virtual and marginal spaces. Participants in our research and health promotion activities indicate the importance of informal knowledge exchange among young people of diverse genders and sexualities. We therefore argue that health and education programmes and interventions should engage with these existing knowledge and communication networks, and consult with young people from these communities of practice.

Given the inherent tensions in attempting to capture complex and sometimes nebulous informal knowledge networks in the rigour and structure of an academic paper, this is an exploratory article. We aim to respect informal knowledge as an interactional accomplishment between young people (Garfinkel 1996), without attempting to 'translate' it into academic language, or reductively treat it as 'lesser than' formal knowledge. In pursuit of this goal, we adopt exploratory and informal research methods, offering reflection and anecdotes around moments where we have been able to witness peer knowledge exchange. These methods highlight how formalised academic ways of 'doing knowledge' do not always sit comfortably with the everyday practices of gender and sexuality diverse young people. By utilising anecdotes, we hope to respect relational ways of knowing (Gallop 2002, 51).

This paper offers examples of how young people informally share information about sex, sexualities and genders. We are not suggesting that formal health and education interventions are redundant, but we do seek to look beyond those, into gender and sexuality diverse young people's everyday practices of learning, teaching, knowing and sharing information. We argue that this often happens at a distance from formal settings, or within these but beyond the instruction or supervision of adults. We offer no models or solutions to health, education and youth work professionals, but share some of our learnings to encourage greater engagement with gender and sexuality diverse young people's needs and experiences.

While we focus on positive examples here, we recognise that these are not the sum of young people's experiences of the spaces we discuss. Instead, positive examples are foregrounded to inspire further consideration of 'best practice' when developing inclusive youth programmes and interventions.

Background

The conservative backlash against the Australian sexuality and gender diverse Safe Schools curriculum resource (Brown 2016; Butler 2016) has raised crucial questions about where and how young people learn to navigate the world from a body or subjectivity that does not map successfully onto normative cisgender[1] and heterosexual models. What we have learned from this backlash is that schools are contested sites (Wood and Lemley 2015, 4) in which young people are unable to formally engage in knowledge exchange or discussion around sex, gender and sexuality (Ullman 2015). In other words, schools cannot easily be demarcated as 'safe spaces'. Given the prevalence of gender and sexuality diverse young people's experiences of mental distress and isolation (Robinson et al. 2014, 36), learning and teaching on diverse identities is needed, but we cannot entirely rely on this kind of knowledge exchange happening in schools. Fortunately, many young people of diverse genders and sexualities have extensive knowledge around their mental health, their safeties and boundaries, and the resources and strategies available to them (Robinson et al. 2014, 17).

We can identify two streams of knowledge exchange around sex, gender and sexuality. The first is formal knowledge, often transmitted in settings like classrooms, and often communicated through hierarchical learning (Mendoza-Denton 2009, 179). Secondly, we can identify informal knowledge, which is communicated in more complex ways that do not fit comfortably into traditional understandings of what constitutes 'learning' or 'legitimate knowledge' spaces. These include via the Internet (Dobson 2014, 98), in spaces such as just after youth group or during lunch at school (Mendoza-Denton 2009, 143), or in other peer-to-peer settings that are largely unmediated by adults.

These two streams of knowledge do not fit comfortably into binaries (Edwards 2016), but share space, may respond to and reference each other, and may communicate the same ideas or materials. Informal knowledges are often nebulous and contradictory, and there may be many accounts of the same truth, or many answers to the same question. What matters most in informal knowledge exchange is not the 'truth' of the anecdote or story or piece of advice, but the creation of the space in which it is shared (Bryson and MacIntosh 2009). That space, whether virtual, or a peer conversation in a youth centre or a school lunch break – is staked out as *safe*. This can be a sharp contrast to environments fostered in some schools, homes and through mainstream media.

In this paper, we deliberately move away from discussion of 'youth risk'. We do so because risk discourse from health and education sectors gives little or no attention to young people's agency in managing their own safeties, and cannot recognise their skills in negotiating discrimination through speaking back, community-building, and resisting the personal and social effects of heteronormativity. When applying a risk framework to young people we easily overlook their 'life skills' (Michaud 2006), and how they understand their own experiences of wellbeing (Spencer 2013). A risk framework often implies that it is the responsibility of adult professionals to educate and inform young people about their risks, giving more attention to adult fears than to young people's specific needs and concerns. In contrast, our own experiences suggest that young people are often adept at managing risks, yet give different language to these (as noted in Spencer 2013), and draw upon informal resources that adult professionals may see as risky, rather than supportive.

Throughout this paper, we deploy the language and terminology used by gender and sexuality diverse young people in the spaces we discuss, including notions of 'triggering' and 'bearing witness'. We wish to foreground the language, politics, and everyday practices of the young people we engage with in our research and education roles. Terms of this discussion are also informed by our own engagements with queer communities, friendships, and activism.

Much research considers young people's informal knowledge practices, peer support and online civic participation (see for e.g. Livingstone, Bober, and Helsper 2005), but little attention has been given to young people's contemporary negotiations of diverse genders and sexualities. While we recognise and draw upon a history of public pedagogies and informal or peer-driven learning and teaching, this paper necessarily foregrounds the experiences and situations of gender and sexuality diverse young people.

Research discussion of gender and sexuality diverse young people

Research on young people of diverse genders and sexualities has illustrated the difficulties faced in practising identities that differ from heterosexual and cisgender norms. Hillier and Harrison consider same-sex attracted and gender questioning young people as space deprived (2007, 82), given their limited opportunities to express their identities in everyday public life (2007, 85, 86). As a result, much of their sexuality work is done online, where safety can be found within anonymity (Döring 2009; Hillier and Harrison 2007) and where a discourse of diverse genders and sexualities proliferates (Robinson et al. 2014; Smith et al. 2014). Alongside everyday social worlds that exclude diversities (including schools, workplaces, and families), the Internet can provide 'liberating alternatives for the building of new forms of culture and community among young people' (Hillier and Harrison 2007, 81).

Gender and sexuality diverse young people's wellbeing is often supported through their everyday use of digital media (GLSEN 2013; Hillier et al. 2010; Robinson et al. 2014; Smith et al. 2014, 15). Our focus does not compare online/offline worlds however, because distinctions between these are less useful today (Hillier and Harrison 2007; Marwick 2013). According to Deuze's theory of 'media life', we do not live *with* but *in* media (2012). To distinguish between online/offline worlds suggests that media spaces are something we can easily move in and out of, rather than something we are always navigating. Young people's friendships highlight this false dualism, given that they operate through multiple communication spaces, where online interactions are no less real than offline. In a media life context, identities and media are co-produced, and one does not simply generate the other. While they have not produced gender diversity, digital media cultures have influenced diversity practices, as well as gender/sexuality discourse, by offering accessible communication channels through which young people can seek identity affirmation and supportive communities.

In the recent *Blues to Rainbows* study, Smith et al. (2014) report that trans and gender diverse young people surveyed found greater support from friends, rather than families. Asked about strategies they used to feel better, 77% stated that they spent time with friends, 70% chatted to friends online, and 66% said they would text or call friends (Smith et al. 2014, 78). Furthermore, when asked about their informational needs, 77% of participants noted that peers provided a good source of information and support (2014, 84). Evidently, friendship and peer support are key to participants' wellbeing, and this is supported through digital media practices.

Driver highlights how digitally mediated communities expand gay, lesbian, bisexual, transgender, queer and questioning identities in helping 'to provide multilayered spaces of self-representation, support, and belonging for youth who are marginalised on the basis of their gender and sexual differences' (2006, 230). In a recent Canadian study, Craig and McInroy isolate five key themes of how online participation influences and supports lesbian, gay, bisexual, transgender and queer young people by providing 'the opportunity to (1) access resources, (2) explore identity, (3) find likeness, (4) come out digitally, and (5) potentially expand identities formed online into offline life' (2014, 100). Discussing online forums for queer young people, Hanckel and Morris also highlight how these can increase a sense of belonging, decrease a sense of isolation, and foster the transfer of subcultural knowledge (2014).

While literature on 'online identities' often focuses on the self-presentations of individuals online, identity is also a key factor in how people interact with each other (Marwick 2013). People conduct themselves differently depending on context and audience (Goffman 1959), and gender and sexuality diverse young people's digital interactions with peers will differ to how they perform identities in family homes, schools, and workplaces, where certain genders and sexualities may be questioned, judged negatively, or be met with unwanted attention. It is in this context that Hillier et al. proposed the Internet as a 'safety net' for same sex attracted young people (2012), and this can be said of young people of diverse genders and sexualities more broadly.

Informal knowledge exchange in formal spaces: creating 'safer spaces'

In this section we offer an anecdote that illustrates young people's ability to construct and demarcate 'safer spaces' within formal learning spaces. Here, participants demonstrate listening skills, skills of disclosure, and reassurance and support skills. These practices can fill a gap in formal learning settings given that facilitators of group work are often advised to

GENDER AND SEXUALITY IN EDUCATION AND HEALTH

discourage or prevent personal disclosures (Tiffany 2012, 35). When personal disclosures occur, they can reveal a slippage of in/formal youth work, where formal codes cannot always contain the informal knowledge exchanges taking place. In such situations, both workers and participants may enact their understandings of safeties (Robinson et al. 2014, 17), thus renegotiating and reconstituting the safety of that space. The anecdote that follows seeks to demonstrate and acknowledge the skills of young people in constantly enacting and instituting safe spaces for informal knowledge exchange within formal spaces. It derives from the second author's experience as a youth worker.

Jessie: Throughout 2015 and 2016, I worked as a Sex & Gender Diverse Youth Access Worker in south western Sydney. Through this time, I worked predominantly with young people of colour, who came from working class backgrounds and who spoke languages other than English at home. These demographics are reflected in statistical data about south western Sydney (Australian Bureau of Statistics 2011). What isn't reflected in official statistics is the number of gender and sexuality diverse people I worked with, or the diverse range of languages those young people used to articulate their sexuality and gender identity. Further, with the exception of Kassisieh's *We're Family Too* report (2011), we know very little about non-white young people navigating multiple marginalised identities in Sydney. Given the absence of data, and to respect the expertise of the young people I worked with in navigating these intersections. I want to share some anecdotes of moments when the young people I worked with became the 'experts', and through which valuable teaching and learning occurred for everyone in the room. These are often moments when I lost control of group discussion, or relinquished control. These are bubbles of informal knowledge exchange that could not be contained by formal knowledge structures.

Anecdote #1

We are nearing the end of a two-hour long gender and sexuality diverse youth drop-in in Sydney's south west. Of the ten young people in the room, all are assigned female at birth or trans-feminine, and eight of the ten are people of colour. I have just finished running a workshop on consent, and I'm feeling emotionally exhausted, slow to react. We are 'checking out', talking about how we feel now and strategies for self-care for when we get home. One participant, Siti,[2] begins talking about how the workshop was hard for her because of her experiences of sexual assault. As Siti begins sharing, I know this is a conversation I should probably 'shut down' – the risks associated with the dreaded disclosure. I feel every inch the new, clumsy youth worker, unsure of how to seamlessly facilitate this moment. But as Siti speaks I see other young people around the room nodding, I see the young people either side of Siti making comforting gestures, I hear the murmurs: 'That happened to me too.' I realise that this space for sharing a story, the gentleness with which other people in the room have held this story, and the solidarity and horizontal support and real empathy given to Siti in this space – afforded by my own ineptitude – could not have been provided in one-on-one counselling, or through a worksheet.[3] I realise that the lessons imparted today – the awareness that other survivors of sexual violence occupy Siti's world, and that we can hold these experiences together – are invaluable.

Jessie: The above moment occurred early in my youth work practice, in a group that had met only three or four times. Theoretically, I was aware that I was supposed to avoid young people making disclosures – and of course, there are very good reasons for this: the sharing of personal stories can be highly triggering or activating for other young people in the room (Dilveko 2015, 9), as well as for the teller themselves. However, there is also an element of risk-aversion in some youth work discourse around disclosure: the idea that acknowledging the existence of sexual assault at all is inherently risky, the idea that being a survivor of childhood sexual assault makes a client an abnormally risky one (Tiffany 2012, 129). Such notions sit uncomfortably with my feminist politics and with my own experiences, and so in this moment of practice I felt highly conflicted. Do I actually intervene to stop the telling of a vitally important story? How do I avoid others in the room becoming activated or triggered? Whilst I was fretting on these questions, the story was told, and I was able to bear witness as young people in the room held the space wonderfully and facilitated an incredible moment of interpersonal caring.

Information sharing and gender and sexuality activism

The prevalence of online support and information for young people of diverse genders and sexualities has been associated with activism around gender and sexuality rights and discrimination (Jones and Hillier 2013; Robinson et al. 2014). Researchers have noted a high uptake of activism among lesbian, gay, bisexual, transgender, intersex and queer young people (Hillier et al. 2010), particularly among young people who are gender diverse (Smith et al. 2014). This can be seen in the value that many gender and sexuality diverse young people place on Tumblr. This social networking site provides significant space for identity-building and knowledge exchange among gender and sexual minorities (Tiidenberg 2014), as noted in recent surveys of gender and sexuality diverse young people in Australia (Byron et al. 2017; Smith et al. 2014).[4] Smith et al. note that many of their participants found Tumblr to be 'a place where transgender and gender diverse experiences, issues and solutions were shared' (2014, 84). Participants from the recent *You Learn From Each Other* study offer similar accounts (Byron et al. 2017). For example, one young person states:

> Tumblr is a platform on which many people can tell their stories and provide resources to others – this often constitutes an exchange of valuable information between young people... that provide support to their members when they aren't getting it elsewhere, or even when they are. It's a microcosm of society, just more up to date when it comes to most info. *(18, agender, asexual)*

This astute articulation of informal knowledge exchange suggests the possibility (and perhaps the need) for health promoters, researchers, and professionals to directly engage with young people of diverse genders and sexualities, rather than devising and delivering interventions without their input. Elsewhere, the same participant discusses the volume of peer-led mental health information available online, and recommends that rather than providing more information to gender and sexuality diverse young people, health professionals could make this existing information more available to young people who need it.

Focusing on queer people of colour, Cho argues that Tumblr's 'networks of passion' also work to destabilise any return to a static understanding of identity politics (2015). Here, community-shared knowledge and discourse of gender fluidity, and opportunities for multiple and non-static sex and gender identities, can challenge traditional projects of 'coming out' and 'gender transitioning'. Seemingly, traditional understandings of young people finding and accepting authentic sexual/gender identities continue to guide formal understandings of how to support young people of diverse sexualities and genders. It should also be noted, however, that Tumblr is not a wholly positive space – gender and sexuality diverse young people we work with note that it can also be a toxic environment when different understandings of sex, gender and sexuality clash and result in disputes.

Young people's engagements with Tumblr and other social media highlight how these spaces can offer and produce new and experimental practices and identities. Arguably this is forged and fostered through active dispute and a politics of space-making for gender and sexual minorities. This highlights how online and identity practices co-constitute each other. As such, one's identities do not simply precede the media, platforms, apps, and other technologies through which these are practiced and articulated.

Mental health and experiential knowledge

Jessie: The following anecdote describes an experience of witnessing mental health stories being shared among gender and sexuality diverse young people in an informal situation of knowledge exchange.

Anecdote #2

I am working at a camp for young people of diverse genders and sexualities. For much of the week I have been supporting a young person who is carrying around some quite traumatic experiences. They have sophisticated analytical language with which to talk about mental health, but are also gifted at talking about their experiences, their uncertainties and insecurities, in a way that invites other folks' sharing. I suggest they run a workshop at the camp, about queerness and mental health. The camp itself, run entirely by volunteers, allows this kind of learning – as a space with lots of autonomy, we are able to facilitate the radical idea of a young person running a workshop about their own experiences of mental health, rather than a professional explaining to us what mental health for young people means. The workshop itself makes me feel lucky to be alive and to be queer and to be present – it is young people who are able to speak with authority about things they have felt and experienced, without having to acquiesce to medicalised languages or accounts of their bodies or experiences. They give trigger warnings – by which I mean they ask permission of, and make eye contact with, every person in the room before talking about self-harm or disordered eating. They speak from their own experiences, never in generalities. I find myself wondering why all kinds of education doesn't look like this. We had to travel hours from these young peoples' homes and schools to allow this space to grow.

This experience is unique in my youth work practice. Though youth workers and health workers have extensive discourses around 'youth led' and 'client led' practices (Caplan 2010; Goodnough 2014, 368), it is uncommon that the term youth led means this particular kind of work. In this workshop, young people's accounts of living with mental health issues or variations were centred. They were not consulted as if they were secondary psychologists, they were not invited to participate in programmes with already-set parameters; young people were the experts. This was not a spontaneously occurring space, as the young person was invited by myself, a figure of relative authority, to give the workshop. But the camp was also removed from more formal learning structures like school: it was voluntary, all workshops were optional, and the young people involved had more autonomy around what they wanted to learn about, and how. The workshop was designed and implemented by young people with mental health diagnoses or variations, as experts on their own experiences

(Gill 2014, 22). The absence of a person 'in charge' enabled the young people to be vulnerable – to openly share accounts of feeling incapable, inferior or bad (Goodnough 2014). This kind of talk is difficult to accomplish in more structured learning environments; it required a space to disclose mental illness without fear or shame (for example, the peer-led environment in which most young people were living with a mental health variation[5]), the option to 'tap out' (for example, the fact that workshops were optional), and the young people's ability to feel ownership of their stories (Batsleer 2008, 96).

Lived experience and relatable feelings

Shared feelings and lived experience are key to young people finding and sharing information about diverse genders and sexualities. For example, many young people have shared their experiences and processes of gender transitioning through producing YouTube videos (Cavalcante 2016; Horak 2014) that generate affirmative response to their experiences, and foster a greater sense of community, solidarity and belonging. Used in this way, social media have also fostered the expertise of trans young people (Horak 2014).

Paul: While considering young people's social media practices, and the examples of Tumblr and YouTube mentioned, I have spent time in these spaces, witnessing much activism, gender identity work, and (often) anonymous storytelling. As an adult, I am aware that these spaces are not for me, that these exclusionary zones are important for the continued safety and trust of these 'networked counterpublics' (Renninger 2015). From my cursory intrusions, I see that these networks can offer significant support through the multiple voices and experiences they offer, and the many stories told from people who have 'been there'. Here, users address audiences that are both fictional and real, often comprised of unknown others whose marginalisations and/or differences are similarly composed. Many conversations I've witnessed seem to be about turning these differences around – from a space of discomfort and non-acceptance, to an accepted experience of selfhood (made more acceptable in light of these experiences being communal). This suggests a practice not restricted to 'finding self', but very much integrated with the practice of 'finding community', where affirmation is sought through shared understandings and experiences. Evidently, these are sites of knowledge and its productions. The following is a question somebody posted on Tumblr.

> I have a very serious question about gender dysphoria. Does anyone else have days where no definition works? Where you cant feel good about your target gender because something is off, and you kinda miss what was before but when you actually think about it or dress like you used to you feel no relief and even more disgust, even though you know [you] could stop and it would make things easier? When you try neutral or bigender or fluid but nothing at all sounds right. It all feels obligatory and pointless …

> Does anyone one else have days they feel this way? This muddled and confused and hurt? I'm worried something is wrong with me [6]

At the time of writing, this post had generated 35 'notes'.[7] This user's posts usually generated between 3 and 8 notes. This high level of engagement might be explained by the questions asked, and/or how the questions are presented. To date, five responses have been made to the post, including the following:

> Yes I do feel that way. There is nothing wrong with you … For me there are days when I can't look at myself because I can't feel like my target gender. Of course [it] may be a little different for me since I am Genderfluid. But I want you to know that you are not alone :)

> i feel that way too sometimes. it's not just you

> YES. I feel stuck. I know I'm not a woman but I feel like I'll never get to the point where I FEEL like a "real" man. For me that's because I'm pre-everything, but I'm pretty sure it's common …

> You are not alone in this. I have not even come out as transgender to my parents but i still feel like this.

Through this question, and the responses to it, the poster's experience of gender dysphoria is neither presented nor responded to as a problem that is solely theirs. Asking 'Does anyone one else have days they feel this way?' not only invites responses, but suggests the poster's knowledge of an available audience of others; a community-at-hand. Only the closing line ('I'm worried something is wrong with me') points to the poster's concern about being isolated and/or abnormal. All respondents rebut this, noting that they too have felt these things, even when their gender identities differ. Unanimously, those who respond indicate that these feelings, while unpleasant, are common (e.g. 'You are not alone in this'/'I'm pretty sure it's common'). Notably, no respondents attempt to solve this problem, and no solution is asked for. Offered instead is evidence that these feelings are heard and are deemed common. Through bearing witness, these feelings are affirmed as a legitimate response to a problem that is larger than oneself.

Jessie: As noted, young people's' connections to online spaces do not exist in a firm binary between offline and online (Robinson et al. 2014, 17), and there are significant points of slippage between young people's online interactions and those that happen in non-virtual spaces (Döring 2009). This is somewhat problematised by moral panics surrounding young people's use of digital technologies (Albury and Crawford 2012, 465), complicating gender and sexuality diverse young people's ability to have open conversations about the intersections between sexuality and digital life. Having been asked to deliver several 'cybersafety workshops' for gender and sexuality diverse young people by directors of youth services – and having been impressed by young people's ability to develop their own strategies for safety and to share experiences – I would like to reflect on young people's uses of liminal spaces to share their experiences.

Anecdote #3

I am packing up after a workshop on online dating and relationships at a youth health service in Sydney's south west. We'd talked about experiences of online dating and friendships, and it had turned out that everyone present used an application or website to meet other gender and sexuality diverse young people, either for romantic relationships or friendships. We'd watched an episode of *Catfish*,[8] about a young transmasculine[9] person who uses a cisgender man's pictures online, and the queer woman who dates him anyway. We had shared frustrated groans when Nev and Max, the show's hosts, misgender the young transmasculine person, but the 'catfishing' itself triggers little or no outrage from the young people in the group – the many and varied ways young trans people work to create online renderings that match their gender identities seem to be just a feature of these young people's landscapes. There are still a few young people around as I pack up, who are trading experiences of making friends or potential lovers online. One young person remarks, 'And then what happened was her *girlfriend* messaged me on Facebook! She'd had a girlfriend the whole time!' Another young person replies, 'Oh yeah, what I do is I lurk their Facebook to see if one person is posting or commenting heaps.'

Rather than occurring outside of formal learning settings, this moment took place nestled alongside one: in the aftermath of a more or less formal youth group. Though I work hard to de-formalise the workshops and the learning settings they provide, young people are accustomed to certain kinds of learning – strict guidelines around who can speak, when, and what counts as 'knowledge' (Batsleer 2008, 7), and sometimes these structures are involuntarily invoked or created by either myself or the young people. Even in such settings, however, there are always moments of what I term 'non-space': whilst other young people are talking loudly, a young person might quietly begin a discussion with me, or several young people may linger to continue their own discussion after the workshop has finished.

The two young people in this anecdote present the 'risk' of engaging in online sexual cultures as an expected and accepted outcome; certainly not shocking enough to avoid online dating. Many young people have devised strategies to navigate these risks – simply examining the romantic prospect's Facebook profile in an attempt to identify who might have an active part in that person's life. Although this risk management strategy is certainly different to those strategies presented by government and non-government education programmes (for example, SXTING 2014), it is a strategy based on experiences of navigating online love, sex and romance. Their discussion, unmediated by any 'adult' or 'expert' presence, takes on different parameters than the facilitated discussion of a workshop. These young people were able to confide and be vulnerable, whilst also presenting harm minimisation strategies that they have developed themselves.

Concluding remarks

According to a survey respondent in the *We Learn From Each Other* study (Byron et al. 2017):

> … non-triggering accounts from individuals with lived experiences has helped me understand what I'm going through and how to deal with it. (*16, agender, grey-asexual/sensual*)

Lived experiences are sought and found in young people's negotiations of sex, sexualities and gender. This happens in online spaces, as well as in peer environments including formal structures which can host informal knowledge exchange. As we've highlighted throughout, sharing lived experience is an educational tool that can elevate the young person from marginalised to expert (Woolley 2015, 37). Young people of diverse genders and sexualities use informal knowledge networks to communicate *in spite of* homophobia and queerphobia, as well as around those discourses that code young people's actions with 'risk' (Albury 2013). Lack of information about how young people are engaging with digital media can generate adult fears about this media and young people's experiences of it (Pascoe 2012); yet, as this paper demonstrates, young people can develop strong informal knowledge networks that support their negotiations of a range of risks. Peer networks often do the kinds of harm minimisation work that adult fears do not.

Informal knowledge networks serve three main functions: first, they carve out space for young people to supplement their formal learning with knowledge grounded in real-world experience; second, they do the kinds of harm minimisation work that adult fears prevent; and third, they render young people experts of their own experiences, in sharp contrast with a culture that positions them as ignorant, wilfully 'risky', and in need of constant surveillance (Batsleer 2008).

Throughout this paper, we have sought to honour the kinds of work that peer knowledge networks do. Informal learning, and the young people who propagate it, contradict dominant cultural narratives of vulnerable gender and sexuality diverse young people, in which young people are perpetually 'at risk' (Kemshall 2008). As informal knowledge differs greatly from academic knowledge in style and format, it seems contradictory to 'translate' this into a formal knowledge setting, as though we are rendering young people as needing someone to speak on their behalf. To properly honour young people's informal knowledge networks, we have explored some alternative methodologies that foreground lived experience and relational knowledges (Gallop 2002). Our aim here is to present an alternative rendering of young people's abilities to communicate and create space, and to bring this discussion into spaces that often foreclose it. We also welcome health and education professionals to question current approaches that do not consider or engage with young people's informal knowledge practices, including gender and sexuality diverse young people's networks of care, support, and information sharing.

Notes

1. Cisgender refers to people whose gender identity 'matches' with their assigned gender at birth. The term, meaning 'on the same side', seeks to disrupt the assumption that cisgender people are 'normal' and transgender people are 'other'.
2. A pseudonym has been used.
3. A worksheet is a paper listing questions or tasks for a client or student to complete, often utilised in social or therapeutic groups.
4. Another of these is the *Scrolling Beyond Binaries* survey (see scrollingbeyondbinaries.com), for which Paul is an investigator. This will not be discussed here because data analysis is in the early stages.
5. Mental health variation is a term used to destigmatise mental health and dislodge the normative assumptions of pathologising language.
6. The url and identity of this user is not referenced here, out of respect for their anonymity and the intended audience of this post. Also, this is one example of many, and it should be noted that these discussions are broad and diverse, along with the engagements they generate.
7. 'Notes' refer to each time a Tumblr post is liked, shared, or commented on by other users. See Dame (2016) and Fink and Miller (2014) for more detailed accounts of Tumblr practices.
8. *Catfish* is an MTV-produced reality television show about people who misrepresent themselves online to attract romantic partners, money or as a joke. The show has popularised the term 'catfishing', a verb used to describe the practice of misrepresenting oneself on the internet.
9. Transmasculine is a broad gender identity, referring to a transgender person who identifies as 'masculine of centre', or on the masculine end of a spectrum. This may or may not mean they identify as male.

Acknowledgements

We'd like to acknowledge the input and influence of Kate Giunta, Angie Kocsisek and Ben Hanckel. Jessie would also like to acknowledge their former supervisor, Andrew Whelan. Paul would like to acknowledge participants and researchers from the LGBTIQ Help Seeking study, and Twenty10 incorporating GLCS NSW.

Disclosure statement

No potential conflict of interest was reported by the authors.

Funding

The *You Learn From Each Other* study mentioned in this paper was funded by Young and Well Cooperative Research Centre, and led by Twenty10 incorporating GLCS NSW.

References

Albury, K. 2013. "Young People, Media and Sexual Learning: Rethinking Representation." *Sex Education* 13 (sup1): s32–s44.

Albury, K., and K. Crawford. 2012. "Sexting, Consent and Young People's Ethics: Beyond Megan's Story." *Continuum: Journal of Media & Cultural Studies* 26 (3): 463–473.

Australian Bureau of Statistics. 2011. Census Quick Stats, "People", Canberra Accessed March 8, 2016. http://stat.abs.gov.au/itt/r.jsp?databyregion

Batsleer, J. 2008. *Informal Learning in Youth Work*. London: SAGE.

Brown, G. 2016. "Safe Schools Judge Co-chair of Gay Youth Group Twenty10." *The Australian*, March 26. http://www.theaustralian.com.au/nationalaffairs/education/safeschool-judge-cochair-of-gay-youth-group-twenty10/newsstory/bf6783a7657069d5ecf4589cdfbe7677.

Bryson, M. K., and L. B. MacIntosh. 2009. "Can We Play Fun Gay? Disjuncture and Difference, and the Precarious Mobilities of Millennial Queer Youth Narratives." *International Journal of Qualitative Studies in Education* 23 (1): 101–124.

Butler, J. 2016. "Government MP George Christensen Likens LGBT 'Safe Schools' Program to Paedophile Grooming." *Huffington Post*, March 26. http://www.huffingtonpost.com.au/2016/02/25/christensengrooming_n_9322362.

Byron, P., S. Rasmussen, D. Wright Toussaint, R. Lobo, K. Robinson, and B. Paradise. 2017. *'You Learn from Each Other': LGBTIQ Young People's Mental Health Help-seeking and the RAD Australia Online Directory*. Sydney: Young and Well Cooperative Research Centre & Western Sydney University.

Caplan, M. A. 2010. "Social Investment and Mental Health: The Role of Social Enterprise." In *Social Work and Social Development*, edited by J Midgley., and Conley Amy, 71–86. New York: Oxford University Press.

Cavalcante, A. 2016. "'I Did It All Online:' Transgender Identity and the Management of Everyday Life." *Critical Studies in Media Communication* 33 (1): 109–122.

Cho, A. 2015. "Sensuous Participation: Queer Youth of Color, Affect, and Social Media." Unpublished PhD thesis., The University of Texas.

Craig, S. L., and L. McInroy. 2014. "You Can Form a Part of Yourself Online: The Influence of New Media on Identity Development and Coming out for LGBTQ Youth." *Journal of Gay & Lesbian Mental Health* 18 (1): 95–109.

Dame, A. 2016. "Making a Name for Yourself: Tagging as Transgender Ontological Practice on Tumblr." *Critical Studies in Media Communication* 33 (1): 23–37.

Deuze, M. 2012. *Media Life*. Cambridge: Polity.

Dilveko, J. 2015. "The Politics of Trigger Warnings." *Journal of Information Ethics* 24 (2): 9–12.

Dobson, A. S. 2014. "Performative Shamelessness on Young Women's Social Network Sites: Shielding the Self and Resisting Gender Melancholia." *Feminism & Psychology* 24 (1): 97–114.

Döring, N. M. 2009. "The Internet's Impact on Sexuality: A Critical Review of 15 Years of Research." *Computers in Human Behavior* 25 (5): 1089–1101.

Driver, S. 2006. "Virtually Queer Youth Communities of Girls and Birls: Dialogical Spaces of Identity Work and Desiring Exchanges." In *Digital Generations: Children, Young People, and New Media*, edited by D. Buckingham and R. Willett, 229–245. Mahwah: Lawrence Erlbaum Associates.

Edwards, N. 2016. "Women's Reflections on Formal Sex Education and the Advantage of Gaining Informal Sexual Knowledge through a Feminist Lens." *Sex Education* 16 (3): 266–278.

GENDER AND SEXUALITY IN EDUCATION AND HEALTH

Fink, M., and Q. Miller. 2014. "Trans Media Moments: Tumblr, 2011–2013." *Television & New Media* 15 (7): 611–626.

Gallop, J. 2002. *Anecdotal Theory*. Durham: Duke University Press.

Garfinkel, H. 1996. "Ethnomethodology's Program." *Social Psychology Quarterly* 59 (1): 5–21.

Gill, K. J. 2014. "Recovery Colleges. Co-production in Action: The Value of the Lived Experience in 'Learning and Growth for Mental Health." *Health Issues* 113: 10–14.

GLSEN. 2013. *Out Online: The Experiences of Lesbian, Gay, Bisexual and Transgender Youth on the Internet.* New York: Gay, Lesbian and Straight Education Network in partnership with Center for Innovative Public Health Research, and Crimes against Children Research Center.

Goffman, E. 1959. *The Presentation of Self in Everyday Life*. New York, NY: Doubleday.

Goodnough, K. 2014. "Examining the Potential of Youth Led Community of Practice: Experience and Insights." *Educational Action Research* 22 (3): 363–379.

Hanckel, B., and A. Morris. 2014. "Finding Community and Contesting Heteronormativity: Queer Young People's Engagement in an Australian Online Community." *Journal of Youth Studies* 17 (7): 872–886.

Hillier, L., and L. Harrison. 2007. "Building Realities Less Limited than Their Own: Young People Practising Same-sex Attraction on the Internet." *Sexualities* 10 (1): 82–100.

Hillier, L., T. Jones, M. Monagle, N. Overton, L. Gahan, J. Blackman, and A. Mitchell. 2010. *Writing Themselves in 3: The Third National Study on the Sexual Health and Wellbeing of Same Sex Attracted and Gender Questioning Young People*. Melbourne: Australian Research Centre in Sex, Health & Society, La Trobe University.

Hillier, L., K. J. Mitchell, and M. L. Ybarra. 2012. "The Internet as a Safety Net: Findings from a Series of Online Focus Groups with LGB and Non-LGB Young People in the United States." *Journal of LGBT Youth* 9 (3): 225–246.

Horak, L. 2014. "Trans on YouTube: Intimacy, Visibility, Temporality." *Transgender Studies Quarterly* 1 (4): 572–585.

Jones, T., and L. Hillier. 2013. "Comparing Trans-Spectrum and Same-sex-attracted Youth in Australia: Increased Risks, Increased Activisms." *Journal of LGBT Youth* 10 (4): 287–307.

Kassisieh, G. 2011. *'We're Family Too': The Effects of Homophobia in Arabic-speaking Communities in New South Wales*. Sydney: Lesbian and Gay Anti-violence Project, AIDS Council of New South Wales.

Kemshall, H. 2008. "Risks, Rights and Justice: Understanding and Responding to Youth Risk." *Youth Justice* 8 (1): 21–37.

Livingstone, S., M. Bober, and E. Helsper. 2005. "Active Participation or Just More Information? Young People's Take up of Opportunities to Act and Interact on the Internet." *Information, Communication and Society* 8 (3): 287–314.

Marwick, A. E. 2013. "Online Identity." In *A Companion to New Media Dynamics*, edited by J. Hartley, J. Burgess and A. Bruns, 355–364. Chichester: Blackwell Publishing Ltd.

Mendoza-Denton, N. 2009. *Homegirls: Language and Cultural Practice among Latina Youth*. Malden: Blackwell Publishing.

Michaud, P.-A. 2006. "Adolescents and Risks: Why Not Change Our Paradigm?" *Journal of Adolescent Health* 38 (5): 481–483.

Pascoe, C. J. 2012. "Studying Young People's New Media Use: Methodological Shifts and Educational Innovations." *Theory into Practice* 51 (2): 76–82.

Renninger, B. J. 2015. "'Where I Can Be Myself ... Where I Can Speak My Mind': Networked Counterpublics in a Polymedia Environment." *New Media & Society* 17 (9): 1513–1529.

Robinson, K., P. Bansel, N. Denson, G. Ovenden, and C. Davies. 2014. *Growing up Queer: Issues Facing Young Australians Who Are Gender Variant and Sexuality Diverse*. Melbourne: Young and Well Cooperative Research Centre.

Smith, E., T. Jones, R. Ward, J. Dixon, A. Mitchell, and L. Hillier. 2014. *From Blues to Rainbows: The Mental Health and Well-being of Gender Diverse and Transgender Young People in Australia*. Melbourne: The Australian Research Centre in Sex, Health and Society, La Trobe University.

Spencer, G. 2013. "Young People's Perspectives on Health: Empowerment, or Risk?" *Health Education* 113 (2): 115–131.

SXTIng. 2014. "The Line," October 6, viewed 21st May 2016. Accessed April 29 2016. http://www.youtube.com/watch?v=HxY8C2ebv1U

Tiffany, G. 2012. "Towards an 'Intelligence Based Approach' to Detached Youth Work Management." In *Critical Issues in Youth Work Management* edited by Ord, 125–134. New York: Routledge.

Tiidenberg, K. 2014. "There's No Limit to Your Love–Scripting the Polyamorous Self." *Journal Für Psychologie* 22 (1): 1–27.

Ullman, J. 2015. *Free2Be?: Australian National Survey of Gender-climate and School Belonging for LGBTQ Students*. Sydney: Western Sydney University. Accessed http://researchdirect.westernsydney.edu.au/islandora/object/uws:32727

Wood, G., and E. Lemley. 2015. "Mapping the Cultural Boundaries in Schools and Communities: Redefining Spaces through Organizing." *Democracy & Education* 23 (1): 1–9.

Woolley, L. 2015. "Anti-oppressive Youth Work with Young People with Disabilities." In *Innovation in Youth Work: Thinking in Practice*, edited by N. Stanton, 34–37. London: YMCA George Williams College.

Responsibilities, tensions and ways forward: parents' perspectives on children's sexuality education

Kerry H. Robinson, Elizabeth Smith and Cristyn Davies

ABSTRACT

Children's sexuality education continues to be plagued with tensions and controversies. In consequence, children's access to sexuality education is severely compromised, especially in terms of the time dedicated to this topic, the content addressed, how it is taught and by whom. Based on a study of 342 Australian parents of primary school aged children we explore: (i) parents' perceptions of the relevance and importance of sexuality education to their primary school aged children and the discourses that inform their perspectives; (ii) parents' views on who should be responsible for the sexuality education of young children; (iii) whether there are certain aspects of sexuality education considered more appropriate for the family to address with children; and (iv) what the implications of these findings are for sexuality education policy and practice in Australian primary schooling. Despite the controversial nature of the topic, the majority of parents in this study believed sexuality education was relevant and important to primary school children and that it should be a collaborative approach between families and schools. However, some parents/carers acknowledged that while that they believed that some topics should only be addressed at home they also indicated that this often does not happen.

Introduction

Children's sexuality education in schools and in families continues to be plagued with tensions and controversies. These social anxieties stem largely from cultural discourses that perpetuate the perspective that sexuality is irrelevant, developmentally inappropriate, risky and dangerous to pre-pubescent children (Renold 2005; Davies and Robinson 2010; Egan and Hawkes 2010; Egan 2013; Robinson 2013). As a consequence, children's sexuality education is severely compromised, especially in terms of the age at which this education should begin, the time dedicated to the topic, the content that can be addressed with children and how it is taught and by whom. The social anxieties encountered by many parents continue to exist despite the demonstrated value of comprehensive sexuality education for young people's health and well-being. Sexuality education is also essential for building young people's informed decision-making around sexuality, and for developing awareness and understandings of the importance of ethical intimate relationships – all of which are critical to the development of their sexual citizenship (Carmody 2009; McKee et al. 2010; Robinson 2013, 2016).

In our discussion, we provide a brief overview about sexuality education in primary schools in two Australian states in which the study was undertaken: Victoria and New South Wales. Second, we outline our study aims and methodology, which involved qualitative and quantitative components. Third, we explore: (i) parents' perceptions of the relevance and importance of sexuality education to their primary school aged children and the discourses that inform their perspectives; (ii) parents' views on who should be responsible for the sexuality education of young children; (iii) whether there are certain aspects of sexuality education considered more appropriate for the family to address with children; and (iv) what the implications of these findings are for sexuality education policy and practice in Australian primary schooling.

Background

Sexuality education has been shown to have many benefits for young people, particularly later in their lives. For example, young people who receive comprehensive sexuality education engage in fewer risky sexual practices (Kao and Manczak 2013), have fewer sexual partners, are more likely to use appropriate protection (Wu 2010), and are less likely to become pregnant in their teenage years (Kirby 2002). However, educating children and young people about sexuality is a contested subject and a site of much disagreement and conflicting perspectives. The anxieties that prevail around children and sexuality education are steeped in sociocultural discourses of childhood and childhood 'innocence' (Meyer 2007; Bhana 2008; Davies and Robinson 2010; Robinson 2013). Within this context, sexuality is considered adults' knowledge, from which children need to be distanced and protected. Broader social taboos about sexuality have led to individual and collective apprehensions that effect many adults talking openly and honestly about sexuality, especially to children and young people (Stone, Ingham, and Gibbins 2013). Consequently, many young people go through life with minimal comprehensive sexuality education in school or within their families. Children and young people have diverse identities and come from a wide range of family backgrounds, which can impact the delivery of sexuality education in the classroom. This can impede the inclusion of certain topics considered inappropriate or controversial by some families. Consequently, difficulties arise meeting the needs of all students, for example young people from gender and sexuality diverse backgrounds (Hillier and Mitchell 2008). Many young people rely on the Internet and peers for their information about sexuality (Hillier et al. 2010; Robinson et al. 2014; Ullman 2015).

In Australia, school education and curricula have traditionally been the responsibility of individual states and territories. More recently, a National Curriculum has been developed, with a Health and Physical Education syllabus that includes relationships and sexuality education, covering primary schools. In this National Curriculum (version 8.3), children in years 1–2 learn about body parts, changing bodies, emotions, and protective behaviours; in years 3 and 4, earlier areas are built on with the introduction of respecting diversity (Including gender, gender expression, sexuality); in years 5 and 6, greater emphasis is given to identity, transitions to puberty, initiating and managing relationships, and valuing diversity (ACARA 2015). However, there has been some opposition to the National Curriculum, including towards the suggested early start of learning about sexuality and valuing gender, gender expression and sexuality diversity (Australian Government 2014).

Children's experiences of sexuality education are not generally reflective of a comprehensive approach and can vary considerably across individual schools, states and territories (Leahy et al. 2016). What knowledge is included in children's sexuality education in primary schools and how much time is devoted to this aspect of their education has not been consistent within or across states and territories. The decisions on these issues are often left to individual schools and made by school principals and individual teachers responsible for teaching sexuality education. These decisions are often influenced by community values and contemporary political debates (for example, the Safe Schools Coalition Australia debate).[1] Parents/carers generally have the right to remove their children from sexuality education classes.

In New South Wales, at the time the research on which this paper is based took place, sexuality education was located in the K-6 Personal Development, Health and Physical Education (PDHPE) syllabus covering four main areas: growth and development, interpersonal relationships, child protection education and personal health choices. However, at the time of writing this paper the PDHPE syllabus is under review and is currently unavailable to the public. The PDHPE syllabus is compulsory, but as pointed out above, programming decisions such as content inclusion and when information is given to children is left up to individual principals, teachers and school communities more generally. Sexuality education in NSW is included within the Controversial Issues in Schools Policy, which states that parents have the right to withdraw their children from a particular session on certain controversial issues (e.g. gender and sexuality diversity).

In the state of Victoria, comprehensive sexuality education in primary schools is compulsory within the Health Education curriculum (DEECD – Department of Education and Early Childhood Development 2009). However, similar to NSW, parents/carers can withdraw their children from the sexual health component of the school's health education. The resource *Catching on Early: Sexuality Education for Victorian Primary Schools* (DEECD 2011) acknowledges the essential role of schools in children's sexuality education and the importance of a whole school approach. The home is identified in this resource as 'the first place' for learning about trust, love, affection, bodies, nudity, privacy, toileting, and values and attitudes (DEECD 2011, 7). Schools are viewed as sites for 'learning the rules for getting on with the rest of the world' and as locations in which everyday interactions intersect with sexuality issues (DEECD 2011, 7). Based on national and international research, the resource identifies why sexuality education is important to primary schools, for example: children want to know; preparation for puberty; some children enter puberty earlier; parents want sexuality education in schools; children are saturated with sexual messages; helps in making healthy choices; gender stereotyping starts early; protection against sexual abuse; addressing family diversity; and for opening up dialogues on sexuality education (DEECD 2011, 12–14).

To what extent sexuality education is taught in primary schools in NSW and Victoria is currently unknown. Minimal monitoring is conducted, often leaving the decisions about what, when, and how sexuality education should be taught, to individual schools, individual teachers and school communities (Duffy et al. 2012). Sexuality education in both states is therefore dependent upon the individual perspectives of principals, the policies prevailing in individual schools and the motivation of parents. Sexuality education policies in both NSW and Victoria point to a collaboration between parents/carers, schools and community health organisations in the development and implementation of sexuality education.

Research demonstrates that parents generally want their children to have good sexuality knowledge – better than what they experienced as children and young people (Davies and Robinson 2010; Dyson and Smith 2011; Robinson 2013).

Australian parents are mostly supportive of the school's role in sexuality education (Berne et al. 2000). However, there is still a vocal minority who has concerns about what and how sexuality education is being taught to their children.

Aims

The study aims outlined below are part of a larger Australian Research Council Discovery (2011–2014) project that explored practices of building primary school children's (aged 5–11) understandings of ethical and respectful relationships, with a particular focus on gender, sexuality and sexuality education. The aims relevant to this discussion are to: (i) identify what discourses and narratives shape parents' understandings of, and approaches to, their children's sexual knowledge; (ii) understand how these discourses affect parents' concerns, anxieties and perceived responsibilities concerning their communication about knowledge of sexuality and relationships to their children.

Methods

The larger study included both quantitative and qualitative components: online surveys (parents and educators), interviews and focus groups with parents and primary school educators, and interviews with children. However, here we discuss the methods relevant to the research with parents/carers only. The online surveys[2] asked parents/carers (49 questions) about a range of questions (closed and open-ended) across the following topic areas: understandings of respect; approaches to building children's understandings of respect and ethical relationships in the home and in school; attitudes and approaches toward primary school children's sexuality and relationships education; the resources they used in the sexuality education of children at home; and perceptions about school and family responsibilities in children's sexuality education. Interviews and focus groups with parents/carers provided the opportunity to explore perceptions and experiences across these areas in more depth.

Discussions in interviews with parents/carers were initiated through the use of images found in magazines, post-cards, newspapers and children's storybooks – we used the same images with both children and parents/carers. Five images were used and included pictures depicting children in what are generally considered 'adult' situations – 'on a date', in a mock wedding, and in a kissing pose; a photo of a male same-sex couple with their baby; and an image of a heterosexual couple in a popular Disney animation. This approach (known as photo-interviewing or photo-elicitation) was used to begin conversations and is especially effective with children and young people (Robinson and Davies 2014). The use of photos and imagery in interviews provides a context in which to explore perceptions of and attitudes about cultural practices (Rose 2001; Hurworth et al. 2005).

Sample

Three hundred and forty-two (342) parents/carers (60.5%, $n = 207$ women and 39.5%, $n = 135$ men). Thirty-one (31) individual interviews and six focus groups were held with parents/

carers. Participants came from a range of family structures, sociocultural and economic backgrounds, and children were from both government and independent schools.

Recruitment

A convenience sample was generated through a multi-pronged recruitment drive. The criteria for involvement in the study included parents of a child attending primary school in the states of New South Wales or Victoria. Twenty primary schools in metropolitan, regional and rural areas in New South Wales were purposively selected (e.g. diversity across urban, rural and regional locations, socio-economic and cultural backgrounds), contacted and sent information about the research. Only two primary schools in a large metropolitan city agreed to participate in the study. The difficulties encountered through this approach led to the decision not to pursue this recruitment avenue in the state of Victoria. The difficulties were largely a result of three main issues: schools having a lack of time; schools being over-researched; and primarily, the perceived controversial nature of the research topic – children and sexuality education.

Other recruitment avenues included social networking sites e.g. Facebook, snowballing, approaching parent and family organisations, and employing a commercial research recruitment agency. The anonymous online surveys also provided information on how to volunteer to be involved in interviews or focus groups. Participants invited through the recruitment agency accessed the online survey through the recruitment agency's server, and interview participants were requested to contact researchers directly to organise a time for an interview, conducted on the university campuses. The selection of parents who participated in this study was diverse across gender, ethnicity, sexual orientation, geographical locations, and different school types (government and independent).

Theoretical framework

Our discussion is located largely within a feminist poststructuralist framework (Burr 1995; Weedon 1997). Within this context, we understand sexuality education as being constituted in socio-cultural, historical discourses, especially those underpinning dominant understandings of childhood and sexuality, and subject to the relations of power inherent within these multiple discourses. As such, sexuality education is mediated through socio-cultural factors, like gender, sexuality, ethnicity, religion/faith, socio-economic class, disability and age. There are multiple discourses of gender and sexuality, but some are imbued with more power, authority and cultural value than others, constituting relations of power within a society (Foucault 1984; Butler 2004). The power inherent in discourses is related to the varying degrees to which they are constituted and perpetuated as 'truth' through individual subjectivity and institutions practices. Feminist poststructuralism and queer theory challenge the binary construction of gender and its implications for normalising and naturalising certain performances of gender and sexuality identities, whilst rendering others unnatural and problematic (Butler 2004). Further, these theoretical perspectives are critical of discursive, taken-for-granted, normative assumptions about childhood, childhood innocence and sexuality that perpetuate the belief that sexuality and sexuality education are irrelevant to children's lives. Developing children's sexuality literacy is a central component of children's sexual citizenship (Robinson 2013).

We understand sexuality education within a comprehensive framework. This includes viewing sexuality as an important aspect of identity from the early years and throughout one's life; and as being critical in the development of a healthy life. This approach incorporates the provision of learning experiences based upon accurate, factual, research-based information related to a broad range of issues, such as bodies and sexual development, pregnancy, contraception (including abstinence), relationships, interpersonal skills, ethical and respectful relationships, sexual pleasure and desire, sexual and gender expression, sexual orientation, sexual health (e.g. STI's, HIV), family planning, and values, society and culture. Sexuality education is both formal (e.g. schooling curricula, health professionals) and informal (e.g. parents/carers, other family members, the Internet, peers).

Data analysis

The interviews, focus groups and open-ended questions from the online survey were digitally recorded, transcribed, de-identified and coded in NVivo 10. The research team developed thematic codes (inductive and deductive) based both on the research aims, and also key themes emerging from the data. An initial thematic analysis was conducted, with a further Foucauldian discourse analysis also undertaken on the data. Discourse analysis provides a linguistic approach to an understanding of the relationship between knowledge, ideology and power (Lupton 1992). This method involves exploring the complex interrelationship between text, discursive practice and social practice – the textual and contextual dimensions of analysis (Lupton 1992). Textual dimensions account for the '*structures* of discourses' whilst contextual dimensions 'relate these structural descriptions of various properties to the *social, political or cultural*' context in which they are located (Lupton 1992, 145). Discourse analysis demonstrates the extent to which the interrelationships between systems of signification and other social systems function in the constitution of subjectivities and the production of meaning. Discourses as Foucault (1974) points out are practices that systematically form the objects of which they speak. Ball (1990, 2) argues that discourses 'embody meaning and social relationships, they constitute both subjectivity and power'. Each of the parent/carer interviews and focus group transcripts were analysed to identify parent/carer positions in discourse.

The quantitative data from the online surveys were analysed using SPSS 21. The surveys were designed to closely resemble the interview and focus group questions so that parents/carers and educators who were unable to attend these could still participate in the research. As such, around half of the survey questions were open-ended and were analysed as per the above. The quantitative questions in the online surveys were mainly nominal and included follow-on questions where participants could explain their responses in detail. Simple descriptive statistics of the former were generated and where applicable, reported on in this paper. Their percentages and frequencies (n) are noted. There were no statistically significant results pertinent to the topic of this paper and therefore it does not report on any inferential statistics.

Ethics and informed consent

Parents consented to their children's participation and relevant educational bodies granted ethics approval (Western Sydney University Ethics No. H9096 – reciprocal ethics was granted from La Trobe University in Victoria; NSW Education Department SERAP No. 12/105714).

Findings and discussion

Parents'/carers' perceptions of the relevance and importance of sexuality education to primary (elementary) school aged children

Despite the perceived public resistance around children's early sexuality education in Australia, often relayed through conservative media (O'Brien 2016; Shanahan 2016) an overwhelming majority of parents/carers in this study considered it to be important and relevant to their primary school-age children. Of the 342 parents/carers who completed the online survey, seventy-one percent (71%, *n* = 242) held this view. Only 13.5% (*n* = 46) indicated that it was not important or relevant, while 15.5% (*n* = 53) were undecided. This perspective is rarely acknowledged in political and media attention in contemporary debates about children's sexuality education in Australia. It is the minority view that sexuality education of children is irrelevant or potentially harmful to children that receives greater media and political attention. This view is often fuelled by moral panic associated with children and sexuality and can influence state and federal election outcomes and decision-making (Taylor 2007; Davies 2008; Robinson 2013). These findings suggest that community education, founded on evidence-based research about the importance of sexuality education to children is required in order to enable best health and wellbeing outcomes for children and young people.

Reasons why sexuality education was considered relevant and important to children

The most frequently expressed reasons parents/carers involved in the survey, interviews and focus groups gave for believing that sexuality education was relevant and important for young children included: the need to develop children's media literacy in order to counteract the sexual narratives children encounter through various media outlets and platforms; to build children's understandings about respect around intimacy and relationships; to try and keep children safe and to reduce their risk-taking behaviours as they grow older; and to correct the misinformation they often receive from peers.

For some parents/carers children's access to sexuality education was primarily a matter of children's rights – a right to access knowledge about their bodies in order to develop a healthy awareness of their own sexuality. For these parents, positive sexuality education was seen as a way to counter negative knowledge about sex and sexuality as shameful or dirty – a discourse that framed the sexuality education experiences of many parents/carers in this research. The following mother's comment typifies these sentiments:

> My children asked me about the whole 'stork' theory last night. I explained to them that when I was a child, it was thought to be dirty to say that a baby came out of a vagina, so the stork story was developed. I think it is important for children to understand how bodies work, how babies are made, including IVF, same sex relationships etc. I think it is important to take the stigma of 'sex' being dirty away. (Mother, aged 44, with two children, a boy 9 and girl 6)

This mother highlights how certain myths have been perpetuated about birth in order to provide children with a fanciful sanitised narrative that shrouds human bodily processes considered by some adults as too 'shocking' for children (Davies and Robinson 2010). This mother's comments also allude to the historical process of the sexualisation and moralisation associated with women's sexual and reproductive bodies. and the perception of vaginal births as being 'dirty' given the association of this process with sex – which has been, and still is for many, related to discourses of stigma and shame. 'Natural' childbirth has become a process that some parents/carers consider to be too difficult, embarrassing and shameful to share with children. In addition, infertility and reproductive technologies are rarely addressed with children in formal and informal educational settings. A dominant public discourse about conception and childbirth is often that it is 'inappropriate' knowledge for children.

A father (aged 44) of a five-year-old considered sexuality education as important to his daughter's and other children's sexual subjectivies, commenting: 'I believe that children have their own experiences of desire/sexuality, and my child has an interest in body and behaviour differences'. This father's response operates as a counter-narrative to dominant discourses about children and sexual knowledge, as he views children as agentic sexual subjects who have the right to access sexuality education. In contrast to this perspective, the dominant discourse of childhood and sexuality is one that constitutes children as largely innocent latent sexual subjects or as asexual subjects, denied a sense of bodily desire, until they reach puberty in early adolescence. Within this discursive framework, sexuality and sexual desire are principally viewed as a component of adolescent and adult subjectivities. While there is still often a panic around sexual knowledge and adolescence because of the fear that young people will engage in sexual activity prematurely, research demonstrates that sexuality education delays sexual debut (Fonner et al. 2014; Haberland and Rogow 2015). Knowledge about sexuality is considered the domain of adults and adulthood (Robinson 2013).

Many parents/carers viewed sexuality education as particularly relevant for girls with some believing that it was important to start these conversations early in their children's lives. This perspective was based on parents'/carers' concerns about the changes in girls' developing bodies, the onset of menstruation, their vulnerability to teenage pregnancy, and the importance of girls' having an awareness of physical safety in the context of sexual violence. In addition, many parents/carers acknowledged that they were anxious about the sexualisation of girls and women's bodies in the media and that it was important to build girls' critical skills and awareness around these issues. Parents/carers determined that girls were more often the targets of media sexualisation than were boys and consequently were considered more vulnerable.

Reasons why parents/carers opposed children's sexuality education

Parents/carers who were opposed to their primary-school children being taught sexuality education at school raised several issues that were central to their fears. There was a strong perception amongst these parents/carers that primary school children were 'too young' to be taught sexuality education. This apprehension was especially linked to fears about the differing maturity rates amongst children and the type of knowledge that they might be subjected to in school-based sexuality education programmes. There was a strong fear that if children accessed certain information about sex and sexuality before they reached 'maturity', this would result in their having too much information, too early, to be able to handle this knowledge appropriately. The following comments typified these sentiments:

> Kids need to remain kids as long as possible. The education makes them teenagers before they need to be. (Mother, aged 46, with one 11-year old son)

> I think it is too early to do so in primary school as sometimes it can give them the idea that it is okay instead of making them just aware. (Father, aged 31, with one 5 year-old son)

GENDER AND SEXUALITY IN EDUCATION AND HEALTH

> I feel children are being exposed to information far too early and the innocence of childhood is being narrowed more and more; what's the hurry? (Father, age not available, with one eight-year-old daughter).

These statements by parents/carers both reflect and reproduce the dominant discourse of childhood and sexuality, in which sexuality is constituted as solely an aspect of adult subjectivity. Within this discursive framework, the relationship between sexuality and childhood is one that is viewed as precarious, dangerous and risky due to children's physical, cognitive and emotional immaturity. It is a relationship in which children are perceived to be innocent, vulnerable and in need of protection (Egan and Hawkes 2008; Robinson 2013; Bhana 2014; Gilbert 2014). Further, in this discourse, sexuality knowledge is viewed as developmentally inappropriate and potentially impacting negatively on children's development.

As the above comments highlight, parents'/carers' fears about children's 'loss of innocence' (Meyer 2007) as a result of sexuality education were profound. Indeed, prolonging childhood innocence for as long as possible was the objective of some parents/carers and primarily underpinned their opposition to sexuality education of children. Childhood innocence is a key discourse used to restrict and regulate children's access to knowledge, especially information about sexuality (Davies and Robinson 2010, 2013; Taylor 2010; Robinson 2012, 2013; Bhana 2014). This discourse of innocence is framed in and reinforced through traditional developmentalist theories of child development such as those by Piaget ([1929] 1973). Within these developmentalist perspectives of childhood, the child is considered too emotionally and cognitively immature (or innocent) to comprehend and deal with complex and abstract concepts associated with maturity and adulthood. However, sexuality, in its broad sense of intimacies, relationships, desires and emotions, is very much part of children's lives and the development of their identities (Blaise 2005; Renold 2005; Robinson 2013; Bhana 2014). Children, often despite some parents' efforts to restrict their access to this knowledge, find this information from other sources, including peers, older siblings, media, books, television, the Internet, and even from watching the sexual practices of family pets and other animals (Davies and Robinson 2010). Restricting access to comprehensive, accurate sexuality education can reinforce the notion that sexuality is a taboo subject that children or young people should not talk about, particularly to adults.

Children's perceived emotional un-readiness is most frequently equated with parental fears about children's access to information about sex, which is often the default understanding of what sexuality education entails. In these instances, sexuality education becomes central to moral and faith based anxieties for some as articulated by the following mother (aged 42) of 2 children, with a boy aged 11, and girl, (age not available):

> There are so many youth out there that know too much about sex and feel they are immune to problems. I refused to let my children go because all of them were not emotionally ready for that. I did not ignore the situation. I bought a Christian book about how the body changes for both girls and boys that was easy for them to read and understand. I believe sex is something sacred for marriage and I felt that letting them learn at school and not at home that they could be taught things that I felt were morally wrong.

As highlighted in these comments, the tensions associated with the sexuality education of children and young people can stem from religious, cultural and moral concerns held by parents/carers, who fear that school-based sexuality programmes clash with their family morals and values (Rasmussen 2015). Conflicts sometimes arise between parents'/carers' and educators' perspectives about upholding values held within a family unit and the desire for children to be given knowledge that would equip them in the future. Some parents expressed that sexuality knowledge was tied to morals and values and that these were specific to family units, rather than tied to a larger ethos or to shared ethical considerations.

The concern that sexuality education might undermine the values and morals taught at home was not only expressed by those parents/carers with more traditional views on sexuality. Parents/carers who wanted their children to have an open and positive outlook about sexuality, and gender and sexuality diversity, were also concerned about school based sexuality education programmes undermining the values and morals they wished to instil in their children. The apprehensions raised by these parents stemmed largely from their own poor experiences of sexuality education at school. Some of these parents/carers were especially weary of sexuality education in schools reinforcing negative attitudes and discriminatory practices toward LGBT identities.

Parents/carers' views on who should be responsible for the sexuality education of primary school children

In this research, the majority of parents considered that sexuality education should be a shared process between the home and school, with 65% ($n = 220$) of parents participating in our online survey believing this to be the case. This was also reinforced in focus groups and interviews. Collaborative approaches between families and schools were generally viewed as the best way for their children to get accurate comprehensive sexuality education. Significantly, 92% ($n = 316$) of parents/carers surveyed believed that they should have at least some input into their children's formal sexuality education in schools. However, the percentage of those who were invited by schools to do so was extremely low.

About one third (35%, $n = 118$) of parents/carers felt their children's sexuality education was their responsibility alone. This finding is significant as it contributes to an understanding of the tensions that exist around sexuality education in schools. Parents'/carers' resistances are often reflected through the withdrawal of their children from sexuality education classes. These parents/carers believed that it was critical to solely provide sexuality education at home because of: the need to control and regulate the information their children received; the centrality of family in developing their children's morals, values and ethics; the importance of passing on family cultural and religious values that may not be held by the school; and also to avoid parent and teacher conflicts around these issues. As one mother (aged 38, with 7-year-old daughter) commented:

> Children learn from their parents. You don't have children to have someone else teach them about life.

Only a few parent/carers in this research considered sexuality education of children to be the primary responsibility of schools. Some parents spoke about feeling unable to talk with their children about sexuality, indicating that it was too difficult and too challenging. These parents/carers did not have relationships with their children that were conducive to having such intimate discussions. Teachers were viewed to be in a better position to talk to children about these issues.

Even though the majority of parents/carers believed that schools and homes should share the responsibility of children's sexuality education, only a third of parents/carers participating in the survey (35%, $n = 118$) had a plan or strategy for talking to their children. Further, only 15% ($n = 48$) of parents had been supplied resources to aid in these discussions with their children. Parents in the focus groups and interviews pointed out that they had planned to talk with their children about sexuality education but had not found the right opportunity or time and/or lacked the confidence, skills and resources to do so (Morawska et al. 2015). Once their children got older, approaching the topic felt even more daunting for some of them.

Are there any aspects of sexuality education parents/carers consider more appropriate for families to address with primary school aged children?

The type of sexuality knowledge that children are privy to in school-based sexuality education programmes is contentious for some parents/carers because it is perceived as a controversial issue. However, there were many parents/carers who expressed the importance of their children having access to a comprehensive sexuality programme in primary school. These parents/carers understood the significance of establishing children's sexuality education literacy early and building their awareness and critical skills around ethical relationships. These are key components of children's sexual citizenship (Robinson 2013, 2016). The following comments made by parents/carers epitomise these perspectives:

> I can't think of anything in particular which I wouldn't like [taught], even as a religious person whose child is in a government school. (Mother, 53, with 8-year-old daughter)

> There is nothing really [I would not want taught in primary school]. They need to know – if they don't find out from someone sensible, i.e. a teacher, they will hear about it from peers. (Mother 37, with six-year-old daughter)

The lack of consistency of comprehensive sexuality education across school sectors, states and territories can result in inequities for students – some topics being covered more than others and some omitted altogether. Imparting certain knowledge to children was considered by some parents/carers to be more appropriate for families. In our study, the majority of parents/carers who had concerns about sexuality education in primary school, identified information about sex, and same-sex attraction as the two areas with which they had most concern. These particular parents/carers' considered these areas more aligned with family discussions with children because of the differing perspectives that prevail around these topics. Other areas identified included: sexual violence and abuse, abortion, STI's, pregnancy, pornography and explicit sexual practices. Many of these topics are not included in the sexuality curriculum in primary school. These anxieties may be a result of some parents'/carers' lack of awareness of what is included in the primary school sexuality curriculum in regards to sexuality education. In terms of same-sex relationships, discussions in the primary curriculum largely relate to respecting diverse identities, family diversity and preventing bullying and harassment of students (Davies and Robinson 2013).

Some parents/carers with concerns about the content of sexuality education believed that issues they perceived to be controversial should be discussed at home. However, many indicated that they did not address these issues with their children due to a lack of knowledge, embarrassment and/or conflict in values. Of importance, in a question asking parents what topics they found the most difficult to talk with their children about, same-sex relationships were mentioned multiple times. Many adults with these concerns perceived information about same-sex attraction as 'difficult knowledge' (Robinson and Davies 2008; Robinson 2012, 2013). Difficult knowledge is perceived as unsuitable information for general discussion with children (Robinson 2013). There is a prevailing perception amongst these parents/carers that children should be sheltered from 'difficult knowledge' largely to preserve their perceived innocence.

A mother in our study felt that while it was difficult to talk about same-sex attraction, it was important to address with children in school and at home due to the fact that these relationships are 'more obvious now' than when she was a child. For some, the difficulty was directly related to personal religious beliefs:

> As a Christian I believe that it is not right. But I want the kids to know that all people regardless of their beliefs should be respected even if we don't agree with them. (Mother, aged 42, with one child aged 11 years)

Another mother explained that talking about same-sex attraction was difficult for her to address because she was uninformed about the topic:

> Perhaps homosexuality, as I don't want to misinform children. People who are homosexual should be treated with the same respect as heterosexuals. (Mother, aged 53, with one son in year two)

While some parents in our study expressed concern about what they perceived to be controversial issues, they also pointed out the contradiction that 'difficult knowledge' was unlikely to be spoken about between parent/carer and child at home. Many children are turning to alternative sources to get this information, including peers and the media because they understood from adults that this knowledge was considered taboo. Recently in Australia, moral panic has erupted, largely fuelled by the conservative press, regarding children accessing information about LGBT matters, or about sex more generally, and also about these topics being included in school settings. This is epitomised by the Safe Schools Coalition Australia furore, in which the debates have been polarised, without much concern for the material affects of this mediation on children and young people. Concerns in these debates have largely focused on not wanting to address gender diversity with children despite the fact gender diverse children attend primary schools and can be subject to harassment, bullying and exclusion (Donnelly 2016a, 2016b).

Conclusion: implications of findings for sexuality education policy and practice in schools

Supporting the development of children's sexuality literacy is key to building sexual citizenship, respectful and ethical relationships early and to fostering children's health and wellbeing throughout their lives. Our research demonstrates that the majority of parents/carers consider sexuality education to be both important and relevant to the lives of primary school children and that it needs to be a collaborative process between families and schools. However, about a third of parents/carers considered children's sexuality education was their responsibility alone. Further, about a third of parents indicated that sexuality education was either not relevant or important to primary school aged children, or were unsure if it was relevant or important. These findings have significant implications for sexuality education policy and practice.

In order to foster more effective sexuality education of children we suggest a number of areas need to be addressed. Sexuality education as a health and well-being issue, as well as an equity matter, would be best to be viewed as a shared responsibility between families, schools and health organisations. We believe that this would provide a more effective foundation for learning for all in this area. Sexuality education needs to target not just children and young people, but needs to address the gaps that exist in adults' learning in this area. State government funding is required to provide community sexuality education programmes run by relevant allied health groups that provide parents/carers up-to-date evidence based information on the importance of developing children's sexual literacy early in life. These programmes would also provide skill development training, resources and support to parents/carers in regards to best practices around talking with children about sexuality education. Allied health sexuality education programmes could also support school-based sexuality education and provide an alternative information service that can be accessed by young people if required.

Schools need to provide parents/carers with more information about the sexuality curriculum and pedagogical approaches to teaching sexuality education to children. Doing so could involve the development of a pamphlet that outlines why it is important to address sexuality education with children, what the curriculum entails for different year groups, and providing other information about frequently asked questions. Inviting parents/carers to an information session to discuss the sexuality education of their children would provide the opportunity to address any concerns they may have.

There also needs to be greater consistency of the implementation and monitoring of a national comprehensive sexuality curriculum across states and territories in Australia, to ensure access and equity for all students. This needs to comprise a focus on building respectful and ethical relationships in the early years of school, including addressing gender, gender expression and sexuality diversity.

Notes

1. Safe Schools Coalition Australia was a national initiative funded by the Australian government, aimed at creating safe and supportive school environments for same-sex attracted, intersex, and gender diverse people by reducing homophobic and transphobic bullying and discrimination in schools. Available at https://www.education.gov.au/safe-schools-coalition-australia Accessed 12 December 2016.
2. Due to the lack of validated questionnaires focusing on parent's perceptions and experiences of communicating sexuality education with their children, the research team developed a questionnaire for the purpose of this study. We aimed to examine parents'/carers' perceptions, experiences and practices in relation to educating children about respectful and ethical relationships and sexuality. The online surveys have not undergone reliability and validity testing.

Acknowledgements

The Australian Research Council funded this study. Project title: The Tensions for Parents, Educators and Children in Building a Sustainable Culture of Ethical and Respectful Relationships Early in Life awarded to Kerry Robinson, Moira Carmody and Sue Dyson. The authors would like to thank Georgia Ovenden, Peter Bansel, Marisa Jane Monagle and Lesley Wright for their research assistance on this project. Thanks also goes to Moira Carmody and Sue Dyson. The authors have no financial interests or benefits to acknowledge arising from the research grant.

Disclosure statement

No potential conflict of interest was reported by the authors.

Funding

This work was supported by the Australian Research Council [grant number DP110104431].

References

ACARA. 2015. *Health and Physical Education: F-10 Curriculum*. Sydney: Australian Curriculum, Assessment and Reporting Authority. http://www.australiancurriculum.edu.au/health-and-physical-education/curriculum/f-10?layout=1

Australian Government Department of Education. 2014. *Review of the Australian Curriculum. Final Report*. Canberra: Australian Government. https://docs.education.gov.au/system/files/doc/other/review_of_the_national_curriculum_final_report.pdf

Ball, S. 1990. *Foucault and Education: Disciplines and Knowledge*. London: Routledge.

Berne, L., W. Patton, J. Milton, L. Hunt, S. Wright, J. Peppard, and J. Dodd. 2000. "A Qualitative Assessment of Australian Parents' Perceptions of Sexuality Education and Communication." *Journal of Sex Education and Therapy* 25: 161–168.

Bhana, D. 2008. "Discourses of Childhood Innocence in Primary School: HIV AIDS Education in South Africa." *African Journal of AIDS Research* 7 (1): 149–158.

Bhana, D. 2014. *Under Pressure: The Regulation of Sexualities in South African Schools*. Braamfontein: MaThoko's Books.

Blaise, M. 2005. *Playing It Straight: Uncovering Gender Discourses in the Early Childhood Classroom*. New York: Routledge.

Burr, V. 1995. *An Introduction to Social Constructionism*. London: Routledge.

Butler, J. 2004. *Undoing Gender*. New York: Routledge.

Davies, C. 2008. "Proliferating Panic: Regulating Representations of Sex and Gender during the Culture Wars." *Cultural Studies Review* 14 (2): 83–102.

Davies, C., and K. H. Robinson. 2010. "Hatching Babies and Stork Deliveries: Risk and Regulation in the Construction of Children's Sexual Knowledge." *Contemporary Issues in Early Childhood* 11 (3): 249–262.

Carmody, M. 2009. *Sex and Ethics: Young People and Ethical Sex*. Melbourne: Palgrave Macmillan.

Davies, C., and K. H. Robinson. 2013. "Reconceptualising Family: Negotiating Sexuality in a Governmental Climate of Neoliberalism." *Contemporary Issues in Early Childhood* 14 (1): 39–53.

DEECD. 2011. *Catching on Early – Sexuality Education for Victoria Primary Schools*. Melbourne. https://www.eduweb.vic.gov.au/edulibrary/public/teachlearn/student/catchingoneyrsv.pdf

Donnelly, K. 2016a. "How Ideology Took over Schools." *The Daily Telegraph*, July 21. http://www.dailytelegraph.com.au/news/opinion/kevin-donnelly-how-ideology-took-over-schools/news-story/9f06e062476a2e04c7999b48d630b043

Donnelly, K. 2016b. "LGBTQI Schools Program Needs Investigating." *The Australian*, February 27. http://www.theaustralian.com.au/opinion/lgbtqi-schools-program-needs-investigating/news-story/c070804e2efbd8710a3cbd530e4e8f01

Duffy, B., N. Fotinatos, A. Smith, and J. Burke. 2012. "Puberty, Health and Sexual Education in Australian Regional Primary Schools: Year 5 and 6 Teacher Perceptions." *Sex Education* 13 (2): 186–203.

Dyson, S., and E. Smith. 2011. "'There are lots of different kinds of normal': Families and Sex Education – Styles, Approaches and Concerns." *Sex Education* 12 (2): 219–229.

Egan, R. 2013. *Becoming Sexual: A Critical Appraisal of the Sexualization of Girls*. Malden, MA: Polity.

Egan, R., and G. Hawkes. 2010. *Theorizing the Sexual Child in Modernity*. New York: Palgrave Macmillan.

Egan, R., and G. Hawkes. 2008. "Endangered Girls and Incendiary Objects: Unpacking the Discourse on Sexualization." *Sexuality and Culture* 12 (4): 291–311.

Fonner, V. A., K. S. Armstrong, C. E. Kennedy, K. R. O'Reilly, and M. D. Sweat. 2014. "School Based Sex Education and HIV Prevention in Low- and Middle-Income Countries: A Systematic Review and Meta-Analysis." *PLoS ONE* 9 (3): e89692.

Foucault, M. 1974. *The Archaeology of Knowledge*. New York: Pantheon Books.

Foucault, M. 1984. *The History of Sexuality. Volume 1, an Introduction*. Translated by R. Hurley. Harmondsworth: Penguin.

Gilbert, J. 2014. *Sexuality in School: The Limits of Education*. Minneapolis: University of Minnesota Press.

Haberland, N., and D. Rogow. 2015. "Sexuality Education: Emerging Trends in Evidence and Practice." *Journal of Adolescent Health* 56: S15–S21.

Hillier, L., and A. Mitchell. 2008. "'It was as useful as a chocolate kettle': Sex Education in the in the Lives of Same-sex Attracted Young People on Australia." *Sex Education* 8 (2): 211–224.

Hillier, L., T. Jones, M. Monagle, N. Overton, L. Gahan, J. Blackman, and A. Mitchell. 2010. *Writing Themselves in 3: The Third National Study on the Sexual Health and Wellbeing of Same Sex Attracted and Gender Questioning Young People*. Melbourne: La Trobe University.

Hurworth, R., E. Clark, J. Martin, and S. Thomsen. 2005. "The Use of Photo-interviewing: Three Examples from Health Evaluation and Research." *Evaluation Journal of Australasia* 4 (1/2): 52–62.

Kao, T. S., and M. Manczak. 2013. "Family Influences on Adolescents' Birth Control and Condom Use, Likelihood of Sexually Transmitted Infections." *The Journal of School Nursing* 29 (1): 61–70.

Kirby, D. 2002. "The Impact of Schools and School Programs upon Adolescent Sexual Behavior." *Journal of Sex Research* 39 (1): 27–33.

Leahy, D., L. Burrows, L. McCuaig, J. Wright, and D. Penney. 2016. *School Health Education in Changing Times: Curriculum, Pedagogies and Partnerships*. Abingdon: Routledge.

Lupton, D. 1992. "Discourse Analysis: A New Methodology for Understanding the Ideologies of Health and Illness." *Australian Journal of Public Health* 16 (2): 145–150.

McKee, A., K. Albury, M. Dunne, S. Greishaber, J. Hartley, C. Lumby, and B. Mathews. 2010. "Healthy Sexual Development: A Mulitdisciplinary Framework for Research." *International Journal of Sexual Health* 22 (1): 14–19.

Meyer, A. 2007. "The Moral Rhetoric of Childhood." *Childhood* 14 (1): 85–104.

Morawska, A., A. Walsh, M. Grabski, and R. Fletcher. 2015. "Parental Confidence and Preferences for Communicating with Their Child about Sexuality." *Sex Education* 15 (3): 235–248.

O'Brien, S. 2016. "Toddlers to Be Taught about Cross-dressing in Controversial Sex Ed Program." *Herald Sun*, March 6. http://www.heraldsun.com.au/news/toddlers-to-be-taught-about-crossdressing-in-controversial-sex-ed-program/newsstory/7b935bb2e1573c1b2e748755d0f18986

Piaget, J. (1929) 1973. *The Child's Conception of the World*. St Albans: Paladin.

Rasmussen, M. L. 2015. *Progressive Sexuality Education: The Conceits of Secularism*. London: Routledge.

Renold, E. 2005. *Girls, Boys, and Junior Sexualities: Exploring Children's Gender and Sexual Relations in the Primary School*. London: Routledge.

Robinson, K. H. 2012. "Difficult Citizenship: The Precarious Relationships between Childhood, Sexuality, and Access to Knowledge." *Sexualities* 15 (3–4): 257–276.

Robinson, K. H. 2013. *Innocence, Knowledge and the Construction of Childhood: The Contradictory Nature of Sexuality and Censorship in Children's Contemporary Lives*. London: Routledge.

Robinson, K. H. 2016. "Children's Sexual Citizenship." In *Introducing New Sexuality Studies*, 3rd ed., edited by N. L. Fischer and S. Seidman, 485–493. London: Routledge.

Robinson, K. H., P. Bansel, N. Denson, G. Ovenden, and C. Davies. 2014. *Growing up Queer: Issues Facing Young Australians Who Are Gender Variant and Sexuality Diverse*. Melbourne: Young and Well Cooperative Research Centre.

Robinson, K. H., and C. Davies. 2008. "Docile Bodies and Heteronormative Moral Subjects: Constructing the Child and Sexual Knowledge in Schooling." *Sexuality & Culture* 12 (4): 221–239.

Robinson, K. H., and C. Davies. 2014. "Doing Sexuality Research with Children: Ethics, Theory, Methods and Practice." *Global Studies of Childhood* 4 (4): 250–263.

Rose, G. 2001. *Visual Methodologies*. London: SAGE.

Shanahan, A. 2016. "Parents Are the Best Judge of Their Kids' Sex Education Needs, Opinion." *The Australian*, February 27. http://www.theaustralian.com.au/opinion/columnists/angela-shanahan/parents-are-the-best-judge-of-their-kids-sex-education-needs/news-story/a4735e9b23790a3769ac99d97d656253

Stone, N., R. Ingham, and K. Gibbins. 2013. "'Where do babies come from?' Barriers to Early Sexuality Communication between Parents and Young Children." *Sex Education* 13 (2): 228–240.

Taylor, A. 2010. "Troubling Childhood Innocence: Reframing the Debate over the Media Sexualisation of Children." *Australian Journal of Early Childhood* 35 (1): 48–57.

Taylor, A. 2007. "Innocent Children, Dangerous Families and Homophobic Panic." In *Outrageous: Moral Panics in Australia*, edited by G. Morgan and S. Poynting, 210–222. Hobart: Australian Clearing House for Youth Studies.

Ullman, J. 2015. *Free2Be?: Exploring the Schooling Experiences of Australia's Sexuality and Gender Diverse Secondary School Students*. Penrith: Centre for Educational Research, School of Education, Western Sydney University.

Weedon, C. 1997. *Feminist Practice Poststructuralist Theory*. Oxford: Blackwell.

Wu, L. 2010. "A Survey on the Knowledge, Attitude, and Behavior regarding Contraception Use among Pregnant Teenagers in Beijing, China." *Clinical Nursing Research* 19 (4): 403–415.

Gender and sexuality diversity and schooling: progressive mothers speak out

Tania Ferfolja and Jacqueline Ullman

ABSTRACT

Although social acceptance of gender and sexuality diversity is growing in Australian society, in schools, visibility and inclusion of knowledge pertaining to those who are gender- and/or sexuality-diverse, such as lesbians, gay men and transgender people, remain marginalised. This may be due, in part, to a belief that parents are opposed to such content inclusions in their children's education; yet, virtually no Australian research supports this belief nor have parental perspectives on gender and sexuality diversity inclusion been specifically examined. This paper draws on a broader research study that examined New South Wales parents' perceptions about the visibility of gender and sexuality diversity and the inclusion or exclusion of related content in school curriculum. It focuses on one particular focus group comprised of only mothers who lived in a specific enclave of Sydney known for its gender and sexuality diversity. The discussion highlights their awareness of gender and sexuality diversity and the dynamics surrounding it; and their perceptions of local school approaches to, and limitations around, gender and sexuality diversity in school curricula, policy and practices, despite potential support for it.

Introduction

Education should be the great instrument for the promotion of equality (Former Prime Minister Gough Whitlam 1972 Australian Labor Party Policy Speech 1972).

Former Australian Prime Minister Gough Whitlam has been heralded as a great visionary for a socially just society and his commitment to the equalising potential of education. Yet, nearly half a century after he made the speech above, inequality still persists in and is often perpetuated by the pedagogies, practices, policies and curriculum constituting school education. One of the most obvious, but perhaps least attended to means whereby injustices are maintained is through the limited inclusion and more often omission of gender- and-sexuality-diverse[1] content, visibility and voice in curriculum, classroom and schooling practices. Despite broader discursive shifts in the nation's sociocultural fabric to embrace such diversities, these changes have not been incorporated into schools in Australia. One contributing reason for this is teachers' perceptions that parents may complain if such issues are broached (Smith et al. 2011); however, this perception has not been substantiated by research and indeed, the research reported in this paper and others by the authors (Ullman and Ferfolja 2016), conflicts with this perception.

To address this knowledge gap, this paper reports on the position of a focus group of parents in relation to their perceptions of in/exclusion regarding gender and sexuality diversity in schools, drawn from a broader qualitative study conducted across New South Wales (NSW) that examined parents' and young people's perceptions about gender- and-sexuality-related content in pedagogy, practice and visibility in schools (Ullman and Ferfolja 2016). This group was comprised of middle-class, educated women with school-aged children, living and schooling their youngsters in what is popularly known as a diverse and liberal area of metropolitan Sydney constituted by a highly visible and celebrated gender-and-sexuality-diverse population. The social milieu in which these mothers were immersed increased their familiarity with the gender- and-sexuality-diverse community, enabling them to demonstrate nuanced understandings of such diversity. It should be noted that their close connection to a gender- and-sexuality-diverse community is unique within the study; hence, it is neither the intent nor the purpose of this paper to generalise their perspectives nor to suggest that their perceptions are in any way universal. Rather, the authors believe that the knowledge and even activism of these mothers in relation to gender and sexuality diversity gave them critical insights and perspectives and that these, at times, intermingled with a range of tensions and complexities located in dominant heteronormative discourse despite their desire to resist the normative. This discussion highlights these parents' keen awareness of gender and sexuality diversity; their experiences of local schools' approaches to in/exclusion of gender and sexuality diversity in curriculum and practices; their frustrations at what they perceived were school limitations regarding these issues; and their observations as to where gender- and-sexuality-related content could be implemented. Before embarking on this discussion, however, it is necessary to first provide some background to the field in which this research is situated.

Background

Gender and sexuality diversity in school education

Students and teachers who are gender- and sexuality-diverse (or who are perceived to be) are frequently subjected to interpersonal and institutional discrimination in schools, a reality that is well reported in the literature (Ferfolja and Hopkins 2013; Hillier et al. 2010; Robinson et al. 2014; Ullman 2015a). Such discrimination undermines equitable practices and equality of access and outcomes through its impact on academic, social, personal and/or professional growth (Blackburn 2012; Ullman 2015b). Despite calls by internationally powerful bodies such as the United Nations (UNESCO 2009) for greater inclusions in school education and local demands for visibility in schools (Ferfolja and Ullman 2014; Hillier et al. 2010; Ullman and Ferfolja 2014), reference to gender- and sexuality-related subjectivities and implementation of associated content in Australia is largely non-existent, *ad hoc* and left to the devices of a few proactive, socially aware, individual teachers.

The reasons for this are complex. Teachers report possessing inadequate understandings or training in these areas (Barbagallo and Boon 2012; Duffy et al. 2013; Milton 2003; Ollis 2010); claim to have limited, if any, appropriate educational resources (Smith et al. 2011); are not necessarily comfortable discussing or teaching 'controversial' issues (Cohen et al. 2004); and/or have moral reservations about the suitability of gender- and sexuality-diverse content inclusion in a curriculum for young people (Cumming-Potvin and Martino 2014; Goldstein, Collins, and Halder 2008). The fear of being labelled gay by association and thus potentially increasing susceptibility to harassment may also contribute to omission (Holmes 2001).

As a result, institutional invisibility is generally the norm. Educational documentation throughout the Australian school system that does refer to gender- and sexuality-diverse subjectivities has been historically poorly constructed, subsumes sexuality into other equity or welfare issues and/or is outdated (Ullman and Ferfolja 2014), although exceptions exist. (See e.g. Victoria's Department of Education and Early Childhood Development which provides more visible and proactive support than other states and territories). Overall, there is little institutional documentation to support the implementation of gender- and sexuality-diverse related content or inclusions, or to relieve teachers' anxieties about the perceived possible negative ramifications for doing this work. For example, although there is mention of LGBT identities in the new Health/Physical Education (HPE) national curriculum, the limited reference provides virtually no guidance to teachers in terms of what type of learning content is required; nor does it mandate explicit teaching or institutional visibility. Indeed, interpreting the document to include gender and sexuality diversities requires teachers to surpass normative constructions of gender and heterosexuality, which is unlikely considering cis-gender and cis-sexual subjectivities are pervasive in dominant discourse (Ferfolja and Ullman 2014; Robinson et al. 2014). Interpretation of the text for implementation may be influenced by a teacher's conservative, cultural or religious beliefs (Mitchell and Walsh 2009); their sense of the un/importance of the issue; their topic knowledge or interest; or 'their comfort teaching these topics' (Cohen et al. 2004, 2). The near invisibility and poor institutional support for the inclusion of this equity issue render it a risk-taking venture for teachers (Cumming-Potvin and Martino 2014). As we have argued elsewhere, curriculum omissions place:

> … responsibility for any potential or imagined negative ramifications on the individual and their school. An institutional mandate that stipulates the importance of this work would provide support for teachers and schools undertaking it and would shift responsibility from the individual to the broader institution (Ullman and Ferfolja 2014, 155).

However, teachers' anxieties pertaining to parental disapproval about the inclusion of gender and sexuality diversities are not grounded in research. Rather, as Martino and Pallotta-Chiarolli (2003) point out, omission or avoidance of the topic seems to be frequently the result of the 'three-parent syndrome'. This is where 'anti-homophobic programmes and teaching strategies are either not initiated or ceased as soon as a few parents complain to the administration' (95). However, the apparent overreaction by teachers and school administrators is also not entirely unfounded considering the way that heterosexuality is 'systematically supported as a preferred and ideal way of life' (Cumming-Potvin and Martino 2014, 310). In Australia, this is epitomised through ongoing political debates about the legalisation of marriage equality. Additionally, contributing to the anxiety is the teaching profession's cumulative memories of government intervention and media hysteria when such issues have been raised in schools with young people. In fact, in 2015, the State Minister for Education banned a highly acclaimed, PG-rated documentary, *Gayby Baby*, which examines the lives of Australian children living in lesbian- and gay-headed families. This occurred just hours prior to its scheduled viewing in a NSW high school on Wear It Purple day[2] and is a case in point. Although there

GENDER AND SEXUALITY IN EDUCATION AND HEALTH

were reportedly no parental complaints to the school (Safi 2015), a polarising paper in the tabloid press appeared to catalyse political intervention. The Minister's rationale, reportedly, was that the film was not part of the curriculum. Of interest here is the fact that in the light of the discussion concerning the HPE curriculum above, viewing this documentary *is* in keeping with the curriculum, which highlights, 'Relationships and Sexuality' as a focus area for all years of learning (Foundations – Year 10) (ACARA 2015). Similarly, a State of Victoria programme, developed and implemented by the Safe Schools Coalition Victoria and rolled out nationally because of its perceived success at reducing homophobic bullying in schools, has had its federal funding for 2017 withdrawn in response to the conservative Christian lobby and federal government backbencher claims that children were 'being bullied and intimidated into complying with a *radical* program' and that 'Our schools should be places of learning, not *indoctrination*' [author's italics] (Anderson 2016). The conservative backlash, filled with hyperbole and misinformation, has been staggering.

Such 'moral and regulatory surveillance' and embellished public debate impact on the professional autonomy of teachers (Cumming-Potvin and Martino 2014, 326) convey messages that marginalise this form of diversity and reinforce the silencing already apparent in schools affirming teachers' fears about addressing such topics. Although some teachers advocate for, and include, gender- and sexuality-diverse content in their teaching, media and political intrusions into teacher professional judgement reinforce the idea that *any* focus on issues that extend beyond or challenge dominant discourses of heterosexual normativity is risky business for teachers and schools and should be broached warily if at all (Cumming-Potvin and Martino 2014; Duffy et al. 2013).

Parental perceptions

Although the literature focusing on parents' attitudes and beliefs about gender- and sexuality-diverse content, visibility and inclusion in Australian school education is sparse, international research examining sex education illustrates that parents generally support the presence of topics pertaining to gender and sexuality diversity in education (Constantine, Jerman, and Huang 2007; Eisenberg et al. 2008). For example, recent research conducted in the USA found that in a survey of 1715 parents, nearly 52% wanted gender/sexual orientation issues included in an age-appropriate way in elementary school and this percentage increased to over 70% in high school (Barr et al. 2014). National research conducted in Ireland, which surveyed the parents of male students aged between 15 and 17, found that 82% of participants approved the inclusion of sexual orientation in the school curriculum and 90% agreed that anti-homophobia education should be taught (McCormack and Gleeson 2010, 391). The reasons for these beliefs largely included a desire to halt homophobic bullying and to have more discussion about gender expectations and stereotypes. Only a minority of parents disapproved of inclusion for fear that 'the school may not transmit the attitudes and values' (392) conveyed at home and that the issues were 'too sensitive' (393) to be discussed at school. However, parents who were uncomfortable addressing these issues with their sons welcomed the topic's introduction by the school – a finding supported by Ollis, Harrison, and Richardson's (2012) Australian site-based research into the teaching of sexuality generally to primary school-aged students.

Parents express confidence that schools will implement appropriate sexual education (Berne et al. 2000). A quantitative study of 177 Sydney-based parents that investigated the attitudes of parents to sexual health education found that 97% thought that homosexuality should be included in the content of sexual health classes and many thought it appropriate to introduce this topic in the late primary years (Macbeth, Weerakoon, and Sitharthan 2009, 328). Although an important finding that supports inclusion, the research does not examine parental notions of visibility and in/exclusion of gender and sexuality diversity in schools more broadly; that is, beyond that linked to sexual health.

Students consider that the exclusion of sexuality and gender diversity in the curriculum does not provide for their educational needs (Clarke 2011). Young people want improvements in both the content and delivery of sexuality and relationships education, which in Australia is frequently presented from a biological perspective focusing on reproduction and safe (hetero)sex (Farrelly, O'Brien, and Prain 2007). Moreover, students report that sexuality and relationships education is largely heterosexist and provides little information about or for gender- and sexuality-diverse individuals (Barbagallo and Boon 2012).

Conceptual framework

Schools in Australia are conservative institutions in which heterosexual subjects are normalised through curriculum, policy and practices. Gender- and sexuality-diverse individuals, on the other hand, generally do not have this luxury. They are often constructed as abnormal, positioned as objects of humour, ridicule or violence and in some contexts are considered non-existent. Ironically, although marginalised, silenced and invisible, these individuals are simultaneously regulated and policed (Foucault 1978) by schools who through both explicit and implicit means endeavour to produce cis-gendered, (hetero)sexual subjects. Discourses pertaining to religion, morality, childhood innocence and developmentalism, among others, support curriculum and schooling practices that reify the production of heterosexual subjects.

Moreover, neoliberalism, which is an economic theory, but simultaneously a dominant discourse in which schools are positioned, situates subjects as commodities. As Griffin (2007) points out, heterosexuality is fundamental to neoliberalism as it provides '"economic" answers to problems of social organisation' (222). Thus, schools are providers of future neoliberal subjects who are work-ready, flexible, globally literate, self-regulating and who assume responsibility for their own future through enterprise and individual effort (Down 2009).

This kind of socially conforming workforce is reinforced by the delivery of a market-driven curriculum in which issues of social justice and equity are considered superfluous, irrelevant to the market and the 'increased technicization of knowledge and knowledge production' (Connell 2013, 108). Additionally, issues of gender and sexuality diversity may be perceived as potentially damaging to a school's reputation in the market. Schools will generally suppress anything deemed 'contentious' as they are competing with other schools for 'students, marks and money', and where parents as consumers can 'exercise "choice"' between schools (Connell 2013, 103). Thus, teachers and schools perform in particular ways to produce desirable products in a competitive market (Ball and Olmedo 2013). These discourses simultaneously intersect with dominant understandings of childhood which position young people as vulnerable, unknowing and in need of protection from adult vices (Kane 2013) of which gender and sexuality diversity is one. As a result, gender and sexuality diversity often remains silent and invisible in school contexts despite the potential negative ramifications on young people. This appears to be buoyed by teachers' and administrators' unsubstantiated and conservative beliefs about what parents desire for their children's education.

Methodology

This paper is based on one focus group discussion from a broader research study examining parent and student perceptions about the visibility and in/exclusion of gender- and sexuality-diverse related content in school education which also aimed to begin the consultation process with parents of school-aged children across NSW. Focus groups were considered the best data gathering tool for this research as they provide a potentially dynamic social interaction and a springboard for ideas (Krueger and Casey 2009). They are also useful when working with people unfamiliar with formal research processes where potential unequal power relations exist between the researchers and participants. The focus groups conducted as part of a larger study were held across targeted areas, selected due to their popularly recognised cultural divergence from each other. Urban regions included the Inner West, Sutherland Shire and Hills District. Four regional/rural centres were also targeted and included Coffs Harbour, Nowra, Maitland and Dubbo. Flood and Hamilton (2005) illustrate that different areas in Australia exhibit different degrees of in/tolerance towards gender- and sexuality-diverse subjects; hence, we felt it imperative to sample across regions to provide a variety of participant voices and perspectives. However, it should be noted that parents are not a homogenous group and discourses pertaining to culture, socio-economic status, religion, age, parental experience, gender and sexuality diversity exposure, education and so forth will constitute the parent subject and the way they position gender- and sexuality-diverse subjectivities.

In total, 22 parents were recruited using advertisements in local newspapers (in the three Sydney regions only), targeted Facebook advertising and advertisements in public school newsletters (in locations outside of metropolitan Sydney). Both the researchers' university and the NSW Department of Education granted ethical approval for the research.

This paper draws specifically on the data from the Inner West parent focus group. This group consisted of six middle-class, educated women in their 30s and 40s who demonstrated a high degree of contextually relevant cultural capital in terms of their knowledge of the education system. They all possessed same-sex attracted friends and/or personally knew of and/or worked with gender- and sexuality-diverse people. Five of the group had primary school-aged children. Of particular interest was the fact that these parents resided, and had their children schooled, in a region of Sydney known for its visible and relatively open gender- and sexuality-diverse community. Because of the social dynamic of the area and participants' particular familiarity with gender and sexuality diversity issues, it was thought that this group could have deep insights into these matters in schools in an area of high gender and sexuality diversity; we wanted to know what these insights were and how might they perceive them in operation. Their networks and experiences enabled them to articulate a consciousness of both the overt and subtle complexities functioning in relation to gender and sexuality diversity in schools.

All focus group interviews were audiotaped with participants' written consent and transcribed by a professional transcriber. The data from the particular focus group were coded and themes identified (Saldana 2009); those reported in this paper include gender and sexuality diversity awareness, perceived visibility in schools with which they had contact and in/exclusion in the curriculum; these themes formed the focal points of discussion in this focus group interview. These were then analysed through the application of feminist poststructuralist theoretical concepts. The voices of the participants quoted in this paper illustrate how the written, spoken and embodied experiences of the participants were constituted within and constitutive of broader social, cultural and/or political understandings (Ezzy 2002), demonstrating at times multiple layers of complexity and tension.

Findings and discussion

Understanding gender and sexuality diversity

This focus group was highly cognisant of the marginalisation experienced by gender- and sexuality-diverse communities, particularly obvious in their response to our opening interview question: 'What do you understand by the acronym LGBTQ?' Rather than simply providing a definition, which was the starting point for other focus groups, these women provided a detailed discussion related to the acronym's politics arguing how 'it's mocked as an acronym - constantly' (Kira), is 'evolutionary' (Kira) in the ways that it has developed and grown over time, that sexual subjectivity is 'fluid' (Marci) and although used for lexical expediency, is at the same time, 'hierarchical' (Kira) in nature – resulting in the 'marginalising of the marginalised by the marginalised' (Kira). Moreover, the notion of labelling was recognised as problematic through its limitations on diversity and the fluidity of subjectivity. The importance of language in the constitution of discourse and participants' awareness of the knowledge it produced and promoted, both in and outside of the gender- and sexuality-diverse community, illustrated the group's highly politicised understandings of gender- and sexuality-diverse subjectivities and their relationship to power and access (Weedon 1987). There was recognition that the acronym represented a 'massive diversity of people' (Anna) who 'want to have the same rights as everybody else' but that these communities had to 'fight for them' (Marci); and that there is a 'huge range of ways of being that are outside the standard norm'; and that these are 'mostly ignored' (Anna) in the broader socio-political milieu.

Perceptions of gender and sexuality diversity in schools

Despite equity for gender- and sexuality-diverse subjects being articulated as 'the biggest civil rights issue of our time' (Judy), equated to histories of racial discrimination, participants felt that gender and sexuality diversity in schools was largely invisible and silenced. Teachers were perceived as actors who normalised heterosexuality in terms of 'monogamous relationships where people only have sex to have babies' (Judy). These approaches reflected a curriculum that focuses on biology rather than intimacy as well as a sanitised and socially idyllic view of heterosexuality. Heterosexuality in schools was seen to form the benchmark by which all else is measured, constructed as 'normal and then everything else is shock, or a change, or something unusual' (Judy) for young people. Even schools located in the culturally alternative areas from which these participants came were considered inadequate in their dealing with gender and sexuality diversity, not from a position of explicit discrimination, but rather a 'lack of awareness, like not thinking about it' (Marci).

Marci: I feel like at my kids' school, that they're quite accepting of the idea of LGBTQ, like for instance, when X donated some money for the school, I suggested that we buy a book for the library that covered one of these topics and the librarian was straight on it and gave me all these suggestions ... and they were really happy to do that so there's not that sort of discrimination. But they're not openly teaching about it either, like it's not part of the curriculum or they're not going out of their way to find ways to teach it.

A number of issues are raised here. For example, Marci points out how the school librarian was able to identify and purchase gender- and sexuality-diverse resources ['she was straight on it and gave me all these suggestions'], demonstrating that locating such teaching resources was neither overly problematic nor difficult – conflicting with claims reported in the literature that indicates otherwise (Smith et al. 2011). Indeed, the librarian was able to provide numerous suggestions. Despite the apparent ease with which gender- and sexuality-diverse resources were acquired, and despite the awareness that omission of such resources in the school equated to 'discrimination', Marci did not think that teachers in her child's school engaged with such content in the curriculum ['it's not part of the curriculum or they're not going out of their way to find ways to teach it'].

It is easy to claim fulfilment of minority representation through artefacts which, in the form of what may be framed as 'contentious' books, are often positioned in the dark recesses of the school library (Ferfolja 1998). Purchase of such resources does imply a tacit support for gender and sexuality diversity but does little to educate or include. Unread books do not challenge the status quo; they do not address the homophobic language rife in schools (Hillier et al. 2010); and they do not empower young people with the language to examine the discursive knowledge and the attendant power relations that exist in relation to difference. Additionally, unless read, they do not educate about or celebrate the social and cultural contributions made by gender- and sexuality-diverse people. Thus, teachers may be 'accepting', but if there is no pedagogical culture to actively engage in these issues nor publicly voiced institutional support, then little changes. It could be argued also that publicly voicing support could incite community hostility and jeopardise the school's position in the market.

The silencing of gender and sexuality diversity that perpetuates the heteronormative culture of schools was articulated by Kira's experience.

Kira: I kind of felt like [names school] … it didn't even occur to them to say on mother's day breakfast, 'bring all your mothers' … I don't think it occurred to them that almost all of the school is in some ways being involved in talking to the [names a gender and sexuality-diverse supportive initiative] or in some way supported or congratulated it.

This extract illustrates a number of issues. It highlights silencing and invisibility in relation to gender and sexuality diversity by the school's language choices and the discursive effects these have. That is, this school seemed to overlook or ignore the fact that some children in the school possessed two mothers; thus, students and parents may feel marginalised by the oversight and Othering of difference which is reinforced through the silence (Foucault 1978). Such omissions work to deny an adult of that subjective space of mother within the school context and deny a child public recognition of a parent's significant role in their life. Furthermore, Kira's frustration was apparent in the school's lack of awareness of its clientele's engagement with gender and sexuality diversity. Thus, despite an apparent openness to diversity, institutional discourse appeared to normalise heterosexual-headed families. Additionally, the discourses operating in the school in relation to family and motherhood were not only heteronormative but also nuclear, failing to be inclusive of blended and/or extended families. Such exclusions, through their silencing, reinforce the dominant but limited discourse of what constitutes family, marginalising alternative constellations.

Both of the above extracts refer to experiences of primary schools, and thus it could be argued that teachers' silencing of gender and sexuality diversity was the result of the students' ages. The dominant Western discourse of childhood, which constructs children in binary opposition to adults and positions them as vulnerable, innocent and in need of protection from adult knowledge, particularly in relation to gender and sexuality diversity may be apparent in these contexts. However, some mothers encountered similar silencing in the education of their high school children.

Judy: So I come at this as a mum of a high schooler … And by ignoring these issues, by self-censoring, by having teachers and their views and certain works censored is extremely problematic as it sets up a status quo, right you know, this is the right history and this is monogamous. … Even my son's experiences in school, there hasn't been, other than sex education, they talk about it there; 'Well you might be this, you might be that' but the discussion is really closed … Even if you look at the prescription for the Stage 6 English in the state, there's not a single text on there that deals with any kind of sexuality. We talk about 'race', we talk about class, we talk about immigration, but we can't talk about sex and sexuality and gender. So I feel like a lot of this is self-censorship that teachers at school engage in – lest they open up the flood for discussion.

In the extract above, Judy acknowledges that gender and sexuality diversity has been raised in sex education but also alludes to the limitations of this ['the discussion is really closed']. She also points to the apparent silences in key learning areas where gender and sexuality diversity could be broached but remains invisible; instead, more socially acceptable notions of difference are offered as senior high school literary texts. Young people possess knowledge about and access to much content once considered for 'adults only' through social media and the Internet. School silences merely enable misinformation and mythologies about sexuality and gender diversity to flourish, fail young people who do or will at some point engage in same-sex intimacy, reinforce the socially constructed normalcy of opposite-sex attraction and infantilise adolescents. Not addressing these issues, other than in sex education classes, means teachers forefront the biological and clinical aspects of sexuality but exclude from young people's learning the histories and contributions of gender- and sexuality-diverse people. In this way, gender- and sexuality-diverse subjects remain defined by sexuality, and this is re-inscribed through their topic's location, if anywhere, within the health classroom.

Gender and sexuality diversity in the curriculum

The question of gender and sexuality diversity inclusions in the curriculum resulted in considerable discussion illustrating that although all focus group participants desired its inclusion, the location and approaches unveiled discursive tensions and complexities. One participant articulated how such content is well-placed in Health/Physical Education classes, although this was not the only space that she felt that learning could occur.

Bonnie: In regards to the formal education, I think that it [Health/Physical Education] is a good factual way of incorporating it into the education. I don't know how, I don't know the nitty gritty of it but I think it's a great way of incorporating the factual way of having it incorporated in. Um, but I also think that through text through the English syllabus and also through the Drama syllabus and also through the HSIE syllabus there's a great history/social sciences that can be a really nonfrightening way for the students to hear about different people that might be helpful for someone who's questioning it, or whether or not just to hear about difference.

Although the Health/Physical Education syllabus makes mention of gender and sexuality diversity, as we have argued elsewhere, explicit incorporation is limited and teachers need to be particularly open, insightful and willing to implement such inclusions in their teaching, especially considering the taboos relating to discussion concerning non-heterosexual relationships and the ongoing public and political surveillance of education (Ullman and Ferfolja 2014). What is of particular interest in Bonnie's quote above is the focus on and tensions produced by reference to a factual approach. Despite being supportive of inclusions, teaching that relies on 'facts' implies a positivist approach based on the biological, suggesting an incontestable and, therefore, safer space for teachers; it simultaneously allays the perceived parental fears of the provision of age-inappropriate information being taught to young people. After all, teaching facts is akin to presenting a singular truth that exhorts the existence of an 'authentic' or singular subjectivity perceived as incontrovertible and therefore defensible; facts are devoid of the complexities, messiness, emotions and intimacies of life. However, teaching facts does not readily enable an exploration of the fluidity of gender and sexuality, or of the complexities of relationships, areas not in-keeping with the current neo-liberal agenda of national testing and league tables, the results of which have impact on a school's reputation, the enrolment of clientele and funding for teachers' positions.

This sanitisation is reinforced by Bonnie's reference to incorporation in the arts and social sciences as providing a 'nonfrightening way for students to hear about different people'. Despite Bonnie's progressive stance and activism in relation to gender and sexuality diversity and her strong belief in inclusion, she too inadvertently constituted through language, discourses that reinforce the marginalisation of gender and sexuality diversity, constructing it as something potentially fearful or threatening. It must be pointed out, however, that her references to 'fear' may have reflected the trepidation she sensed in more conservative parents in the community.

Bonnie's suggestion that gender and sexuality diversity should be included in various areas of the curriculum was reinforced by other participants. Marci, for example, stated:

Marci: I think the social sciences are a good way [to address LGBTQ content] because their lessons are all about investigating controversial subjects and things that are in the community and current affairs so this can be explored so much just under that curriculum already, I think.

Although an important suggestion that aims to normalise gender and sexuality diversity and legitimise it through curriculum outside of the health/physical education classroom, positioning this content in disciplines that investigate 'controversial subjects' and 'current affairs' re-inscribes the constructed abnormality and social problematic of individuals who transgress cis-gender and cis-sexual identities, again illustrating the tensions that arose for these mothers in terms of how gender and sexuality diversity is discursively positioned. Although important to include such subjectivities in the curriculum to equally educate about a range of achievements, contributions and histories, this positioning as special event simply re-inscribes gender and sexuality diversity as Other. Locating gender and sexuality diversity in such reductive curricular spaces positions it outside of the everyday and in contrast to the relatively unspoken spaces dominated by socially constructed and publicly endorsed heterosexual normalcy. Those who identify as gender- and sexuality-diverse are perceived to provide a provocative or 'exciting' topic to be investigated, analysed and debated, undermining the normality of these subjectivities.

The focus group participants recognised that parents played a significant role in the education of their children in relation to content related to gender and sexuality diversity.

Bonnie: In one respect I think that schools, depending on where your children are or where you live, schools are already part of the community, possibly and probably, where some of the students are coming from families where the caregivers or parents are in same-sex relationships or marriages or identify as one of these other words [LGBTQ] in part, and so there's a place already for informal education because other children are coming home and saying 'X has two mums', 'X has two dads', 'X only has one mum and X sometimes has two mums' and so the information is filtering out. So if it's filtering out and coming into the home, then guaranteed it's coming out into the school and so I think in that aspect there's already a place for informal education to be taking place.

Bonnie raises two important points here. The first point is that the awareness referred to above illustrates that young people are often already exposed to this knowledge in some form; thus, schools broaching these issues are addressing content with which children have familiarity. The second point that gender and sexuality diversity at school will inevitably be raised as a topic in the home is critical and formed part of a complex discussion in the broader study in relation to the rights (or not) of parents to veto their child's participation in related lessons (see Ullman and Ferfolja 2016). Of special interest, though, is that children's and young people's awareness, experience and anecdotal knowledge provide parents with an opening for what many consider difficult or even embarrassing conversations to initiate; parents are not likely to broach such topics very frequently (Calzo and Ward 2009) and moreover, a young person's sex and ethnic background impact on the types of messages that they receive about sexuality diversity (Fine and McClelland 2006). Thus, it cannot be assumed that young people are uniformly receiving access to quality information in the home.

Conclusion

This paper has illustrated that perceptions of gender and sexuality diversity inclusion in education are complex and multilayered. Despite the political awareness of this particular participant group and their overwhelming support for inclusivity and equity in education, they were at times constituted within dominant discourses of normalised gender and (hetero)sexuality. This meant that they too, inadvertently re-inscribed gender and sexuality diversity as 'Other'. Yet, it could be argued that it was their political astuteness that enabled them to recognise the perceived shortcomings of the schools with which they had contact as parents. Despite the progressive region in which they lived, and the diversity of its demographic characteristics, these mothers argued that the schools that their children attended provided little, if any, support for, or education about, gender and sexuality diversity. However, these findings cannot be generalised and large-scale research would be useful to provide a representative picture of parental understandings and desires; not all parents would agree with the perspectives of these mothers. Such research would inform where work was needed to move beyond the limitations of hetero and gender normative understandings that continue to negate so many young people's rightful place in education (Robinson et al. 2014; Ullman 2015a). In Australia, at the time of writing, gender and sexuality diversity in education remains a hotly debated issue where tensions are daily fuelled by uninformed conservative, political interference, religious agendas and the media.

All children, regardless of background, gender or sexual orientation or preference, have a right to be fully informed. Paul Clarke (2011) argues that young people possess a moral 'right to this kind of education' (84). This moral 'right flows from the notion that students are separate persons. Respect for this separateness means that as emergent sexual beings, they are entitled to age-appropriate information about human sexuality as they develop and grow' (86). It logically flows that schools are potentially the best places to educate about gender and sexuality diversity. No student should be denied a comprehensive education which provides them with better understandings of, and the opportunity to celebrate, difference; the ability to critically think about power and in/justice; and the necessary information to make educated choices. Teachers and schools could provide this education yet this can only be achieved if educational leaders and their institutions provide greater support through policy and curriculum documentation, and explicit direction for inclusion; without this, teachers, who understand its importance for the welfare and future of young people, and individually incorporate it in the curriculum, will continue to feel vulnerable. Funding for teacher education programmes could enhance understandings, and greater collaboration with parents could clarify any misconceptions about what might be addressed in school education. As Clarke (2011) points out, if parents do not want their child to receive such information, other educational options such as home-schooling and private institutions exist. However, adults must realise that all young people are entities unto themselves and have a right to knowledge; parents are guardians of young lives but children are not property. As individual agents, tomorrow's adults have a right to a full and complete education.

Notes

1. Throughout this paper, we employ the term gender- and sexuality-diverse rather than the more commonly used LGBTQ acronym (lesbian, gay, bi-sexual, trans*, queer) which is ever-evolving yet limiting. As young people are increasingly rejecting labels, the term gender- and sexuality-diverse allows for greater fluidity and is more inclusive and respectful of all aspects of gender and sexuality. This discussion only employs LGBTQ and its variations when referencing, citing or quoting others who have used it.
2. Wear It Purple day aims to support young people to be proud of themselves regardless of sex, sexuality or gender identity. Individuals wear purple in support on Wear It Purple Day which is held annually in August. See http://www.wearitpurple.org/

Disclosure statement

No potential conflict of interest was reported by the authors.

Funding

This work was supported by Western Sydney University.

ORCID

Jacqueline Ullman ⓘ http://orcid.org/0000-0002-6999-423X

References

ACARA (Australian Curriculum, Assessment and Reporting Authority). 2015. *The Australian Curriculum. Health and Physical Education, Foundation to Year 10.* http://www.australiancurriculum.edu.au/healthandphysicaleducation/Curriculum/F-10

Anderson, Stephanie. 2016. "Safe Schools: Malcolm Turnbull Requests Investigation into Program Helping LGBTI Students." *ABC News Online*, February 23. http://www.abc.net.au/news/2016-02-23/turnbull-requests-investigation-into-safe-schools-program/7192374

Ball, Stephen J., and Antonio Olmedo. 2013. "Care of the Self, Resistance and Subjectivity under Neoliberal Governmentalities." *Critical Studies in Education* 54 (1): 85–96.

Barbagallo, Milena, and Helen Boon. 2012. "Young People's Perceptions of Sexuality and Relationships Education in Queensland Schools." *Australian and International Journal of Rural Education* 22 (1): 107–124.

Barr, Elissa M., Michele J. Moore, Tammie Johnson, James Forrest, and Melissa Jordan. 2014. "New Evidence: Data Documenting Parental Support for Earlier Sexuality Education." *Journal of School Health* 84: 10–17.

Berne, Linda A., Wendy Patton, Jan Milton, Lynne Y. A. Hunt, Susan Wright, Judith Peppard, and Jenny Dodd. 2000. "A Qualitative Assessment of Australian Parents' Perceptions of Sexuality Education and Communication." *Journal of Sex Education and Therapy* 25 (2–3): 161–168.

Blackburn, Mollie. 2012. *Interrupting Hate: Homophobia in Schools and What Literacy Can Do about It.* New York: Teachers College Press.

Calzo, Jerel P., and Monique Ward. 2009. "Contributions of Parents, Peers, and Media to Attitudes toward Homosexuality: Investigating Sex and Ethnic Differences." *Journal of Homosexuality* 56 (8): 1101–1116.

Clarke, Paul T. 2011. "Sex Education and Students Rights: Including the Missing Actor." *International Journal of Education Reform* 20 (2): 84–110.

Cohen, Jacqueline N., Sandra E. Byers, Heather A. Sears, and Angela D. Weaver. 2004. "Sexual Health Education: Attitudes, Knowedge, and Comfort of Teachers in New Brunswick Schools." *The Canadian Journal of Human Sexuality* 13 (1): 2–15.

Connell, Raewyn. 2013. "The Neoliberal Cascade and Education: An Essay on the Market Agenda and Its Consequences." *Critical Studies in Education* 54 (2): 99–112.

Constantine, Norma A., Petra Jerman, and Alice X. Huang. 2007. "California Parents' Preferences and Beliefs regarding School-based Sex Education Policy." *Perspectives on Sexual and Reproductive Health* 39 (3): 167–175.

Cumming-Potvin, Wendy, and Wayne Martino. 2014. "Teaching about Queer Families: Surveillance, Censorship, and the Schooling of Sexualities." *Teaching Education* 25 (3): 309–333.

Down, Barry. 2009. "Schooling, Productivity and the Enterprising Self: Beyond Market Values." *Critical Studies in Education* 50 (1): 51–64.

Duffy, Bernadette, Nina Fotinatos, Amanda Smith, and Jenene Burke. 2013. "Puberty, Health and Sexual Education in Australian Regional Primary Schools: Year 5 and 6 Teacher Perceptions." *Sex Education* 13 (2): 186–203.

Eisenberg, Marla E., Debra H. Bernat, Linda H. Bearinger, and Michael D. Resnick. 2008. "Support for Comprehensive Sexuality Education: Perspectives from Parents of School-Age Youth." *Journal of Adolescent Health* 42: 352–359.

Ezzy, Douglas. 2002. *Qualitative Analysis. Practice and Innovation.* Crows Nest: Allen & Unwin.

Farrelly, Cathleen, Maureen O'Brien, and Vaughan Prain. 2007. "The Discourses of Sexuality in Curriculum Documents on Sexuality Education: An Australian Case Study." *Sex Education* 7 (1): 63–80.

Ferfolja, Tania. 1998. "Australian Lesbian Teachers – A Reflection of Harassment in NSW Government High Schools." *Gender and Education* 10 (4): 401–415.

Ferfolja, Tania, and Lucy Hopkins. 2013. "The Complexities of Workplace Experience for Lesbian and Gay Teachers." *Critical Studies in Education* 54 (3): 311–324.

GENDER AND SEXUALITY IN EDUCATION AND HEALTH

Ferfolja, Tania, and Jacqueline Ullman. 2014. "Opportunity Lost or (Re) Written out: LGBTI Content in Australia's New National Health and Physical Education Curriculum." In *Contemporary Issues of Equity in Education*, edited by Margaret Somerville and Susanne Gannon, 69–87. London: Cambridge Scholars.

Flood, Michael, and Clive Hamilton. (2005). *Mapping Homophobia in Australia*. The Australia Institute. http://www.tai.org.au/documents/downloads/WP79.pdf

Fine, Michelle, and Sara McClelland. 2006. "Sexuality Education and Desire: Still Missing after All These Years." *Harvard Educational Review* 76 (3): 297–338.

Foucault, Michel. (1978). *The History of Sexuality. Volume 1: An Introduction*. Translated by R. Hurley. New York: Vintage Books.

Goldstein, Tara, Anthony Collins, and Michael Halder. 2008. "Anti-homophobia Education in Public Schooling: A Canadian Case Study of Policy Implementation." *Journal of Gay & Lesbian Social Services* 19 (3–4): 47–66.

Griffin, Penny. 2007. "Sexing the Economy in a Neo-Liberal World Order: Neo-liberal Discourse and the (Re)Production of Heteronormative Heterosexuality." *The British Journal of Politics & International Relations* 9 (2): 220–238.

Hillier, Lynne, Tiffany Jones, Marisa Monagle, Naomi Overton, Luke Gahan, Jennifer Blackman, and Anne Mitchell. 2010. *Writing Themselves in 3 (WTi3): The Third National Study on the Sexual Health and Wellbeing of Same Sex Attracted and Gender Questioning Young People*. Melbourne: Australian Research Centre in Sex, Health and Society, La Trobe University.

Holmes, John. 2001. "'If There Was Any Hint': An Analysis of the Perceptions That Lesbian and Gay Educators Have of Teacher Sexuality and Education." *Leading & Managing* 7 (1): 61–75.

Kane, E. 2013. *Rethinking Gender and Sexuality in Childhood*. London: Bloomsbury.

Krueger, Richard A., and Mary Anne Casey. 2009. *Focus Groups: A Practical Guide for Applied Research*. 4th ed. Thousand Oaks, CA: SAGE.

Macbeth, Allison, Patricia Weerakoon, and Gomathi Sitharthan. 2009. "Pilot Study of Australian School-based Sexual Health Education: Parents' Views." *Sexual Health* 6 (4): 328–333.

Martino, Wayne, and Marina Pallotta-Chiarolli. 2003. *So What's a Boy? Addressing Issues of Masculinity and Schooling*. Maidenhead: Open University Press.

McCormack, Orla, and Jim Gleeson. 2010. "Attitudes of Parents of Young Men towards the Inclusion of Sexual Orientation and Homophobia on the Irish Post-primary Curriculum." *Gender and Education* 22 (4): 385–400.

Milton, Jan. 2003. "Primary School Sex Education Programs: Views and Experiences of Teachers in Four Primary Schools in Sydney, Australia." *Sex Education* 3 (3): 241–256.

Mitchell, Anne, and Jenny Walsh. 2009. "Sexuality Health Education Today: Towards a National Curriculum?" *Education Today*. Accessed August 8, 2015. http://www.educationtoday.com.au/article/Sexual-health-education-today-500

Ollis, Debbie. 2010. "'I Haven't Changed Bigots but . . .': Reflections on the Impact of Teacher Professional Learning in Sexuality Education." *Sex Education* 10 (2): 217–230.

Ollis, Debbie, Lyn Harrison, and Anthony Richardson. 2012. *Building Capacity in Sexuality Education: The Northern Bay College Experience*. Geelong: School of Education, Deakin University.

Robinson, Kerry, H. Peter Bansel, Nida Denson, Georgia Ovenden, and Cristyn Davies. 2014. *Growing up Queer. Issues Facing Young Australians Who Are Gender Variant and Sexuality Diverse*. Melbourne: Young and Well Cooperative Research Centre.

Saldana, Johnny. 2009. *The Coding Manual for Qualitative Researchers*. Phoenix, AZ: SAGE.

Safi, Michael. 2015. "Sydney School Received No Complaints from Parents about Gayby Baby Film." *The Guardian*, August 26. http://www.theguardian.com/world/2015/aug/26/sydney-school-received-no-complaints-from-parents-about-gayby-baby-film

Smith, Anthony, Marisa Schlichthorst, Anne Mitchell, Jenny Walsh, Anthony Lyons, Pam Blackman, and Marian Pitts. 2011. *Sexuality Education in Australian Secondary Schools 2010*, Monograph Series No. 80. Melbourne: La Trobe University, the Australian Research Centre in Sex, Health & Society.

Ullman, Jacqueline. 2015a. *Free to Be? Exploring the Schooling Experiences of Australia's Sexuality and Gender Diverse Secondary School Students*. Sydney: Centre for Educational Research, School of Education, Western Sydney University, Penrith.

Ullman, Jacqueline. 2015b. "'At-risk' or School-based Risk? Testing a Model of School-based Stressors, Coping Responses, and Academic Self-concept for Same-sex Attracted Youth." *Journal of Youth Studies* 18 (4): 417–433.

Ullman, Jacqueline, and Tania Ferfolja. 2014. "Bureaucratic Constructions of Sexual Diversity: 'Sensitive', 'Controversial' and Silencing." *Teaching Education* 26 (2): 145–159.

Ullman, Jacqueline, and Tania Ferfolja. 2016. "The Elephant in the (Class)Room: Parental[1] Perceptions of LGBTQ-Inclusivity in K-12 Educational Contexts." *Australian Journal of Teacher Education* 41 (10): 15–29.

UNESCO (United Nations Educational, Scientific and Cultural Organization). 2009. *International Technical Guidance on Sexuality Education. an Evidence-Informed Approach for Schools, Teachers and Health Educators.* http://unesdoc.unesco.org/images/0018/001832/183281e.pdf

Weedon, Chris. 1987. *Feminist Practice and Poststructuralist Theory.* Oxford: Blackwell.

Whitlam, Gough. 1972. Australian Labor Party Policy Speech, 1972. http://whitlamdismissal.com/1972/11/13/whitlam-1972-election-policy-speech.html

IN CONVERSATION

Young people, sexuality and diversity. What does a needs-led and rights-based approach look like?

Simon Blake in conversation with Peter Aggleton

In 2015, the *Australia Forum for Sexuality, Education and Health* (AFSEH) held its inaugural conference in Sydney on the grounds of Western Sydney University. The conference aimed to increase the public profile of work on equity and justice particularly in relation to contemporary issues of gender, sexuality, health and education and their intersections.

Simon Blake, OBE, delivered one of the key note addresses at the conference. Simon is the Chief Executive of the National Union of Students (UK), an organisation which works to shape education and empower individuals with the ultimate goal of contributing to a just and sustainable future. As the former Chief Executive Officer of Brook, the UK's largest young people's sexual health charity, his insight and expertise into the sexual health and education needs of young people is unparalleled. In his earlier role as Assistant Director of Children's Development and Director of the Sex Education Forum at the National Children's Bureau in England, Simon built collaborations across education, health and social care that provide excellent models as well as inspiration and direction for those working in similar fields internationally. Simon possesses real-world insight and strategic experience in forging alliances, promoting equity and bringing about change.

Editor-in-chief of *Sex Education*, Professor Peter Aggleton, interviewed Simon about his understandings of sex and relationships education and the shifting policy landscape. It is no longer a matter of *whether* adults should provide sex and relationships education for all children and young people, but rather, *how* adults should focus on building knowledge and understanding in terms of what makes a positive educational experience for children and youth, and what kinds of innovative approaches can be implemented to ensure the needs of all children and young people are addressed.

What follows is an excerpt from this conversation.

PETER: I'm so pleased that you could present the keynote address for the AFSEH conference this morning. As we know all too well, sex and relationships education –SRE – has long been a contested area of the school curriculum. I think that many of us agree that this is unnecessarily so. Why do you think this is the case and what might we achieve through SRE?

SIMON: Although there is broad based consensus that SRE is a positive and important part of a young person's education, it does continue to be contested on thoroughly misguided grounds – namely the idea that SRE promotes early sex engagement and that it somehow corrupts children's innocence. Family rights campaigners, despite evidence to the contrary, continue to argue that SRE promotes early sex and an unhealthy curiosity about sex, homosexuality and 'promiscuity' – whatever that is. Take for example a recent article by the psychiatrist Miriam Grossman; the headline read something like 'government funded sex education groups promote promiscuity and homosexuality while downplaying the health and psychological risks associated with premature sexual activity'. This sort of nonsense is insidious.

Such attitudes have hampered the development of SRE in England and interestingly, similar policy and public debates happen in English speaking countries across the world – to a greater or lesser extent. SRE, done well, can equip children and young people with the information, skills and values they need to have safe, fulfilling and enjoyable relationships and to take responsibility for their sexual health and well-being.

You see, unlike other subjects such as maths and science, SRE is not universally believed in, trusted and valued. It's seen as scary by some, optional by others and, thus, its inclusion is still viewed as a valid subject of debate, despite it being 2016 and all the research showing its importance.

PETER: So, in your experience, what is the position of those who support SRE?

SIMON: The evidence tells us that the vast majority of children, young people, parents and professionals support good quality school-based SRE. In England, we have a national Sex Education Forum which is a broad based coalition that seeks to build consensus on sex and relationships education across health, education, children and youth, and specialist organisations. The Forum defines sex and relationships education as learning about the emotional, social and physical aspects of growing up; about relationships, sex, human sexuality, sexual health and so on. Supporters of sex and relationships education argue that, for children and young people, such education promotes awareness and understanding of their bodies, protects them from abuse and actually *delays* sex. The evidence from international reviews supports this and shows that school based SRE, when linked to contraceptive services, can have a positive impact on young people's knowledge and skills.

Personal Social, Health and Economic Education – or PSHE education – is the curriculum subject in schools where much of the content of SRE is provided in England. The PSHE Association in England, for example, has demonstrated the full extent of support for PSHE education. Over 120 organisations expressed their wish that PSHE education included teaching about sexual consent, and that it be a statutory part of the national curriculum. These organisations ranged from the National Union of Teachers to Girl Guides to the Royal College of Paediatrics and Child Health, to National Union of Students, to the National Society Prevention of Cruelty to Children, to the Royal College of General Practitioners; the support was immense.

PETER: A lot of the research demonstrates that SRE contributes to sexual competence. What are your thoughts about this?

SIMON: I firmly believe that SRE contributes to sexual competence. The evidence tells us so. It is good that it does. However the drive to prove the effectiveness of SRE has often driven experts to focus on measuring and proving SRE has *health* benefits, rather than *educational outcomes*, which is in fact how we measure the outcomes associated with other subjects.

GENDER AND SEXUALITY IN EDUCATION AND HEALTH

So while the evidence demonstrates there are health outcomes and that SRE can contribute to sexual competence, it is absolutely imperative that we take a *rights-based* and *needs-led* approach to SRE. This approach focuses on educational experience and educational outcomes and links to other issues that affect children and young people such as emotional health, body image, alcohol and other drug use.

PETER: So, what does the evidence tell us about SRE and its effectiveness and what does good practice looks like?

SIMON: Well, in 1997, the UK government undertook a review of all the evidence about what would help reduce our unacceptably high teenage pregnancy rate. SRE was identified as one factor and became a core plank of the very successful teenage pregnancy strategy. In fact, almost 20 years on from the UK government's publication of Teenage Pregnancy Strategy for England we now know a lot about what works. We know that children and young people learn about sex and relationships, whether we teach them about these or not, and that ever easier access to pornography makes it urgent that we ensure children and young people are, as they say, taught not caught.

We know, unequivocally, that children, young people, parents and professionals actually *do* support comprehensive SRE. We have a rights-based mandate from the United Nations Convention on the Rights of the Child and relevant global organisations including UNAIDS, UNESCO, UNFPA and World Health Organisation.

We have a clear understanding that teaching and learning must use active learning methods, start from where children are at, involve them in planning and delivery, differentiate the learning outcomes so everyone can achieve at their own pace, and ensure assessment is a core part of the learning experience. We also have enough evidence to know that, done well, SRE contributes to reductions in teenage pregnancy, HIV and improved sexual health. In addition, we understand how to combine the range of legal, health, faith and secular perspectives to deliver a strong educational entitlement.

PETER: With all that in mind, who do you think should deliver SRE? Should it come from a single person, or from an array of sources? What are your thoughts about this?

SIMON: No one person can or should be responsible for delivering SRE. Learning about sex and relationships happens every day in a range of places through both formal and informal sources. Given that sex, relationships and sexuality are central to children and young people's experience as they grow up, all adults should ideally be able to talk about the issues positively and openly.

However, the reality is that we are a long way from that ideal, so unless adults are trained and feel confident dealing with the issues it's best advised to stay well away from SRE to avoid confusing, misrepresenting or reinforcing negative stereotypes and prejudices. Children and young people want SRE that is positive and empowering that doesn't focus on telling them not to do things – which all the evidence suggests doesn't work anyway – as we know. Parents and carers have a responsibility to educate their children. Ideally, they should be the first educators and ensure they talk about their own values and beliefs.

PETER: But what about if they don't feel confident in doing this? As you've just said, many adults are uneasy about broaching these issues with young people …

SIMON: There are a number of resources to help parents. One of these, from the Family Planning Association, is *Speakeasy: Talking to your children about growing up*. In the UK, lots

GENDER AND SEXUALITY IN EDUCATION AND HEALTH

of schools will hold sessions to help parents and carers understand the school curriculum and help them think about how to talk to their children.

If parents and carers know and understand the school's programme and approach to SRE they are more likely to support it, and to be able to reinforce the learning. Too often when discussing sex and relationships education with parents, the content is pitched at convincing them that it is the right thing to do, rather than discussing the how and the what. Schools can provide a base level of education for all children and young people that is sex-positive, empowering and inclusive. Owing to time, expertise and class size, they will be unlikely to meet the specific needs of all different groups; they can, however, bring in specialist agencies who have expertise in working on particular issues.

For example in the UK, Brook is often invited into schools to work on a wide range of issues; most often, it is around the issues that teachers feel uncomfortable with such as sexual consent, online pornography and sending sexually explicit messages or images online. Some staff at Brook were concerned about only having a short amount of curriculum time to implement education sessions, and most often being asked to talk about 'problem issues'. In response, the teams developed a programme called *Bitesize Brook* which was designed to be used with big groups who are divided into smaller groups and rotate across a number of zones that cover different issues such as contraception, stereotypes, decisions about sex, being LGBT, alcohol and other drugs. The programme aims to offer a high energy, memorable session and make sure that young people know they can access confidential community services if they want help and advice.

Two different LGBT organisations in the UK – Diversity Role Models and Stonewall – take LGBT people and straight allies into school to talk about their lives to help tackle homophobic bullying and promote a positive understanding of LGBT people and the importance of straight allies. Evaluation shows that children and young people value the experience and learn from it because it focuses on the positive, and on everyday experience, creating visibility of LGBT people rather than simply telling children not to bully or hurt others.

School based SRE, of course, can also form the basis of more targeted or additional education for particular groups of young people, either on the basis of characteristics such as LGBT youth groups, friendship groups or single gender sessions.

PETER: So there's quite a lot that can be done by parents and within the school. What about externally, outside of the school context, what kinds of things might be available?

SIMON: Youth and community settings can provide more specialist education and support for example through working in single gender groups, working in friendship groups or providing SRE for people with disabilities. Youth and Community settings have the advantage of being informal so generally people will be attending of their own accord and therefore want to participate which can really enhance the learning. Contrary to what some believe, churches also have a role to play in promoting understanding of their values and beliefs, including promoting positive respect, tolerance and understanding.

Other educational sites such as colleges of further education and universities can also do work in this area but of course, it must be relevant to the age and maturity of the students. For example, Brook, FPA and Durex undertook some research with further education students who said they really wanted education about issues that were relevant to them and that it must not feel too like school. The National Union of Students Women's Campaign developed and launched sexual consent sessions across universities. Despite initial protestations from

GENDER AND SEXUALITY IN EDUCATION AND HEALTH

some who said they did not need to be taught about sexual consent, these have now become incredibly popular and well received. Done well, SRE in these settings can be engaging and feel relevant, and it can build on what has been taught earlier in a young person's life, focusing on rights and consent.

PETER: What about people with particular experiences, different abilities or special needs?

SIMON: Specialist colleges for people with disabilities can provide tailored SRE programmes that will meet the range of needs of their populations. Similarly, residential care providers can deliver one-to-one and small group work with children in care, taking account of the background and experiences of those children and young people. Most children's services departments in the UK will have a policy for working with children in care.

PETER: Is there wisdom that you might be able to share in relation to curriculum development and inclusion?

SIMON: Wherever you are intending to deliver SRE, the curriculum must be planned with children and young people at the heart of it. Too often children and young people tell us that the information they receive is too little, too late and too biological. We need to ensure that children and young people are asked to input into the curriculum at planning stages. The Sex Education Forum has published a series of questions for different age groups to help guide the curriculum design in line with the stage of maturity and development of different groups. Research and evidence can be used to inform the development of curricula.

As society changes so does the need to develop the curriculum so it integrates and explores a wider range of issues in the classroom. In the UK, the government last published guidance on sex and relationships education in 2000 and despite attempts by Government to get schools to tackle issues such as child sexual exploitation, pornography and sending explicit images and texts – all issues which have either emerged or we have greater knowledge of since then – the UK government has not yet published updated SRE guidance to help schools develop inclusive curricula that takes account of current issues.

So Brook, the PSHE Association and the Sex Education Forum joined forces to produce supplementary advice for schools which outlines how to address current and emerging issues which children and young people face and provides a summary of how to integrate the issues into the curriculum. We learned through that process how important it is to keep thinking about how the curriculum needs to develop and evolve as knowledge and understanding changes.

All curricula should enable everybody to participate at their own level. Within any one room there will be a range of experiences, abilities and disabilities, and curricula should be structured to allow for this. They should include positive values of respect and tolerance, avoid assumptions about beliefs and behaviours and be linked to other real life issues that are relevant such as mental health, body image, identity and alcohol and other drugs.

When I worked at the Sex Education Forum over a decade ago representatives from the six major world faiths came together as part of a project I led, called Faith, Values and SRE, to discuss and agree how best to talk to young people about sex and sexuality. They agreed that SRE should include legal perspectives – what is the law on an issue such as homosexuality or abortion and health understandings combined with faith, cultural and secular perspectives in order to create a curriculum that inclusive works.

133

I guess it is probably important to say that we often wait for Government to legislate and make innovative practices around SRE happen, but Government is invariably cautious. Innovation in curriculum development comes from practitioners on the front line, such as the work done by the Clarity Collective (1985) to produce *Taught Not Caught*, or community projects run by Brook and FPA to develop resources that target particular groups such as boys or people with disabilities.

PETER: So, in a nutshell, what does good practice look like?

SIMON: A summary of evidence and understanding of best practice has been published by the Health Development Agency (2001). It suggests that SRE should start early before puberty, before sexual feelings and before sexual activity. The most effective approaches involve children and young people in planning and start from where children and young people are at. It should also be positive about sex and sexuality, be rights based and be continuous, developmental and relevant.

Additionally, we need to use inclusive language, distancing techniques and methodologies that make it safe for everyone to participate without talking about personal experience; include information, skills, values and attitudes as well as emotions; include the law, health perspectives, faith and secular views. We need to use active learning methods and ensure we have differentiated learning outcomes. SRE needs to be provided by educators who know about teaching and learning, and are confident talking about relationships, sex and sexuality; peer educators may be part of this but having the skills is more important than who is doing the educating. It should be linked to confidential one-to-one advice and sexual health services. Finally, it is good practice for everyone to know what they are trying to achieve and how they will know if they have got there; so there also needs to be robust assessment of learning and evaluation of the teaching.

Two really good UK based websites which have loads of advice about good practice are www.sexeducationforum.org.uk and www.brook.org.uk

PETER: Is that in a nutshell?!

SIMON: I would like to finish by saying, we have a mandate from the United Nations through to medical colleges, from teaching unions to parents, carers, children and young people. We know what works. We know what children and young people tell us they need. So the time has come to stop talking about whether and when, and to move to what and how. SRE in schools should be taught like any other subject, by trained and confident teachers and specialist contributors who know about teaching and learning. We need to measure effectiveness against educational objectives safe in the knowledge that good SRE contributes to health outcomes.

PETER: Thanks so much Simon. It has been great having this opportunity to talk.

References

Blake, S., and J. Laxton. 1998. *Strides: A Practical Guide to Sex and Relationships Education with Young Men*. London: Family Planning Association.

Blake, S., and Z. Katrak. 2002. *Faith, Values and Sex and Relationships Education*. London: National Children's Bureau for the Sex Education Forum.

Brook. 2012. "Sex and Relationships Education Fit for the 21st Century: We Need It Now." https://www.brook.org.uk/images/brook/professionals/documents/press_releases/sreforthe21stcenturyreportfinal.pdf

Brook, PSHE Association and Sex Education Forum. 2014. "Sex and Relationships Education for the 21st Century: Supplementary Advice to the Sex and Relationship Education Guidance DfEE." (No. 0116/2000). https://www.brook.org.uk/data/SRE-supplementary-advice.pdf

Clarity Collective. 1985. *Taught Not Caught: Strategies for Sex Education*. Wisbech: Learning Development Associates.

Family Planning Association. 2009. *Speakeasy: Talking with Your Children about Growing up*. London: Family Planning Association.

Grossman, M. 2010. "You're Teaching My Child What? The Truth about Sex Education." *The Heritage Foundation*, August 9. http://www.heritage.org/research/lecture/youre-teaching-my-child-what-the-truth-about-sex-education

Grossman, M. 2015. "Promiscuity is Hidden Agenda of Sex Education." February 17. http://henrymakow.com/2015/02/Promiscuity%20is%20Hidden-Agenda-of-Sex-Education%20.html

Health Development Agency. 2001. *Teenage Pregnancy: An Update on Key Characteristics of Effective Interventions*. London: Health Development Agency. http://www.lemosandcrane.co.uk/bluesalmon/resources/HDA%20-%20Teenage%20pregnancy.pdf

Image in Action. 2010. *Going Further: Sex and Relationships Education Course: For Learners with Additional Needs at Colleges of Further Education*. High Wycombe: Image in Action. http://www.imageinaction.org/pdf/GF_SREcourse-6.12.10-1.pdf

Oringanje, C., M. M. Meremikwu, H. Eko, E. Esu, A. Meremikwu, and J. E. Ehiri. 2009. "Interventions for Preventing Unintended Pregnancies amongst Adolescents." *Cochrane Database of Systematic Reviews* (4). doi:10.1002/14651858.CD005215.pub2

Personal, Social and Health Education Association. 2016. "Support for PSHE Education." Accessed August 30, 2016. www.pshe-association.org.uk/campaigns

Redrup, S. 2015. "Why I Needed Consent Lessons." *Huffington Post*, October 20.

Santelli, J., L. D. Lindberg, L. B. Finer, and S. Singh. 2007. "Explaining Recent Declines in Adolescent Pregnancy in the United States: The Contribution of Abstinence and Improved Contraceptive Use." *American Journal of Public Health* 97 (1): 150–156. doi:10.2105/AJPH.2006.089169

Sex Education Forum. 2015. *SRE – The Evidence*. London: National Children's Bureau. http://www.sexeducationforum.org.uk/media/28306/SRE-the-evidence-March-2015.pdf

Sex Education Forum. 2016. "Curriculum Design: What to Include in SRE." Accessed August 30, 2016. www.sexeducationforum.org.uk/resources/curriculum-design.aspx

Social Exclusion Unit. 1999. *Teenage Pregnancy* (no. Cm 4342). http://dera.ioe.ac.uk/15086/1/teenage-pregnancy.pdf

United Nations. 2016. "UN Committee on the Rights of the Child: Concluding Observations on the Fifth Periodic Report of the United Kingdom of Great Britain and Northern Ireland." http://www.crae.org.uk/media/93148/UK-concluding-observations-2016.pdf

Index

Note: **Boldface** page numbers refer to tables and *italic* page numbers refer to figures. Page numbers followed by "n" refer to endnotes.

Abbott, Tony 14
academic self-concept 48, 51
Academic Self-Description Questionnaire II 48, 49
ACARA *see* Australian Curriculum, Assessment and Reporting Authority
AFSEH *see* Australia Forum for Sexuality, Education and Health
Aggleton, P. 5, 58, 60, 129
All of Us teaching kit 10, 13–15
Altman, Dennis 13
anal cancer 23
Ansara, Y. G. 9
anti-discrimination legislation 16
anti-homophobia education 47, 57, 63, 64, 117
Attitudes Towards School Survey 48
Australia: education policy, homophobic language 58; National HPV Vaccination Program 22, 23; Safe Schools Coalition Australia 111n1; school education and curricula 100–1; sexuality education in 101–2; *see also* homophobic language; LGBTIQ+ student experiences; sexuality education, in primary schools
Australia Forum for Sexuality, Education and Health (AFSEH) 1, 6n2, 129
Australian Curriculum, Assessment and Reporting Authority (ACARA) 29
Australian Education Union 58
Australian Health and Physical Education (F-10) curriculum 10
Australian queer-affirming learning materials 3; *All of Us* teaching kit 10, 13–15; controversy 11–12; diversity 10–11, 15–16; *Gayby Baby* (2013) 9, 12–13, 16–17; LGBTIQ youth in 14; overview 8–10; politicisation of 16–18; Safe Schools Coalition 13–15, 17
Australian Research Council Discovery (2011–2014) project 102

Baird, Mike 13
Ball, S. 104
Bennett, J. 78
Bernardi, Cory 14, 17
bisexuals 71
Bitesize Brook 132
Blake, Simon 5, 129
Bolch, Megan B. 45
broad-based biopsychosocial model 27
Butler, J. 71, 77, 80
Byron, Paul (anecdote) 4, 92–3

Catching on Early: Sexuality Education for Victorian Primary Schools 101
Catfish 95n8
cervical cancer 23, 24
childhood innocence 107
children's sexuality education *see* sexuality education, in primary schools
cisgender 16, 44, 49–50, 86, 95n1
Clarke, Paul 125
'coercive queering', of transgender 9
community sexuality education programmes 110–11
Controversial Issues in Schools Policy 101
Cox, Laverne 16
Craig, S. L. 88
cultural knowledge 69
cybersafety workshops 93

Daily Telegraph, The 12–13
Dame, A. 95n7
Davies, Cristyn 3, 5
Davis, Alexander K. 77
Deuze's theory of media life 88
Diaz, Elizabeth M. 46
digital media 88–9
diversity 10–11; concept of 15; notion of 15; problematising 15–16; rhetoric of 15; sexual and gender 15; 'tolerance' of student 15

137

INDEX

education intervention 29; facilitators and barriers 31–2, 34; implementation of 29–30; teachers/ school nurses in 34
England: Personal Social, Health and Economic Education 130; Sex Education Forum 130, 133; Teenage Pregnancy Strategy for 131
equity and justice 1–2
Equity and Justice–in Gender, Sexuality, Education and Health (2015) 1
experiential knowledge 91–2

Facebook 49, 59, 94, 103, 119
far-right political parties 15
"feeling safe" at school 45
Ferfolja, T. 5, 9, 11, 16
Fink, M. 95n7
Flood, Michael 119
formal knowledge 86 *see also* informal knowledge
Foucault, M. 71, 104
From Blues to Rainbows report 14, 17, 88
Fulcher, Karyn 4

Gayby Baby (2013) 2, 3, 9, 12–13, 16–19, 42, 116
gay, lesbian, bisexual and transgender (GLBT) 58
gender and sexuality activism 90–1
gender climate 47, **48**
gender non-conformity 16, 17
Ghaziani, A. 70, 71, 80
GLBT *see* gay, lesbian, bisexual and transgender
global gag rule 1
Goodenow, Carol 45
Greytak, Emily A. 46
Grossman, Miriam 129
Guerin, B. 58, 63

Hamilton, Clive 119
Hanckel, B. 88
Harrison, L. 87, 117
HAVIQ *see* HPV Adolescent Intervention Questionnaire
Health Belief Model (HBM) 27
heteronormative values 72; of monogamy and same-generation pairings 71; of sexuality and gender 9, 12
heterosexuality, in schools 116, 118, 120
Hillier, L. 87, 88
homonormativity 69, 72, 77, 80
homophobic jokes 58
homophobic language 4; anti-homophobia initiatives 57–8, 64; asynchronous online discussion 59; in Australian education policy 58; as form of homophobia 62–3; functions of 57; heterosexual study participants 60, 63; interview data, analysis of 59–60; masculinity and 57; methods of 59–60; racism/racist

behaviour 58; reinforce masculine gender norms 61–2; social context in determining meaning 60–1; student-led gay–straight alliances 64; word choice, regardless of 60
homophobic violence 70
homosexuality 58, 117–18, 130
HPV Adolescent Intervention Questionnaire (HAVIQ) 27, 28, 30
HPV.edu study group 25, 27–9, **33**
Human papillomavirus (HPV) vaccination 3; Advisory Board 28; Australian Curriculum, Assessment and Reporting Authority 29; blinded analysis 28; conceptualisation and design 27; decision-making and 28; education intervention implementation 29–32, 35; education resources 28, 29, **30**; ethics and informed consent 28; HPV Adolescent Intervention Questionnaire 27; implementation of 24; intervention 27; mixed methods evaluation design 27; overview 22–3; research-based information 24; School Based Immunisation Program 34; sexual health and relationships education 34; strengths and limitations 36; student knowledge and understanding 24, **32**; study design 26; thematic analysis 28
Hunt, Jessie (anecdote) 4, 89–94

Index of Community Socio-Educational Advantage (ICSEA) ranking 31, 36
individual and collective identity 8
informal knowledge 4; activism, gender and sexuality 90–1; *Blues to Rainbows* study 88; *Catfish* 95n8; creating 'safer spaces' 88–90; digital media, use of 88–9; exchange 85, 87; formal *vs.* 86, 94; friendships and false dualism 88; functions of 94; homophobia and queerphobia 94; Jessie's anecdote 89–94; lesbian, gay, bisexual, transgender and queer young people 88; mental health and experiential knowledge 91–2, 95n5; nebulous and contradictory 87; networks 85, 94; online identity 88; online/offline worlds 88; Paul's anecdote 92–3; *Scrolling Beyond Binaries* survey 95n4; shared feelings and lived experience 92–4; Tumblr, young people's engagements with 90–2; *We Learn From Each Other* study 94; *You Learn From Each Other* study 90
informed consent, ethics and 28, 104
Internet 87, 88, 107, 122

Jenner, Caitlyn 16

Kassisieh, G. 89
Kehily, Mary 47

INDEX

knowledge exchange 85, 86 *see also* informal knowledge
Kosciw, Joseph G. 44, 46
K-6 Personal Development, Health and Physical Education (PDHPE) syllabus 101

Lalor, T. 60, 63
Lamb, S. 18
Leonard, W. 58
lesbian, gay, bisexual, transgender, intersex and queer (LGBTIQ) 9–10, 14, 16, 52n3
LGBTIQ+ student experiences 4, 81; authenticity 71–2; cultural knowledge 69; in educational settings 69, 70; hetero/homo/trans-normativity 69, 71–2; holding queerness 78–9; knowing queerness 75–7; marginalisation and isolation 70–1; methods of 73–5, **74**; non-binary transgender 79; participants, demographic characteristics of 73, **74**; performing queerness 77–8; queerness 68–9, 77, 78; tertiary educational institutions 80, 81; transnormativity 72, 79, 80
Lichterman, P. 70, 79

Martino, Wayne 116
McCann, P.D. 57
McGregor, Cate 16
McInroy, L. 88
Melbourne Declaration on Educational Goals for Young Australians 10
mental health: and experiential knowledge 91–2; variation 95n5
Meyer, A. 70
Miller, Q. 95n7
Minichiello, V. 57
Minus18 10, 14, 17
monogamous relationships 120
Morris, A. 88
Morrish, L. 15
Murdock, Tamera B. 45

National Curriculum 100–1
National HPV Vaccination Program 22, 23
National School Climate Survey 44, 46
neoliberalism 118; political framework of 15
Newell, Maya 12
New South Wales (NSW) 10; Personal Development, Health and Physical Education 11; Piccoli, Adrian 13, 17; radio media outlets in 13; sexuality education 101–2
NVivo 10 software 59, 75, 104

Ollis, Debbie 117
O'Mara, K. 15
OMG resources 14
online identity 88

Pallotta-Chiarolli, Marina 116
parents/carers, children's sexuality education and 5, 111; comprehensive sexuality programme 109; content of sexuality education 109–10; emotional un-readiness 107; importance 105–6; 'loss of innocence' 107; opposition to 106–8; perceptions of 105; responsibility of 108–9
penile cancers 23
Personal Development, Health and Physical Education (PDHPE) curriculum 11
Personal Social, Health and Economic (PSHE) education 130, 133
phpBB3 open-source software 59
Piaget, J. 107
Piccoli, Adrian 13, 17
Plummer, D. 57
preventive education strategy 3
PSHE education *see* Personal Social, Health and Economic (PSHE) education

queer-affirming learning materials 9

racial discrimination 120
randomised controlled trial (RCT) 25
'Relationships and Sexuality' 117
Rendle-Short, J. 60, 63
Renn, Kristen A. 70
Richardson, Anthony 117
Robinson, Kerry 5
Roffee, James 4

Safe Schools Coalition 13–15, 17–19
Safe Schools Coalition Australia (SSCA) 2, 42, 111n1
Safe Schools Coalition Victoria 58, 117
same-sex couples 12
SBIP *see* School-based Immunisation Program
school-based harassment 43, 47
School-based Immunisation Program (SBIP) 23, 34
school-based vaccination programmes 23, 36
school climate 52n4; concept of 47; negative 43; positive 44; research 44–5
school engagement 45
schooling, gender and sexuality diversity 5, 114–15, 124–5; conceptual framework 118; curriculum development 122–4; educational documentation 116; focus group discussion 119–20; institutional discrimination 115; institutional documentation 116; interpersonal discrimination 115; New South Wales context 115; parental perceptions 115, 117–18; perceptions of 120–2; 'right to this kind of education' 125; school education context 115–17; "silenced and invisible" 118, 121–2; understanding 120; Whitlam, Gough 114

INDEX

Scrolling Beyond Binaries survey 95n4
Seelman, Kristie 45
sex and relationships education (SRE) 129–34
sex education 11, 122, 130; fact-based approach to 18
Sex Education Forum 130, 133
sexual diversity 11, 14
sexual health and relationships (SHR) education 34
sexuality education, in primary schools 99, 100, 110; in Australia 100–2; benefits 100; comprehensive sexuality education 101; discourse analysis 104; ethics and informed consent 104; online surveys 104; positive sexuality education 105; recruitment avenues 103; research methods 102; samples 102–3; theoretical framework 103–4; *see also* parents/carers, children's sexuality education and
Shannon, B. 3, 11
Shelton, Lyle 14, 17
SHR education *see* sexual health and relationships education
Smith, E. 5, 88, 90
Smith, S. J. 3, 11
Social Cognitive Theory 27
social conservatism 17
South Australia (SA) 11, 28, 29
Speakeasy: Talking to your children about growing up 131
SPSS *see* Statistical Package for the Social Sciences
SSCA *see* Safe Schools Coalition Australia
Statistical Package for the Social Sciences (SPSS) 49
Szalacha, Laura 45

Talking Sexual Health (Ollis & Mitchell) 6n1
teacher positivity towards gender diversity 4, 42–3, 51–2; academic self-concept 48; Academic Self-Description Questionnaire II 48, 49; anti-homophobia education 47; Attitudes Towards School Survey 48; Australian school context 42–3; cisgender students 46, 49–50; descriptive statistics and Pearson's product moment correlations **48**; emotional support, perceptions of 45; lesbian-, gay- and bisexual-identifying students 45; National School Climate Survey 44, 46; negative school climate 43; positive school climate 44; predicting school

engagement 45; regression model 45, 46; Safe Schools Coalition Australia 42; school-based harassment 43; school climate research 44–5, 47, 52n4; 'sexuality and gender diversity', notion of 52n3; student outcomes 50–1, **51**; study limitations 52; study participants 49; teacher/student relationship 46, 50; theoretical framework 46–7; three-item subscale 48, **48**; transgender students 46; transphobia 49–50; *Writing Themselves In* series of studies 43, 44
teachers' anxieties 116
teaching programmes 10–11
Teaching Sexual Health 11
Teenage Pregnancy Strategy for England 131
Theory of Planned Behaviour (TPB) 27
'three-parent syndrome' 116
TPB *see* Theory of Planned Behaviour
transgender: coercive queering of 9; toilets, in schools 1
transmasculine 93, 95n9
transnormativity 69, 72, 79, 80
transphobia, teacher positivity and 49–50
Trump, Donald 1
Tumblr, young people's engagements with 90–2, 95n7
Turnbull, Malcolm 14

Ullman, Jacqueline 3–5, 52n5

Valentine, David 71
Victoria state 2, 100, 103; comprehensive sexuality education 101; Safe Schools Coalition Victoria 58, 117

Waling, Andrea 4
Warwick, I. 58, 60
Wear It Purple Day 12, 13, 116, 125n2
Weedon, C. 9
We Learn From Each Other study 94
Wentzel, Kathryn R. 45
We're Family Too report (2011) 89
Western Australia (WA) 28, 29
Westheimer, Kim 45
Whitlam, Gough 114
Writing Themselves In 3 14, 43, 44, 56, 57

You Learn From Each Other study 90
'youth risk' 87
YouTube, young people's engagements with 92